AFRICA
TODAY—AND TOMORROW
An Outline of Basic Facts and Major Problems

by

John Hatch

FREDERICK A. PRAEGER
Publishers
NEW YORK

BOOKS THAT MATTER

Published in the United States of America in 1960
by Frederick A. Praeger, Inc., Publishers
64 University Place, New York 3, N.Y.

Library of Congress catalog card number 60-7964

AFRICA TODAY—AND TOMORROW
is published in two editions:

A Praeger Paperback (PPS ▶17)
A clothbound edition

The British edition of this book was published by Dobson Books Ltd., London,
under the title *Everyman's Africa*.

Manufactured in the United States of America

CONTENTS

647809

ACKNOWLEDGEMENTS

Most of the typing of this manuscript was done by Miss Jean Damer, Miss Marjorie Sapt, and Mrs G. Hollings. I am very grateful to them for their valuable assistance.

My thanks are also due to Mrs Hollings, Miss Joan Wicken and Miss Maureen Pledge for their help with Appendix 2.

Finally, I should like to express my gratitude to all those students in my classes and friends in Africa whose stimulating discussions have so greatly helped to clarify my own ideas.

Responsibility for the opinions of the book rests, of course, with me alone.

PREFACE

DURING the past ten years I have conducted many Extra-Mural courses on the African peoples for the universities of Glasgow and London. I have also given scores of individual lectures on the same subject. It has become increasingly common for students to ask me to recommend a simple outline book which provides the basic facts of the African continent. I have never been able to discover a satisfactory book of this kind; so I decided to write one myself.

I have based this little book on the series of lectures I have given, mostly to adult students. I have attempted to concentrate on those aspects of African problems which seem to have interested my students most, based on a factual foundation, and concentrating on British Africa. I hope that it may prove a useful introduction to a study of Africa for the rapidly increasing number of students of all ages whose interest is attracted towards that continent. Its object is no more than this.

JOHN HATCH

During the past ten years I have conducted many literature courses at ... the Author, penalties for the universities of Glasgow and London. I have also given many of individual courses of the some subject to Blackwood ... study of many to students ... my transactions and simple text book which ... upon the ... days ... After a long time I have used ... to have made strong text of this ...

I have based this little book on the same as of lectures. ... having, however, proposed to club sets as ... I have attempted to reproduce all these aspects of ... as problems ... work needed in preparation ...

...

1912

I: THE AFRICAN BACKGROUND

THE most important single factor dominating the history of the African peoples is the isolation of their continent from outside contact. It was not until the second half of the nineteenth century that any serious attempt was made to discover what lay within the continent and to bring the majority of the African peoples into contact with the rest of the world. Even today, in the mid-twentieth century, much of Africa still remains difficult to penetrate, whilst a large proportion of its peoples remain outside world society. Africa is, indeed, the last continent in the world to be brought into relation with that human development which has been in progress for the last 9,000 years. Whilst the peoples of the other four continents have been engaged in constant social experiments which have brought them ever closer into contact with each other, the African peoples have remained outside and are now, for the first time, beginning to enter the portals of this world-wide human society.

It is therefore both interesting and significant to begin a study of the peoples of the African continent by first spending a few minutes in drawing a broad back-cloth of human development before which we can spotlight the characters of the Africans themselves. If we first paint a picture of human history with broad sweeps of a wide brush we shall be able to see more clearly, distinctly, and relevantly the perspective of African life within it and understand many of those features which profoundly influence the African situation of today. So much of the character and reactions of a people depend upon their relations with others that without some knowledge of the development of these other peoples, much of African character and problems remain inexplicable.

So far as our present knowledge extends, human social life, in the form of settled societies, began about 7,000 B.C. in four river valleys. In Egypt beside the Nile, in Mesopotamia beside the Tigris and Euphrates, in India in the valley of the Indus, and in China alongside the Hwang Ho, man first found an opportunity to develop the earliest forms of co-operation from which the whole of human history has sprung. In each of these areas there was fertile land, naturally irrigated, and protection against the savages and wild animals in the shape of surrounding mountains, deserts, rivers and seas. Here it was possible to work out the first primitive forms of social life, the growing of crops, domestication of animals, production of pottery, the division of time and the first primitive forms of transport. Foresight and organization were stimulated by the necessity to anticipate the seasons, to know when to plough, sow and reap, and to learn how to store for the barren months.

Perhaps the most important of the experiments conducted and of the achievements made was in the field of travel. The natural features, which had proved a protection for these little islands of social life in the midst of a wild and barbarous world, had eventually to be overcome if man was to make contact with his fellow beings in other areas. Indeed, one of the most significant methods of studying human history is to trace the successive means by which, from these first societies, man has steadily overcome the natural boundaries which limited him and harnessed them to his own purposes.

The river which at first was a protection became a communication. These first courageous pioneers of exploration built their primitive coracles, learnt how to float them and steer them, in spite of tides and currents and wind, and, eventually, no doubt after many casualties and many hazards, found their way to the mouths of the rivers. Here they faced a new and much more difficult obstacle. Now they had to adapt what they had learnt from river sailing to mastering the sea.

Note at this point the profound and far-reaching effect of the simple differences in the environmental experience of the various primitive peoples. Take the contrasting experiences of the Nile dwellers and the Chinese. When the primitive Egyptians reached the mouth of the Nile they found waiting for their conquest a convenient inland sea dotted with islands to which they could sail like stepping stones. When the early Chinese reached the mouth of the Hwang Ho they faced a completely different prospect. There they met the mighty Pacific Ocean. Nothing in their previous experience of river sailing could serve them to conquer this entirely different hazard. As a consequence, broadly speaking, whilst the Nile dwellers continued their adventures, eventually bringing into being the great Mediterranean and European civilizations, the Chinese looked mainly inward and remained largely within their own land mass until the nineteenth century when the Europeans sailed in their steamships to make contact with China from the outside.

From these early adventures, settlement, knowledge and experience were gradually spread around the shores of the Mediterranean through the Near and Middle East and into Asia. Some few tenuous lines of communication were always maintained between European and Asian societies even though distance and the hazards of travel kept the two continents in almost complete isolation. Yet these weak communications became increasingly important, not only as a cultural link, but, more importantly, in trade. The goods exchanged had a significance far higher than the quantities involved. Take one example. As the standard of living gradually rose during the Middle Ages, so greater quantities of meat were eaten in Europe. But winter feeding was not yet known and the only preservative was salt. Each autumn therefore, all the cattle, except a few for breeding, had to be killed off. One can imagine what the meat smelt and tasted like by the following spring. It was essential to eat something with it to make it at all palatable and this need was supplied in the form of spices from the East. The demand for such spices was thus essential to the ordinary life of European society and the trade of the merchants between Europe and Asia formed a vital lifeline for European economy.

At the end of the Middle Ages however, by the beginning of the fifteenth century, came the threat that this lifeline would be cut. The southward advance of the Ottoman Turks, who had no interest in European civilization, who were anti-Christian and who destroyed trade wherever they established their power, threatened to cut off all communication between Europe and Asia. But by this time man's ingenuity and adaptability had developed to the point at which he was not prepared to accept the inevitable and he concentrated his thought and energies on finding a way round this impending disaster. The astronomers, the geographers, the sailors and the philosophers combined to search for a new trade route between the two continents. They recalled the heresies of former centuries, the revolutionary suggestion that the world was round rather than flat, that one would not fall off the end of it by travelling southwards along the African coast or westwards across the Atlantic. Portuguese, Spanish and British sailors began to make adventurous expeditions to the north-west and the north-east, farther and farther down the west coast of Africa, searching for a new passage to Asia. Eventually, after a succession of expeditions, at the end of the fifteenth century, Bartholomew Diaz reached the Cape, Vasco da Gama sailed round it into the Indian Ocean and Columbus crossed the Atlantic. Only a few years later Magellan had circumnavigated the world. The Mediterranean era was ended and henceforth there was but one ocean linking the shores of every land and bringing all peoples into contact with each other.

Here starts our own modern historical period, in which the peoples of Europe find the new continents of North America and Australasia, gain power and influence over the old civilizations and the wealth of South America and Asia, and lay the material basis of a world society. Having overcome and brought into his own use the rivers, the seas and the oceans, man now proceeded to devise means of transforming the land masses into means of communication between peoples by the use of roads, railways and the internal combustion engine. He took the further step of conquering and using the air. All those natural elements which originally protected the primitive societies have been transformed from barriers into channels of communication. It needs little imagination to suggest that we have now reached the end of the first period of human history. We have conquered and tamed the natural forces of our universe. We have brought all its shores and waters into our human knowledge and control. We have linked all peoples and we are now on the threshold of a new age in which we leave our universe to go and search for the civilization of other planets.

Yet, from this inclusive movement of humanity over the past 500 years the continent of Africa was excluded until very recently. The European political and religious refugees and those seeking a new society made their way to the Americas and to Australasia, but not to Africa, with the exception of the small settlement made at the Cape in the middle of the seventeenth century. It was not until the twentieth century that any considerable number of European peoples was attracted to this obscure continent.

Two questions are immediately raised by this fact. First, why is it that Europeans were not attracted to Africa? Secondly, why have the Africans never developed to the stage at which they would break out of their own continent and take the initiative in contacting peoples of other countries?

The major explanation for both these queries lies within the field of geography. A glance at a physical map of the African continent will show that it is largely composed of a great central high plateau and a very narrow belt of low coastal land. To this should be added wide areas of swamp and desert. Now the usual way of penetrating a new land has been to sail up the rivers from the coast. In Africa this was impossible, for, within a short distance of the coastline, all the main African rivers become torrents dashing their waters down huge precipices and thus useless for navigation. When to this physical fact is added the widespread European belief in the barbarity of the African peoples, the poverty of the soil and the heavy incidence of tropical diseases, it can be understood that there was little attraction or opportunity for Europeans to explore or settle in the continent.

The answer to the second question is to be found mainly in environment and the influence of climate. In the temperate zones there has always been the stimulant of necessity to force mental development. The estimate of flood seasons; the compilation of calendars, the division of time by year, season, month, week and day; the organization of production and division of labour; the storing of resources and the making of clothes, are all essential elements in the making of life in the temperate regions. In the tropics, on the other hand, and particularly in the heart of a large tropical land mass, subsistence is easy, though a radical increase in the standard of living is very difficult indeed. Without seasons or the necessity for clothes, with no need to store food or plan production, life could be sustained with very little effort or organization. But to raise society out of this static subsistence level into a higher degree of organization and plan an attack upon the basic poverty of the continent essential for a modern standard of living were far beyond the resources developed in such an environment. It required a stimulus, guidance and knowledge of the peoples from the outside with their upbringing in the temperate zones to initiate this revolutionary change in African society.

Whilst it is true that in general the African continent, with the exception of the Mediterranean and Red Sea coastlines, was almost unknown to the rest of the world until modern times, there had been certain contacts which have had a slight effect upon the African peoples. The Greek historian Herodotus recorded that in the year 600 B.C., a Phoenician expedition circumnavigated the continent. ('The sun to the north at midday on their right hand as they sailed westward round the Cape.') Herodotus doubted this story, but it is certainly true that the Phoenicians explored the north African coasts and built trading posts there, including Carthage. They also made some contact in the west reaching as far as the Gambia and possibly even Sierra Leone. The objects of their trade were the same commodities as those which attracted merchants for the next 2,000 years, slaves, gold dust and ivory.

The Greeks also took their cultural impact to North Africa, whilst their Roman successors found in their North African empire an important wealth of agricultural produce, including wheat, olives and a variety of fruits.

In the seventh century A.D. there began a series of invasions which were to bring to North and East Africa their most lasting contact with the outside world until modern times. This emanated from the growth of the militant Mohammedan religion carried by the Arabs through Egypt and North Africa, destroying Greek and Roman influence and introducing the Moslem faith. Meanwhile the Arabs also penetrated down the East African coast as far as Zanzibar and later were to extend even farther south to Sofala in what is now Portuguese East Africa. This Moslem influence has remained in north and east Africa right down to the present day.

The Arabs brought not only their religion to Africa but greatly extended the slave trade. It was from them that came the term 'kaffir', the Arabic word for unbeliever, which has now become a term of abuse for the Negro in southern Africa. It was the Arabs too who introduced rice and sugar plantations from the East to the African tropics.

After the age of discoveries the demand for labour in the Caribbean areas and in the Americas greatly increased the value of the Arab slave trade and stimulated the Western European nations similarly to engage in it. The Portuguese explored the West African coast and eventually rounded the Cape. For a time they drove out the Arabs on the eastern coast, but their weakness at home soon enabled the latter to re-establish their sway. The Portuguese were succeeded by Dutch, English and French, though the latter two nations concentrated mainly on the west littoral.

Apart from some exploration by the Arabs in the east and the Dutch settlement in the Cape in the middle of the seventeenth century, the outsiders were interested only in the coastlines and paid little attention to the interior of the continent. Most of the actual capture of slaves remained in the hands of African chiefs who brought their prisoners to the ports and there exchanged them for paltry goods.

Nevertheless, when the serious contact between the Europeans and the African peoples began in the eighteenth century, this primary factor in the relationship between the two peoples was already established. To the African the European was traditionally a slave trader and slave owner. To the European the African was a pagan and barbarian.

It was with this background that the Dutch expedition set sail in 1652 under Jan van Riebeeck to establish the first European settlement on the continent. This was to be not a colony but simply a half-way station on the route between Holland and the East Indies, where the ships of the Dutch East India Company could put in for water and refreshment. From it has grown the modern Union of South Africa.

The Dutch pioneers no doubt expected to find a land full of hostile barbarians. In fact they found the country empty except for small numbers of Bushmen and Hottentots. At this stage, as we shall see in more detail later, the question of colour did not enter into the consciousness of European or African and this first settlement knew nothing of colour prejudice. All that was recognized, as in any other part of the world, was that those who were outside the Church could be enslaved or killed at will. Yet, very early in the history of the settlement, Hottentots and converted slaves were admitted as members of the community and considerable inter-marriage and many extra-marital unions were known. From them have developed the Cape Coloured people, now over a million strong.

The two first influences therefore in the relations between Europeans and Africans were the tradition of slavery and the importance of the Christian Church. They have remained to this day as central factors in this relationship. Yet, in spite of the fact that the African continent was circumnavigated in 1497, with the exception of the Dutch settlers at the Cape, its interior remained almost unknown until less than one hundred years ago. The main reasons for this continued isolation we have stated above. Even the Cape settlement which was established by Jan van Riebeeck on behalf of the Dutch East India Company in 1652 was less of a colony than of a maritime station. It only gradually expanded as land was taken in for farms and its outposts did not come into direct contact with the tribes of Africa until the eighteenth century. Apart from this, and a few trading posts around the coast, Africa remained almost as remote from Europe as it had been before the voyage of Vasco da Gama.

Exploration within the continent only began towards the end of the eighteenth century. Its main purpose was to discover the sources of the Niger and the Nile. In 1788 the African Association of London was founded to encourage African exploration and its most famous explorer, Mungo Park, made a series of ventures around the turn of the century in West Africa. In the 1820s an expedition crossed the Sahara and made contact with Timbuc-tu and Lake Chad. This work was carried on by the German, Dr Barth, particularly in the Sudan, but it was left to David Living-

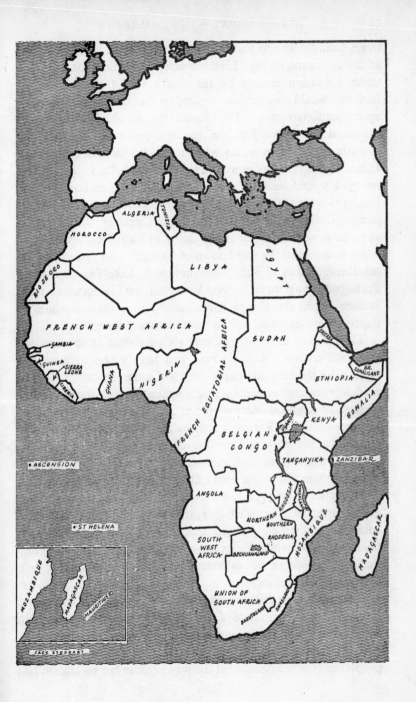

stone, John Speke and Richard Burton to penetrate the real heart of the continent. It was Livingstone's firm belief that the slave trade, organized mainly by the Arabs with the assistance of Africans, would only be destroyed when the continent was opened up to legitimate trade. He crossed the Kalahari in 1849 and examined the upper Zambezi reaches, eventually reaching the Atlantic coast. It was on his way back across the continent to the Indian Ocean that he discovered the Victoria Falls. In 1858 he set out on a second series of explorations under the authority of the British Government and made his way to Lake Nyasa. On his last journey, during which occurred his famous meeting with Stanley in 1871, he penetrated as far as the shores of Lake Tanganyika.

By now something was known of the great lake systems of the continent. Speke and Burton had discovered Lake Tanganyika and Speke got through as far as Lake Victoria. After Livingstone's death Stanley traced the Congo River and by now vague outlines of Central, East and West Africa were becoming recognized.

The paths of the explorers were soon followed by the missionaries and traders. Slave trading, still largely organized by the Arabs with the help and participation of some African chiefs, was gradually fought and killed. The missions brought the first glimmerings of learning, some medicine and the Bible, though often their application of European standards and habits to the primitive societies produced tragic results. Customs which to Europeans appeared immoral or barbaric were often like the sap of a tree. Without them the whole social life of the society was destroyed. The practice of polygamy, for instance; lobola, or the custom of giving cattle to the bride's father; the dances and music of African tribes, were often condemned and, where possible, destroyed by the missionaries whose European religious values were so absolute that they prevented an understanding of the significance of such elements of African society.

Meanwhile, the traders and eventually commercial companies recognized the importance of this new continent to the European commercial world. By the second half of the nineteenth century the effects of the industrial revolution had begun to be evident to many peoples of Europe. Britain led the way because her revolution had taken place before that of any other European country and its effects were correspondingly more severe. Yet, it was not long before Germany, France, Belgium and, to a lesser extent, Portugal, were following the same path.

The industrial revolution removed large numbers of people who previously had been producing their own food, clothing and other necessities into the factories, mines and workshops of the new towns. The agricultural revolution which accompanied that in industry increased the nation's food production, but not sufficiently to provide the cheap food necessary for the large and rapidly increasing urban population. The new factory aids turned out masses of cheap textile goods, but they required raw materials which could not be found in Britain nor in the European continent. At the same time the rapidly increased mass production of various manufactured goods eventually outstripped the purchasing ability of the home population and manufacturers were tempted to search for fresh and profitable markets abroad.

Consequently, the latter part of the nineteenth century gave colonial expansion a new significance to the European nations. They saw the possibility in comparatively virgin lands of securing cheap food for the industrial workers, raw materials like cotton, timber and rubber for their factories, and new customers who would buy their goods. Moreover, the peoples of the colonies seemed to provide them with an inexhaustible supply of completely unorganized workers whose wages would be almost negligible. Slavery might be killed, but forced labour and virtual serfdom could easily take its place.

As the industrial race became more bitter in Europe, so there developed an added incentive to gain colonial possessions which could offset the newly developing demands of European trade unionists, increase the national industrial potential in competition with neighbour states, and offer strategic advantages in the event of warfare. Inevitably, in this kind of Empire building, the variety of motives was quickly canalized into that of national prestige. The possession of empires raised national power and became a national pride. Eventually, it was itself a cause of increased tension between the European imperial states.

The opening up of Africa to Europe, therefore, was more conditioned by European than by African factors. Boundaries were drawn in the African continent with no relation to African societies, to economic units or geography. European political power determined European imperial influence. Portugal, for example, was prevented by Britain from joining her East and West African colonies because of Britain's ambition to develop northwards from South Africa. Britain was able to do this simply because she was so much more powerful than Portugal in Europe.

Meanwhile, the industrial systems of the European powers continued to reap the benefit of economic and human exploitation in the African continent. Control was in the hands of the minority European capitalists, yet benefits were gained by the whole population. In Britain the gradual rise in the standard of living of the working class, which by the end of the century had reached a higher point than that of any other people, was largely made possible by the exploitation of colonial and semi-colonial peoples. Indeed, it is no exaggeration to suggest that much of the freedom from class warfare in Britain, which allowed the gradual but steady development of political democracy, was only possible because the ruling class was able to pass on economic improvement and political and social reforms gained from colonial exploitation.

African history in the second half of the nineteenth century was therefore largely determined in Europe. What of the people with whom these first European pioneers in Africa came into contact? In a book of this size it is, of course, impossible to attempt any profound analysis of the differences amongst African peoples, but it is as well to note that those differences are at least as great as the varying features found amongst European or Asian peoples. Some broad divisions of the African peoples can however be drawn and we can begin by pointing out that the vast majority of African peoples comes within the bounds of the negroid race.

The negroid peoples may be divided into four main categories. First, there are the Bushmen, Pygmies and Hottentots who are amongst the least socially developed of African communities. Bushmen were found in the Cape when the Dutch first settled there in the seventeenth century. They are short people with tufty hair and wrinkled yellowish skin. They are mainly hunters and refused to be assimilated into the Cape Settlement. A few of them still exist in the Northern Cape and in South-West Africa, but they are today almost extinct.

The Pygmies are also hunters and are found mainly in the tropical forests of the equatorial regions. They are even shorter than the Bushmen, usually about 4 ft 6 in high, and they also have never been assimilated into European society.

It was the Hottentots who mostly encountered the early settlers in the Cape and many of them became servants within the Settlement. They found European life easier to tolerate than did the more primitive Bushmen, and some of them even inter-married or had extra-marital relations with Europeans, forming the basis of the later Cape Coloured population. A few pure Hottentots still remain in South-West Africa.

The second category of negroid peoples is variously known as Guinea or Sudanese negroes. These form the majority of the West African population, are fairly tall, very dark-skinned, with woolly hair, broad noses and thick lips. They were mainly cultivators rather than pasturalists, growing oil palms, beans and millet, and inhabited the West African forests right across to the Sudan. Considerable mixture had, of course, taken place within these people, particularly as a result of the Hamite invasions from the Sahara.

The third classification of people is called the Bantu, which is a word variously used in different parts of the continent. Sometimes it is used to describe languages, at others the people, though originally it simply meant human beings. The Bantu negroes occupy at least one-third of the African continent, including most of southern Africa. They might be subdivided into the Eastern Bantu, living between Uganda and the Zambezi, Southern Bantu in South Africa, and the Central Bantu of central and west-central Africa. They are largely a cattle-owning people and, though they speak different languages, these are really dialects derived from a common tongue. Similarly common social and cultural traits are to be observed amongst all their people.

Finally, there are the Hamitic negroid people of eastern Africa, formed through the crossing of Hamites and negroes. Their features vary, but generally the mixture is to be observed by the lighter complexion and finer facial characteristics of the Hamites and the woolly hair of the negro. Most of them are a pastoral people.

It may be noted at the same time that there are two non-negroid peoples in northern Africa, the Hamites and the Semites. The Hamitic peoples lived along the Mediterranean coast and in the Sahara before the Arab invasions of northern Africa, and although the culture and religion of the Arabs became dominant in this area, the invasions had little effect on the racial characteristics of the people. It is the Arabs who present the main Semitic features of the North African population and their influence has been extended down the East African coast at least as far as Zanzibar. It was they who were principally responsible for bringing the Mohammedan religion to North, West and East Africa, where it still remains a dominant influence in each of these societies.

These are the broad classifications of the African peoples. There has of course been a great deal of inter-mixture amongst them and some introduction of non-African bloods. Thus today wide varieties are to be seen amongst the people of different parts of the continent.

Variety is also seen in social life. South of the Sahara in particular, the African negro may be a primitive hunter, though few of these still survive, a member of a tribe, a citizen of a new nation or a detribalized urban worker. Where permanent European settlement has been difficult or impossible African society is usually developing towards a national consciousness as in West Africa or Uganda and is normally marked by some progress towards western political forms. Where the Europeans have settled, however, different and often contrary social patterns have evolved. The tribal system of life is usually maintained where the European influence has not penetrated too deeply or it may be deliberately maintained by European rule. At the same time the activities of the European settlers tend to break down tribal society even despite the intentions and policies of the Europeans. In some parts of central Africa, for example, tribes have been left virtually intact, whilst in

South Africa specific provision has been made for areas to be allocated to the continuation of tribal life. It is indeed the defined policy of the South African Government to maintain, strengthen and even reimpose a tribal pattern of life on the African population. Yet, first by taking land, then by confining the tribe to a limited area, thus ending its nomadic habits, and finally by creating a demand for labour, the white man has unwittingly torpedoed the foundations of tribalism. In spite of their declared policy, the South African Nationalists have been unable to prevent their white community from continuing to recruit African labour from the tribal reserves to serve them on farms, in domestic service, in the mines, and in industry. There has inevitably grown up an urban African community which gradually loses its contact with tribal origins.

At the same time the white man's medicine has brought about steady increases in population which cannot be maintained within the tribal community on their limited land allocation. This in its turn has forced increasing numbers of Africans to migrate to the urban areas adding to the breaking up of tribalism.

The peoples of Africa are thus living in an age of deep disturbance, of transition from tribal society to new and unknown forms of social life. Varying influences are to be seen in different parts of the continent, often with very different results. Political and economic groupings are taking place, some transitory, others of longer duration, forming constantly changing kaleidoscopic patterns across the continent. What is written today may be an anachronism tomorrow. The understanding of Africa and Africans should therefore start from a knowledge of history and background, from an attempt to recognize the permanent scenery before which these varying acts are being played out. For every scene in the African drama affects and is related to each of the others, whilst the whole dynamic play and its players are rapidly becoming of dramatic significance to the world outside their own continental stage.

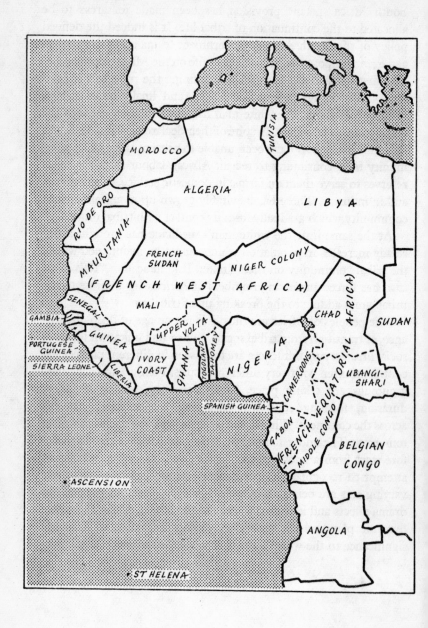

II: BRITISH WEST AFRICA

SOME Europeans look at the development of white nationalism in South Africa with hesitant admiration. Many more Africans regard it with fear and anger. These feelings are completely reversed when whites and blacks look towards West Africa. It is often said that the white nationalism of the Union is counterpoised against West African black nationalism, with its spearheads in Ghana and Nigeria. This judgement is not quite accurate. It is true that the Afrikaners of the Union are trying to build a new nation. Their efforts, therefore, can justly be described as nationalistic. It is also true that most white people living in Africa feel something in common with each other through the similarity of their skin colour. This is more accurately described as a form of white racialism.

The Africans, however, take a different position. Some degree of black racialism is latent amongst many of them—at least partly as an instinctive reaction to the racial communalism of the dominant white communities. To a degree all black Africans feel that they have something in common, but this is not yet a powerful continental emotion. It is felt rather as a form of resistance to the aliens who have come from outside the African continent, taken the land, and imposed their own form of society. This emotion is growing and can be expected to increase rapidly as Africans become more socially conscious, unless the Europeans and Asians quickly drop their colour consciousness and open their doors to people regardless of race or colour.

Nationalism, however, hardly exists amongst Africans as yet. This is hardly surprising, for almost the whole of the African continent is arbitrarily divided solely according to European considerations. The political boundaries of Africa were drawn by the European states during the period of African colonization. They were fixed according to the power and interests of the various

European imperialists. These boundaries are, therefore, more closely related to the nineteenth century balance of power in Europe than to the realities of African life. The political frontiers have no relation to the geography, economics or tribal organization of Africans. In many cases they cut right across tribal communities and economic units.

Within the present African states, therefore, very little common history, tradition, custom or even language exist amongst the African peoples themselves. Even in Ghana, where Dr Kwame Nkrumah and his party have been trying to instil a spirit of Ghanaian nationalism, this unifying nationalist emotion is constantly weakened by rivalries and suspicions based partly on a sense of loyalty to the different tribes.

It is more accurate, therefore, to recognize in the Africa of today a growth of the rival forces of black and white racialism. Africans all over the continent increasingly resent, not the presence, but the privilege and the domination of the immigrant communities. The white racialists are attempting to preserve their privileged position and their power to control the development of the continent. Whilst the white racialists are led by the European community of South Africa, the spirit of racial independence spreading amongst black Africans looks to Ghana and Nigeria for leadership.

It is the still vague continental emotion of black comradeship which has led Africans from all over the continent to watch with expectant hope the progress of Ghana towards independence. 'Gold Coastism' has become a militant term for all Africans throughout the continent. They want to believe that they can emulate the rapid progress towards independent African statehood which has marked the recent history of Ghana. At the same time, the fear that this development will inspire Africans in other countries to demand the same control over their own affairs has led 'Gold Coastism' to be viewed with fear and abhorrence by a large proportion of the white people who have settled in the continent.

*   *   *   *   *

West Africa has the longest contact with the outside world of any area south of the Sahara. The age-old caravans crossed the great desert and brought trade from the east to the northern areas of the West African bulge. Cities, markets and a certain social organization grew up, giving this area a wealth of known African history which does not exist farther south. This contact also brought with it the northerners' religion, for the Moors, who took Mohammedanism across North Africa and into Europe, also found their way southwards into West Africa. As a consequence, in the northern areas of such countries as Nigeria and Niger, experience of trade and social contact, strength of organization and the well established Moslem religion have provided the people with a continuity and cohesion unknown in most parts of Africa.

It was also West Africa which received the first contact from the European maritime explorers of the fifteenth century. Portuguese first settled in West Africa in 1471 and, although penetration from the coast inland was never considerable until the nineteenth century, trading contact has been maintained with this part of Africa ever since. The trade in slaves was of particular importance, and for four centuries West Africa remained the principal source of the slave trade of the world. It is estimated that about 100,000 slaves a year were exported from the west coast in the second half of the eighteenth century. The English, French, Spanish, Portuguese, Dutch, and Danes all took part in this trade.

Two principal factors resulted from this history. The first was that the relation between European and African became deeply rooted on a basis of slave trader and slave. The second was that the people of the coastal area became much more sophisticated and detribalized than those of the interior. This second feature was considerably strengthened after the abolition of slavery, when liberated slaves were taken back from England and America to the coastal areas of Sierra Leone and Liberia. The ex-slaves had become almost completely detribalized and had an experience quite different from those who had avoided slavery and remained at home. The repatriates formed a new class after their return. Down to the present day the difference between the coastal people and those of the interior is still strongly noticeable throughout West Africa and often marked by considerable hostility.

*   *   *   *   *

In spite of the historical relationship of slavery, British West Africa demonstrates one of the healthiest examples of race relations in the continent. Although white superiority and colour prejudice have often been shown in the past, today very little colour prejudice remains in any of these territories. Indeed, Europeans are increasingly welcomed, as are citizens of other continents. The only condition for the acceptance of immigrants is they should come with the purpose of contributing to the development of these new countries. In particular, they are welcomed if they will come to pass on their knowledge to Africans, who can then, in their turn, teach their fellow-countrymen.

The main reason for the difference in race relationships between West Africa and most of the rest of the continent is the virtual absence of white settlers from this area. The unhealthy climate proved disastrous to European life in previous ages, and, even with the aids of modern science, it is still unsuitable for permanent European settlement. As a result, there is no racial competition for land or for skilled employment, and no organized alien political groups to seek domination. Europeans who go to West Africa are usually administrators or traders, or the teachers of some skills, and all these are variously welcomed.

It is partly as a result of this absence of racial conflict that the British West African states have made such rapid advances in constitutional development, particularly since 1945. Indeed, members of one Nigerian political party wear a badge with a mosquito painted on it, symbolizing their thankfulness that the presence of this insect has kept away European settlers and thus facilitated African political progress.

It is difficult to estimate just what circumstances and influences produced political advance in any society. British colonial policy since 1839 has been based vaguely on the supposition that eventually colonial peoples should rule themselves. This principle led to the eventual establishment of the white dominions as independent members of the Commonwealth. Only more recently has it been held to apply in a similar manner to the non-white colonies. Again, there has been constant pressure in recent times by various political groups in Britain to speed up the process of granting self-government. At the same time, one wonders to what extent the swift developments towards self-government seen in Ghana and Nigeria over recent years stem from the riots in Accra of 1948 and those in Enugu in the following year. Both these disorders brought the Gold Coast and Nigeria to the notice of British and world opinion. They were at least partly due to nationalist political movements, eventually resulting in enhanced political influence for their leaders. Perhaps the most we can say is that the complementary pressure of anti-imperialism in Britain and political nationalism in the colonies is a significant combination. Its significance emerged into political practice when a small cadre of African politicians like Nkrumah, Awolowo, Azikiwe took the opportunities offered to West Africans to gain education and experience in Europe and America, fitted themselves for leadership, and seized the occasion to organize their people behind national policies.

For convenience and clarity we may now describe briefly the position in each of the four British West African colonies. Each of them demonstrates different stages of the advance towards self-government and the problems which are met on this road.

The Gambia

The Gambia is a small, narrow territory, situated on each side of the River Gambia. Its width varies between fifteen and thirty miles on each side of the river, totalling in all just over 4,000 sq miles. Two hundred and eighty-nine thousand people live here, mainly engaged in the growing of ground nuts. The country is divided into the coastal Colony, ruled directly by the British Colonial Office, and the inland Protectorate, which is administered by Britain as the protecting power. Nine out of ten people in the Gambia live in the Protectorate, and most of them are Moslems.

In 1946 elections were first introduced, and seven years later it was judged that they had been conducted so successfully that a new constitution was introduced. Under this constitution elected members were given a majority rule; fourteen of the members of the Legislative Council are elected, two are nominated, and the other five are official members. The Executive Council, which is the real government of the territory, consists of the Governor, five official members, and seven unofficial members, who come from the legislature. Certain government departments have now been taken over by ministers from within the executive.

Thus the Gambia is already under the majority influence of members elected by and responsible to the people. Perhaps the two major obstacles to constitutional advance towards complete self-government are the smallness of the territory and the contrast between the Colony and the Protectorate. It is doubtful whether such a tiny territory could ever become completely viable as an independent state. Meanwhile, the difference between the two sections of the Gambia is reflected in the fact that, whereas all persons over 25 in the Colony have the right to vote, the more backward Protectorate still uses the electoral college system for its elections.

Sierra Leone

Sierra Leone has some similarities with the Gambia, though, of course, it is very much larger. It has a population of over two million people, again divided between the coastal Colony and the interior Protectorate. People of the Colony are largely descended from repatriated slaves and are now known as Creoles. They are generally more advanced than those of the interior, and certainly consider themselves to be much superior. So far they have managed to maintain a political influence much greater than their numbers alone warrant. Although there are only about 30,000 real Creoles, the Colony elects fourteen of the fifty-one elected members to the House of Representatives.

It is interesting to note here that even in an all-black society strong social prejudices can exist which are reflected in the economic and political life of the country. Although colour does not enter into this situation, there are some similarities between the attitude of the Creoles in Sierra Leone towards the more primitive people of the interior, and that of the white settlers towards Africans in other parts of the continent.

It was in 1951 that for the first time an unofficial majority was introduced into the Legislative Council. Twenty-one of the thirty-one members were elected, seven in the Colony and fourteen in the

Protectorate. The Colony elected its members directly, but of the fourteen from the Protectorate, twelve were chosen by District Councils and two by the Protectorate Assembly. There were also seven ex-officio members of the Assembly, along with two unofficial members who were nominated by the government to represent trade and commerce, and one vice-president, who acted as Speaker.

In 1957 the old thirty-two-member Legislative Council was replaced by a House of Representatives of fifty-one elected members, two nominated members without voting powers and four ex-officio members and a Speaker. The franchise was also extended to include virtually all adult men and women taxpayers or property owners.

In the Executive Council nine of the fourteen members were appointed from the elected members of the House of Representatives. These nine are all Ministers.

In August 1958 the first Cabinet, led by a Premier, was formed. The Premier was Dr M. A. S. Margai. The Governor now had to consult the Government and act on its advice, subject to his ultimate responsibility for peace and good government. He retained responsibility for external affairs, internal security, police and public services, but all other responsibilities have been passed over to the Government.

Shortly after this new constitutional development, Dr Margai's brother, who had been Chairman of the Sierra Leone People's Party, supporting the Government, announced that a new party was to be formed called the People's National Party. It included other Government supporters and may take a somewhat more progressive line than that of the Government.

Sierra Leone seems likely to press on towards independence in the next few years. There have previously been doubts as to whether the country is big enough or sufficiently populated to maintain an independent state. Yet now that French Guinea has shown the way the Sierra Leone leaders are likely to follow suit. Whether it will be possible to sustain anything like genuine statehood and establish a progressive society is still to be proved. It may well be that Sierra Leone will be one of the smaller territories looking with particular interest on the proposals to set up some form of West African Federation. This wider association would lend her people more hope of establishing a form of society in which they could reasonably expect the services and standards of modern life.

The division between the Colony and the Protectorate is reflected again in the political organizations which have grown up. The Sierra Leone Peoples Party, at present the majority party, is in office, and it is from this party that the ministers are drawn. It secures its main support from the Protectorate, and its policy is to secure a united country. On the other hand, the National Council of Sierra Leone consisted almost entirely of Creoles from Freetown, and it is this party which is leading the demand for Creole privilege and a representation from the Colony greater than is warranted by its population. Recently there has also been formed a Sierra Leone Labour Party, which has so far not had the opportunity of showing its strength. It is perhaps significant, however, that this Labour Party was associated with the National Council in agitating against the growth of a constitution which would spread representation more democratically amongst the whole population.

The principal products of Sierra Leone are palm extracts, iron ore and diamonds. In some parts of the country, particularly in the Protectorate, diamonds are found very readily, and this has led to a great deal of illicit diamond mining and trading, often resulting in the seduction of many rural workers from their employment into the search for quick wealth.

Nigeria

Nigeria is the largest British dependency in the colonial empire. It is four times as large as the United Kingdom, and its population of thirty-two million is almost as great as that of the whole of the rest of the colonial territories.

Nigerians, however, have very little common history. It was only as late as 1914 that the country was first administered as a single unit, and consequently, even today, loyalties tend to be stronger towards tribes and regions than to a central state. This has led to the development of a federal as opposed to a unitary constitution.

The new constitution of 1946 divided the country into three legislative regions, with a central assembly superimposed. These three regions, North, East and West, roughly corresponded to the areas inhabited by the three main tribes, Hausa, Ibo and Yoruba, though there are many subdivisions of these tribal groups and some other tribes outside this general grouping. The 1946 constitution gave each region a council, with a legislature at the centre also. It was originally intended that the constitution should last for nine years, but by 1948 the Governor was so satisfied with the progress which had been made that he announced that he was prepared to consider further changes in 1950-1951. Accordingly a select committee of the Legislative Council was formed to initiate a new constitution, and it is significant to note that this committee proposed greatly increased powers for the regions. Two years after the constitution came into operation in 1951, however, the Nigerian leaders expressed themselves as dissatisfied with the powers accorded to the regions and another conference took place to discuss increasing regional powers at the expense of the central government. A new constitution was devised, which came into force in 1954. At the same time, the British Government declared that a further constitutional conference would be held in 1956, when full self-government for those subjects which are regional responsibilities would be granted to any region which desired it. On account of the dispute in the Eastern Region, however, this conference was postponed until 1957.

Under the 1954 constitution, each region had its own constitution and the differences between them reflected the various political outlooks. In the North, the legislature consisted of two Houses, a House of Chiefs and a House of Assembly. In the Assembly there was a Speaker, 131 elected members, four officials, and five special members representing various interests and communities. Franchise was confined to men, reflecting the strong Moslem tradition, and elections were conducted through electoral colleges. The Executive Council was composed of the Governor, who acted as President, three officials, and thirteen ministers, one of whom was the Premier. Provision was also made for some of these ministers to be drawn from the House of Chiefs.

The West also had a House of Chiefs and an Assembly. The latter consisted of a Speaker, eighty elected members, and three special members. Full adult suffrage operates in this region. The Executive was composed of the Governor, who acted as President, and nine ministers, one of whom was Premier, with provision for some of the ministers to be drawn from the Chiefs.

In the East, the constitution was somewhat simpler, consisting only of a single House, the House of Assembly, with a Speaker and eighty-four members elected on adult suffrage. The Executive again had the Governor as President, with nine ministers, including the Premier, drawn from the elected members of the Assembly.

In addition to the regional Parliaments, Nigeria also has a federal legislature, known as the House of Representatives. This consisted of a Speaker, three official members, six special members, and 184 elected members. Of the latter, ninety-two were elected in the Northern Region, forty-two each in the West and East, six from the Southern Cameroons and two from the municipality of Lagos. Lagos is the federal capital, although it is situated in the Western Region which has agitated strongly to retain it as an integral part of the region. The same method of elections is employed in each region as for the elections to the regional Parliaments.

The federal Executive consisted of a Council of Ministers, three from each region, and one from the Southern Cameroons.

As might be expected in these circumstances, the development of political parties has been based mainly upon the regions. In the North, the main party is the Northern People's Congress, led by the Sardauna of Sokoto, who is the regional Premier. It is opposed by the Northern Elements Progressive Union, an organization largely led by young westernized politicians who are pressing for more democratic elections and for a break in the strong traditional control of the Moslem emirs. In the West, the Action Group led by the Premier, Dr Awolowo, is the majority party, although there have been a number of break-aways, usually based upon personalities. In the East, the National Council of Nigeria and the Cameroons is led by Dr Azikiwe, widely known as 'Zik'.

It is difficult at present to discern any general political policy amongst these parties, for most of them are, for the time being, concerned with the domestic problems of administration and with local issues. Each of them, however, is anxious to strengthen the powers of their respective regional governments. The N.C.N.C. approaches most nearly to a national party, and has considerable influence in the other two regions. Other parties, including a new Nigerian Labour Party, have been formed, but none of them so far can challenge the strength of those already established.

The first federal elections were held in 1954, and in the North and East the ruling parties also won the federal elections in their regions. In the West, however, Dr Azikiwe's N.C.N.C. gained a larger number of seats than Dr Awolowo's Action Group. When the Governor-General came to appoint his federal Council of Ministers at the beginning of 1955, therefore, he was faced with a dilemma. The constitution left him either to appoint a cabinet on the advice of the leader of the majority party, or, if there were no such majority, on the recommendation of the leader of the federal majority parties in each region. Because of the preponderance of the North the N.P.C. held the majority of the seats in the House of Representatives, but could not command an absolute majority over all other parties. The Governor-General, therefore, decided to appoint three ministers from each region. As the N.C.N.C. held a majority in both the East and the West, Dr Azikiwe's party was given six of the ten ministerial appointments, the N.P.C. three and the Cameroons one.

The major problem facing Nigeria, therefore, still remains the relationship between the regions and the federal state. Is Nigeria to become a great new central state, strongly influential in the affairs of the African continent, or is it to be divided virtually into three separate states ? The Northern Region contains more than half the population of the country, with nearly 17 million people; the East, with a population of about 8 million, is comparatively poor, but many of its Ibo people go to work as clerks and officials in the other regions; the West is, at present, the wealthiest, though its population of 6½ million is the smallest. The North, however, is much more backward than the other two regions; it is mainly dominated by Moslem tradition and its feudal emirs still continue to control much of the life of their people. Yet the North is cut off from the sea and its progress would be severely impeded if it were to be separated from the other two regions. Meanwhile, of course, the whole country, which, in spite of its large population, is still meagrely developed and very poor, has to bear the cost of four administrations. It may be that this federal structure will become permanent. Certainly, at present, people in Nigeria look much more often to their regional than to their federal government, and their loyalties are more strongly rooted in their regions. Though a unitary Nigerian state is not on the horizon and may never appear, very important developments occurred in 1957. In the first place, the Federal Assembly unanimously approved a motion asking for complete Nigerian independence in 1959. This was a tremendous step forward. Although the Eastern and Western Regions had adopted such a policy for some time the North had remained adamant in opposing the complete removal of British control. Now, however, the Northern representatives took the courageous step of dropping their previous opposition and joining with their fellow members from the South in naming 1959 as independence year.

These were the problems faced by the Constitutional Conference which met in May 1957. After a month's deliberations it adjourned until the end of September 1958, eventually concluding its work in the following month.

This Conference achieved spectacular results. Not only did it study and resolve the most complicated problems relating to the regions and their relations with the Federation; even more remarkable, Nigeria's various and contrasting leaders came to a joint agreement on basic principles which will allow Nigeria to become an independent state in 1960. The instincts of division which were so evident in the past were set aside in the search for formulae which would allow them the emergence of the new state. This was a triumph of tolerance in negotiations shared between the Colonial Secretary, Mr Lennox-Boyd, who acted as Chairman, the Federal Prime Minister, the Hon. Alhaji Abubakar Tafawa Balewa, the three regional Prime Ministers, the Sardauna of Sokoto, Dr Awolowo and Dr Azikiwe, and the Prime Minister of the Southern Cameroons, Dr E. M. Endeley.

In the 1957 session of the Conference both the Eastern and Western Regions claimed and were granted regional self-government. The effect of this was to remove from the Governors of the two regions almost all their reserve powers and their right to preside in the Executive Councils. The Northerners did not feel themselves ready for full self-government and still felt some fears of the influence in their regional administration of the better educated Southerners. They decided to delay regional self-government until 1959.

During this earlier session two changes were made in the Federal Government. Although the Governor-General remained as president and retained his reserve powers, the ex-officio members of the Council of Ministers were removed. A Federal Prime Minister was appointed for the first time on 30 August, and he immediately formed a national Government, bringing two members of the Action Group into his Council.

The Colonial Secretary did not agree that he could accept the claim for federal independence by 1959, but promised that if after the next federal elections a request were made for independence in 1960 the British Government would then fix an independence date. Federal electoral law was to be uniform throughout the regions, except that women were still to be excluded from the franchise in the North because of traditional Moslem custom. Second chambers were to be introduced in the Federation, in the Eastern Region, and in the Southern Cameroons. Constitutional progress was to be speeded up in order to catch up with the other regions through the introduction of a premier, a majority of unofficial members in the Executive Council, and a larger House of Assembly.

Finally, the Conference set up a number of commissions to deal with the problems of minorities, the delimitation of federal constituencies, and the allocation of revenue between the Federation and regions. The reports of these commissions were to be considered when the Conference resumed its sittings.

When the 1957 session adjourned a slight note of bitterness was expressed by the leaders, who had staked much on securing agreement for a declaration of independence. This feeling may

have had a salutary influence, for, during the fifteen months before
the Conference resumed, greater efforts than ever previously were
made to secure national unity and the spirit of compromise
essential to a united demand for an independence date. Much
was achieved during this interim period. A Federal Prime Minister
was appointed, with a national Government reflecting national
unity and with no British representative in his Council other than
the Governor-General. The Eastern and Western regions attained
full self-government; the Northern Region declared March 1959
to be its date for self-government. The ministerial system was
extended to the Southern Cameroons. 2 April 1960 was agreed
in Nigeria as the date for national independence.

Meanwhile the reports of the commissions were published,
proposing solutions to some of the thorniest problems to be faced
in constituting the new state. The most controversial was that on
minorities. The three big regions were largely dominated by the
main tribes in each; Hausa in the North, Ibo in the East and Yoruba
in the West. Smaller tribal groups felt the danger of oppression
and agitated for the creation of new states corresponding to their
communities. There was also some feeling in the Western Region
that Yoruba districts in the North should be added to the West.

Further political disturbances had also occurred in the East.
Dr Azikiwe has often in the past had to face revolts against his
dominant position in the N.C.N.C. He has always succeeded in
overcoming them by representing himself as the leader of the
masses. On this occasion, however, he was faced with a more
serious revolt, arising partly from the demand that he implement
his promise of universal free education for the children of his
region. This was followed by an attempt by leading members of
his own party, including N.C.N.C. Federal Ministers, Dr K. O.
Mbadiwe and Chief K. Balogun, to overthrow him. The rebels,
however were expelled from the N.C.N.C. and formed a new
party which they called the Democratic Party of Nigeria and the
Cameroons.

When the Constitutional Conference resumed in September
1958, in spite of various political manoeuvres and rumours of
alliances and counter-alliances between the three main regional

parties, a sense of unified momentum had been created. This enabled the three regional leaders together with the Federal Prime Minister and the Premier of the Southern Cameroons to subordinate their personal or regional ambitions to the common aim of laying the foundations for independence. They therefore found it possible to agree on the controversial issue of minority protection, setting aside claims for new states and boundary revisions, but making provision for further consideration in the future. It is likely, for instance, that Dr Awolowo will make this claim an important feature of his election appeal in the Federal general election of 1959. It was also possible to reach agreement on the other vexed problem of police control. A single force is to be created under an inspector-general responsible to the Federal Government. In each region contingents will be recruited, with some degree of control exercised by the regional governments. The fiscal and electoral arrangements were agreed in the expectation that the North will move gradually towards the introduction of women to franchise rights. Assuming that the people of the Southern Cameroons approve at a referendum, its constitution will be amended and it will attain the status of a fully self-governing region within an independent Nigeria. The division of powers between the regions and the Federation has also been laid down.

Finally, and most important, the Secretary of State, whilst not accepting that Nigeria will be ready for independence on 2 April, 1960, nevertheless agreed that 1960 is a reasonable year for the attainment of independence and fixed 1 October as the date on which the new state will be born.

Thus in 1960 Nigeria will become an independent African state and a full member of the Commonwealth. This event will be of momentous significance for the whole African continent. Nigeria, with a population of 32 million and likely to increase steadily, is by far the largest state in the continent. It will also be the fourth largest state in the Commonwealth.

It is bound to be some time before this great state realizes all its potential and makes a profound impression on African and international life. Yet its leaders combine the profundity of the ancient world with the width of knowledge drawn from the modern. It is certain that Nigerian opinion, and ideas yet to be born within this new nation, will have a steadily increasing impact on the whole African continent. So far British black Africa has looked more to Ghana than to Nigeria for its inspiration. Much of the future will depend on the relations between these two West African states and their leaders. Neither any other people in the continent nor the European powers will ever again be able to ignore the views of the Nigerians. In the new age which is so rapidly awakening for the African peoples, the state of Nigeria is likely to become the major influence and it is satisfying to know that racialism hardly exists amongst its people, whilst, on the other hand, they have a profound regard for the Commonwealth. These facts could be decisive in the continent.

Ghana

Ghana was born on 6 March 1957. Its birth was celebrated by Africans throughout the continent as a triumph for the principle of African self-rule and a proof of its efficacy. All over the continent Africans saw in the birth of Ghana a defeat for European colonization and a blow at the dogma of South Africans and racialistic white settlers that the black man is incapable of ruling himself and conducting good government. Beyond Africa, too, in Asia and in the Caribbean the birth of this state was heralded with enthusiasm.

At the same time the emergence of Ghana to statehood was not accompanied by anti-white racial feelings. Many Britishers, some of whom have played an important part in the creation of an independent Ghana, were honoured guests at the celebrations in Accra. Dr Nkrumah and his government also made it clear that they intended to retain their membership of the Commonwealth and when the new Prime Minister attended his first Commonwealth Prime Ministers Conference in London in June 1957, he was given a great welcome. Political commentators in Britain and other parts of the Commonwealth were not slow to recognize the significance of the fact that for the first time a state ruled by Africans had entered the circle of independent members of the Commonwealth. The independence of India, Pakistan and Ceylon in 1947 and 1948 had changed the character of Commonwealth membership from that of a white man's club into that of a genuine multi-racial comity of nations. The appearance of Ghana developed that character still further by adding Africans to the Asians, Europeans and European-descendants already members.

It is important, therefore, to examine something of the recent history which has so quickly changed this colony into an independent state.

Ghana has set the pace for constitutional development in British Africa since the Second World War. In 1946, under the terms of the Burns constitution, the first Legislative Council in British Africa with a majority of African members was set up. In 1948 its government accepted a large proportion of responsibility for its own finance. In 1949 Mr E. C. Quist became the first African president of the Legislative Assembly. A commission of inquiry, appointed to investigate the riots of 1948, recommended an increase in the membership of the Legislative Council and greater African responsibility in the Executive. This was followed by the appointment in 1948 of a representative all-African committee under an African judge, Mr Coussey, to examine the whole constitutional position. The report of this committee formed the basis for the new constitution which came into effect in February 1951. The Legislative Assembly was now largely composed of members elected directly by the people. In the following year a cabinet was appointed, with an African Prime Minister and ministers approved by the assembly in charge of government departments. For the first time the real powers of government had passed into the hands of Africans.

Once such steps have been taken and a genuine transfer of power has begun, there can be no turning back. The only danger of a reversal or pause in this process is the failure of the new administrators or the seizure of power by extremists with the object of eliminating their opponents. Neither of these disasters has occurred in Ghana. It is true that Dr Kwame Nkrumah was serving a term of imprisonment on a charge of sedition when he was released in 1951 in order to take charge of government business. But Nkrumah and his supporters who were in gaol, many of whom have played a leading part in public life since, were not extremists. They were nationalists who had been imprisoned for the part they were playing in the agitation to secure independence and because of the fear that their methods would lead to violence. Indeed, imprisonment has become a badge of honour in the political life of Ghana. Those who were imprisoned during this period have since worn special caps with the letters 'P.G.' printed on them, representing the term 'Prison Graduate'. This has almost become *sine qua non* of political influence. But they had all taken their political training from Britain and America, and were prepared to take the opportunity of working a westernized democratic machine.

Nor has this experiment in responsibility failed through lack of administrative ability. Most of the ministers who have taken charge of government departments have shown extraordinary skill in administration, considering their complete lack of training and experience. Mistakes have been made, of course, and some men in the public service have taken advantage of the opportunities for personal gain found in their new posts. There has also been criticism of some members of the civil service, and, indeed, this has been particularly severe against some of the European permanent civil servants. Nevertheless, there is no doubt that since 1951, under the guidance of these new African ministers, the country has made tremendous strides, socially, economically, and politically.

One of the major factors in the success of this experiment was the personality of the Governor, Sir Charles Arden-Clarke. It was clear from the beginning that the venture in developing self-government would depend largely upon the personalities of the Governor and the Prime Minister, and the character of their relations with each other. All the ministers came to their new offices without training or experience. Only meagre efforts had been made in the past to provide training facilities for Africans in branches of the administration. Political pressures, suspicions and personal considerations were bound to play an important part in the development of the new state. The guidance of the Governor through these troubled waters, therefore, would be of paramount importance. Only if he could establish a position of complete confidence with the Prime Minister could the experiment succeed. Sir Charles Arden-Clarke accomplished this task magnificently. He has set an example to the rest of the colonial service in how to pass over responsibility gradually but with certainty to the new politicians, still offering sound advice, but increasingly recognizing that he must be prepared on occasion to have it rejected without feeling rancour or resentment.

As a result, after 1951 Ghana made tremendous strides towards complete self-government and in 1957 became the first African colony to be transformed into a completely independent state. In 1954 further amendments were made to the constitution. They provided for a cabinet almost entirely responsible for the internal government of the country, with only final reserve powers left to the Governor. The cabinet was to be presided over by the Prime Minister and to consist wholly of Africans drawn from the Legislative Assembly. The Assembly itself, with 104 members, was to be entirely and directly elected. In the use of his reserve powers, the Governor was to have an advisory committee of African ministers to assist him. In short, the Gold Coast was to become almost completely self-governing in its domestic affairs, and, once its ministers and members were prepared themselves to accept the responsibility, external affairs, defence, and the police would also be handed over to them.

In May 1956 the Secretary of State for the Colonies announced that he would be prepared to fix a date for independence after another General Election had been held and if a motion were passed by a reasonable majority in the new Legislative Assembly asking the British Government to declare the Gold Coast an independent state. This General Election was held in July 1956. Dr Nkrumah's Government party, the C.P.P., gained an absolute majority over all other parties, winning seventy-one of the 104 seats. In the new Assembly the motion asking for independence was passed by seventy-two votes to none, the Opposition abstaining from voting. On 18 September the Secretary of State announced that in response to this motion he had agreed that the Gold Coast should become an independent state on 6 March 1957, and, at the request of the Assembly, that its name should be changed to

'Ghana'. On that date, for the first time, a British colony was transformed into an independent state ruled by Africans.

*   *   *   *   *

Political opinion in Britain has generally been divided between the Imperialists, who consider that we should retain our authority over the colonies at all costs and the anti-Imperialists, who believe that we ought to relinquish our control immediately. Both approaches are facile and naive. It is perfectly obvious in the present age that no imperial power can hold on to its colonial authority against the wishes of the colonial peoples without provoking warfare; it has become equally clear that the simple withdrawal of imperial authority, without careful preparations, creates problems which can exacerbate relations between the colonial peoples themselves to the point of civil war. Both these shallow attitudes spring from emotion rather than from reason based on knowledge; both express a passive attitude in place of the dynamic thought and action which every imperial power is challenged to discover if it is to meet the colonial problems of the mid-twentieth century.

The dangers of these two attitudes are well illustrated in the present situation of British West Africa. Any thought of maintaining British control in Nigeria and the Gold Coast had to be abandoned towards the end of the 1940s, as soon as determined nationalist movements developed in both countries. To have attempted to withstand the forces of nationalism would have provoked a major colonial war with the West African peoples. On the other hand, no sooner had the British intention to withdraw her control become clear, than unforeseen problems arose which cannot be solved simply by granting self-government to these states.

These new problems are taxing the political wisdom of colonial administrators and African politicians alike. In both Nigeria and the Gold Coast considerable sections of the African people were so shocked by the impact of the British intention to withdraw that they organized an agitation to retain British control, at least for some time to come. Some of the inhabitants of the Northern Region of Nigeria, where more than half the Nigerian peoples live, were openly frightened of British withdrawal. Many feared that an independent Nigeria would bring the chiefs and the northern tribes under the control of the modern politicians of the two southern regions. They feared, too, that they would become dependent upon the larger proportion of educated people in the two southern regions to carry on the technique of modern government, once the British left the country. These fears were strengthened by the federal victories of the N.C.N.C. in both West and East, giving that party a majority in the new Federal Government.

There are still fears in the Northern Region that its traditional way of life and long established disciplines and authorities may be undermined. In general these have been protected under British rule. Even now, when adult suffrage is established in the rest of the country, only men are allowed the vote in the Moslem North. Yet Britain is asked, on the principle of democracy, to hand over power. Is it democratic to pass authority to one-half of the adult citizens? These traditions are likely to be treated sympathetically by the westernized politicans of southern Nigeria. Some of the younger men in the Northern Region, most of whom have some experience in Europe or in the other two regions, are anxious to see a change in the traditional pattern of northern life. So far, however, they represent only a minority of the northern people. Until 1957 there was, therefore, a distinct possibility that the Northern Region would decide to retain British control for the time being, and if the other two regions insisted upon complete self-government, the North might have decided to separate itself from the rest of the country. The experience of Nigeria should show us some of the difficulties to be faced in creating a new nation out of a wide variety of tribes, all at different levels of development, with varying customs, prejudices and outlooks, united mainly through the single medium of British rule.

* * * * *

The Ghana example is somewhat different, but it has a basic similarity which is significant. In the General Election of June 1954 the C.P.P. gained an overwhelming victory, and it appeared that Dr Nkrumah and his party were set fair to guide the country to independence almost without opposition. Yet, only four months later, not only had an opposition sprung up, but the situation in Ashanti was so tense and hostile that no member of the government dare visit that province. Ever since then a strong opposition to Dr Nkrumah's government has developed, and even the prospect of independence did not lessen its hostility.

Ashanti is the central province of Ghana and was a great military nation. In fact, the Ashanti still believe that if it had not been for British intervention and the wars which Britain fought against them, they would have conquered the whole country. Tradition is still strong in this province; they maintain their own culture and tribal chieftainship is still revered. After the election of 1954 many of the Ashanti suddenly awoke to the fact that Britain seriously intended to surrender control of the Gold Coast and that they would be left under the authority of Dr Nkrumah's government. Dr Nkrumah and his party have drawn their strength mainly from the coastal Colony, the people of which are somewhat looked down on by the Ashanti. The prospect of the whole country being dominated by these new politicians aroused profound concern.

Many of the Ashanti people believed that their tribal customs, their chieftainship system, and their ancient traditions were endangered by the Nkrumah government. It is this fear which lay at the root of the opposition, which came to be known as the National Liberation Movement. It was joined by many from the Northern Territories who shared the same fears. 1954, moreover, was a propitious moment for an opposition to develop, for it was not only the traditionalists who feared the policy of the Government. The cocoa farmers were discontented when the Cocoa Marketing Board, its statutory body, continued to fix the price of cocoa at 72s. a load at a time when world prices were very high. Some of the cocoa farmers accepted the Government's policy of building up reserves, both for lean times and to use in order to develop the country. Many did not accept these arguments, having been led to believe during the election that a higher price would be paid.

To these nationalist and economic discontents was added the element of political disappointment. A number of politicians formerly associated with the C.P.P. had either been discarded or had not received the offices to which they believed themselves entitled. The fusion of these various elements of discontent lent a distinctly inflammatory character to the new opposition movement.

There were undoubtedly legitimate reasons for criticism of the Government, and, if a genuine democratic spirit was to be created in the country, there was an obvious need for strong and well-organized opposition. The tragedy of the situation was that the Government, on its part, showed some signs of identifying opposition with treason, whereas opposition elements began to use petrol and sticks of dynamite in place of argument. The lesson that democracy demands more than an electoral system, elected ministers, and a sound administration was thus early demonstrated.

The Opposition had some legitimate criticisms to make. It had become clear that some politicians used their new power in order to gain personal wealth. The conduct of the statutory boards, such as the Cocoa Marketing Board, its subsidiary, the Cocoa Purchasing Company, and the Industrial Development Corporation, were often managed in such a way as to show political favouritism. The charge of corruption and nepotism was borne out, and, although this would probably have occurred whatever individuals were in government, it is far healthier to be brought out in open criticism, for these types of malpractice can so easily poison and distort a political movement.

The attitude of the Government to the chiefs also was often tactless. To secure national unity requires more than a simple goal of independence. Statesmanship in recognizing the susceptibilities of different sections of the population is essential.

Then again, it is a legitimate objective to attempt to preserve the cultural traditions of a people. Political unity is strengthened rather than weakened by the preservation of cultural variety. If the Government had recognized the genuine fears of people both in Ashanti and in the Northern Territories, and had made it clear that they had no desire to interfere with cultural life, much conflict could have been avoided.

Above all there were legitimate grounds for criticism of the character of the C.P.P. itself. It is based on what is known as 'democratic centralism', which left real power in the hands of a small group. During the last few years it has been this group which has controlled both Party and Government, with the obvious danger of oligarchic tendencies.

These are the legitimate criticisms, and democracy in the Gold Coast would have been strengthened if they had been put forward rationally and persuasively by a coherent opposition. Here, however, the Opposition failed; it began by using violent emotions, and the weapon of violence, either in practice or in threats, has never been entirely discarded by it. It even threatened to use it as the final arbiter against the Government if their constitutional demands were not met before independence was achieved. By adopting these tactics the Opposition, unfortunately, lent some justification to the early tendency of the Government in identifying all opposition as treason. What is more when the Government began to make concessions to the Opposition demands, albeit somewhat belatedly, these overtures were always rejected. In 1955, for instance, the Government called in Sir Frederick Bourne to make a constitutional inquiry and report. Sir Frederick's report went a long way towards satisfying the demand of the Opposition for a federal constitution which would safeguard the local wishes of the different regions. The Government issued its own White Paper, which largely accepted the recommendations of the report. Not only did the Opposition refuse to give evidence to Sir Frederick Bourne, but it boycotted the debate on the White Paper, thus casting much doubt on the genuineness of its critical arguments. It declared that it would be satisfied with nothing less than calling a constituent assembly to frame the constitution, and, even when defeated in the 1956 General Election, stubbornly maintained this attitude. Even when it seemed, late in 1956, that Government and Opposition had more nearly reached agreement than ever before, mistrust again destroyed the chance of agreement. The Opposition chose this moment to produce a scheme for the secession of Ashanti and the Northern Territories. It thereby prejudiced its whole claim to be a constitutional opposition.

In reality these arguments and criticisms are largely a cloak for the political activities which lie beneath. The fact is that the Convention People's Party is a westernized political organization, designed to transform the Gold Coast into a modern political state. It may have taken some of its philosophy and organization from the United States, and there are even influences drawn from Communist structure. Its attitude to opposition, or to potential opposition, from organizations like the trade union movement, is often brusque and intemperate. Nevertheless, it is organized as a political party, and it has accepted parliamentary forms as its method of operation.

No other such party has developed; the National Liberation Movement claimed to be a national movement until forced by the Government to form a party to maintain its opposition. Its use of the Asantehene, and the Asanteman Council, the traditional ruler and his council of Ashanti, of tribal forms and associations, and of the chiefs, has demonstrated clearly that this was no political party in the westernized sense. Basically it was a traditionalist movement attempting to block the development of a modern political state.

Although its members have never publicly admitted as much, there seems little doubt that the Opposition would have preferred British rule to continue in Ghana until it had secured its constitutional aims. This means, in brief, that the leaders of local opinion in Ashanti and the Northern Territories would have liked the British to retain control in the country until they had established domination in their own regions. They still turned to the British Government and the British people to intervene, rather than concentrating their case amongst their own people. There are similarities here with the situation in the Northern Region of Nigeria.

Ghana is now set firmly on the path to modern political statehood. It will still have to face many profound problems and difficulties. The fluctuations in the price of cocoa continually hit the economy of the country very shrewdly, for cocoa is their main economic asset. Much will depend on its ability to attract international finance in the building of the great Volta River scheme, providing power for modern needs. This in its turn will depend largely on the ability of the Government to control the country, prevent violence, and rid itself of suspicions of corrupt practices.

E.A.–D

A tremendous social and economic revolution in the lives of the people is demanded if modern standards are to be achieved. The challenge is great and historic; the difficulties are many and complex. Can a people whose history has been so conditioned by tribalism and colonialism transform themselves into modern statehood, taking their place as a new star in the international firmament? All Africa is now looking to Ghana to set an example which can be followed throughout the Continent, thereby proving that the South African racialists are wrong.

Since independence, Ghana has on several occasions been the butt of hostile criticism in the British press. Much of this has been malicious, expressed by the same people who have never been reconciled to accepting the Indians or other non-Whites as full and equal members of the Commonwealth. At the same time, many of Ghana's closest friends have been worried about certain trends evidenced in her internal affairs. When people are deported, lawyers barred from defending their clients, meetings of the Opposition banned, trade unions controlled by the state, and opponents imprisoned without trial under the new Preventative Detention Bill, those most anxious to see Ghana become a full parliamentary democracy are naturally concerned. Above all, when Mr Krobo Edusei, who was Minister of the Interior, made speeches threatening the whole existence of the Opposition, such fears seemed well founded.

The Ghana Government has yet to learn the importance of public relations overseas, and the necessity of explaining the background and purpose of its actions, particularly to its friends. The three men who are principally responsible for Government policy, Dr Nkrumah, Mr Gbedemah and Mr Botsio, have too often allowed those with little experience or interest in overseas opinion, like Mr Edusei, to give a false impression. There are welcome signs that this lesson has been learnt.

What has to be recognized is that the state of Ghana was established during a period of tension which amounted almost to civil war. The two groups represented by the Convention People's Party and the National Liberation Movement were locked in combat for eighteen months before Independence Day. Murders,

riots and terrorism marked the struggle. It would have been sheer
romanticism to expect all this to end and be forgotten as soon as
Ghana became an independent state. It will be a long time indeed
before the C.P.P. forgets that as a result of this violent opposition
independence was postponed from 1956 to 1957.

It is not surprising, therefore, that powers have had to be taken
to remove undesirable characters, some of whom were certainly
using their money and influence to undermine the new state. The
methods used may have been rough and ready, hardly conforming
to the suavity of mature democracy. Nevertheless, the essential
and surprising fact of this situation has been that the foundations
of parliamentary democracy have been preserved during this
period of tension, violence and intrigue. During the same period
the parliamentary system has suffered eclipse—one hopes temporarily—in Pakistan, Burma, Indonesia, and the Sudan. Ghanaian
democracy for a long time is likely to resemble that of India, in
which a strong centralized party with its symbolized leader is
seen as the personification of the national struggle. So long as
parliamentary practices are maintained, the opportunity will be
there for a genuine critical opposition to grow and to express itself.
It is likely, however, that most discussion and debate on national
affairs will for a long time take place within the Convention
People's Party rather than between it and its opponents. It is
likely that Ghana will become a republic in 1959 or 1960, with
Nkrumah as first President. The constitution has already been
amended so that this may be done quickly by a simple majority.
This will give Nkrumah even greater power, but should not
damage parliamentary democracy.

The influence of Ghana in the African continent and in the
rest of the world is still to be seen. What seems certain is that
under Dr Nkrumah's leadership this newly independent African
state will take a positive initiative in the development of the
continent. Dr Nkrumah for many years, long before he was a
recognized leader of Ghana, has made it clear that he is concerned not only for his own people but for all Africans. He has
long preached the necessity of a West African Federation to
combine the strength of the small states in this area and perhaps to

rectify the divisions arbitrarily made by European interests in the past. His move for closer union with French Guinea immediately after the latter refused the de Gaulle constitution and became independent, is one sign of his continuing interest in this project. Many of the small West African states may well be prepared to accept his leadership. It is highly unlikely, however, that the Nigerians will do so, and the time may come when Nkrumah will be faced with the choice of surrendering West African leadership or seeing Nigeria remain outside such a community.

In continental affairs Ghana's Prime Minister is perhaps a little more cautious, though he has shown already a clear determination to play a leading role. In the spring of 1958 a conference of the independent African states was held in Accra, and though there was little practical result, it was a significant occasion. The Governments of these states decided to consult together in something approaching the Commonwealth method, particularly in their policies within the United Nations. Dr Nkrumah followed this conference by visiting the participating states, clearly demonstrating that he is not going to keep his eyes fixed inside Ghana's boundaries alone.

In December 1958 another conference was held in Accra, attended by most of the nationalist leaders of colonial Africa. Nkrumah made it clear in his opening address that he will not be content until every shred of imperialism is removed from the continent. He advised his listeners to rely on non-violent means of fighting colonialism, and warned them at the same time that imperialism might come from other places than Europe. Probably he was thinking of Egypt, Russia and America.

Thus, although Ghana's Prime Minister and his Cabinet have not actively interfered in the affairs of other parts of the continent, nor yet made any distinctive mark in international affairs, the first two years of independence have shown that they regard themselves as Africans with a distinctive contribution to make. Nkrumah himself talks of a specific 'African personality'. He believes that Africans have a unique contribution to make to world society, and that he and his people are specially fitted to adopt a leading role. Though he has been meticulous in his relations with the Union of

South Africa, whose policy he detests, and with the European imperial powers, there is no doubt that he will give support to those whom he considers to be fighting oppression and colonialism in the African continent. He may find rivalry from Egypt or from Nigeria to his leadership ambitions. It may be that he will persuade his rivals to unite, at least until colonialism has disappeared. What is certain is that both in Africa and in the rest of the world the personality of the African, represented by Kwame Nkrumah and the state of Ghana, is going to be seen more clearly than ever before in world affairs.

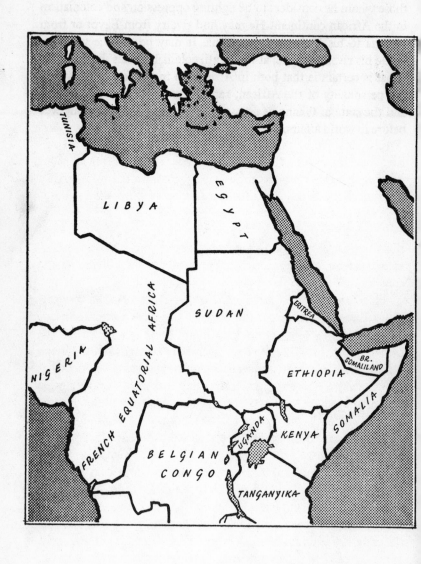

III: BRITISH EAST AFRICA

Uganda

THE Protectorate of Uganda is usually classed as one of the three main British East African territories, along with Kenya and Tanganyika. Geographically this may be reasonable, but its administration and its future seem to lie closer to those of the West African colonies than to the East. This assessment of Uganda's position stems largely from the fact that, as in West Africa, European settlement plays no significant part in the territory. The latest estimates show that the African population is about 5,300,000 and that there are only 7,000 Europeans, many of whom are in Government service. There are also about 50,000 Asians living in the country.

This absence of any large white settler element in the community relieves Uganda from the political pressures and divisions of its Kenyan neighbour. It has been deliberately said by the British Government that the future of Uganda is as a primarily African state, and though this phrase is by no means defined in detail, it is obvious that constitutional development will follow more closely that of the Gold Coast and Nigeria than the example of Kenya. Already Africans have a powerful influence in the Legislative council of the country and experience little European political competition.

The interest of the British people in Uganda was deeply stirred by the exile of Kabaka Mutesa II at the end of 1953, and it was the present Kabaka's ancestor, Mutesa I, that European explorers first contacted. Speke and Grant were the first white men to reach the capital of Kabaka Mutesa, ruler of the Kingdom of Buganda. It was in 1862 that they achieved this feat, and, to their surprise, discovered a closely-knit, well-organized social system and a people proud of their history and ancestry, considering themselves to be the aristocrats of East Africa. It was not until fifteen years later, after Stanley had visited Uganda, that the Christian Church realized its opportunity and sent out Protestant missionaries from England, and Catholics from France, to begin the conversion of Mutesa's people to Christianity. The Kabaka welcomed the missionaries, but after his death in 1884, his son, Mwanga, reversed his father's attitude, persecuting and massacring supporters of the Church.

By 1888, the traders had been attracted to the market which this well-organized kingdom could provide, and the Imperial East African Company received its Royal Charter. Lugard, the famous British administrator, found an early opportunity to begin his important work in Africa when he was sent to Uganda by this company and concluded a treaty with Mwanga. By this time, however, widespread political tension had developed throughout the Kingdom of Buganda. The Kabaka had once had to flee from his own people and it was only by military means that the company established its control over the kingdom. Even after its military victory the company found the cost of controlling Buganda so heavy that it decided to evacuate Uganda completely, and, somewhat reluctantly, the British Government stepped in to take over its responsibilities in 1893. The Protectorate was established in the following year, and, in 1896, extended to almost the whole region of present-day Uganda.

Further troubles were experienced in 1897 when Mwanga raised a revolt against the authority of Britain, and, later in that year, a mutiny of Sudanese troops broke out. Finally, Dandi Chwa, Mwanga's infant son, was proclaimed Kabaka of Buganda, and, in 1900, the Uganda Agreement settled the basis of the administration which has lasted ever since. This infant Kabaka was later knighted, ruled until his death at the end of 1939, and was then succeeded by his son, the present Kabaka Mutesa II.

It was chiefly to Buganda that British eyes were turned at the end of the nineteenth century when the British interest in East Africa first developed. The railway from Mombasa, out of which modern Kenya has developed, was begun as a link between the coast and the Kingdom of Buganda. There were obvious advantages in trading with a settled and established kingdom with a sufficient degree of organization to guarantee some protection and to offer an established market. It was found, moreover, that important crops such as coffee, sugar cane, tea, tobacco, and sisal could be cultivated in this area, and it was hoped that minerals would be discovered, as they had been in other parts of the continent. The introduction of cotton-growing was also found to reap considerable benefits, supplying the factories of Lancashire and laying deep foundations for economic progress in the Protectorate.

Most of the social services, particularly the educational system, were introduced by the Christian missions. Moved by their attack upon the ancient slave-trade across East Africa into Uganda, the Christian Churches secured a warm response from the peoples of the Protectorate, and both the Protestant and the Catholic Churches found many adherents there in spite of their hostility to each other.

The Protectorate is divided into four main Provinces; Buganda, the Eastern, Western, and Northern Provinces. Buganda, however, has always been on a different footing from the rest, for its ancient traditions—the present Kabaka claims to be the thirty-fifth in direct line of succession—has given its people a cohesion and a national consciousness unknown elsewhere. Three other districts—Toro, Ankole and Bunyoro—show some similarities to the Buganda administration, but none of them has either the proud history or the status-consciousness of the Baganda. Moreover, the Baganda have a population of over a million, about 17 per cent of the total population of the Protectorate, and almost twice as large as that of any other of the thirteen main tribes. It is not surprising, therefore, that most of the history, the problems, and the development consequent upon the British connexion with Uganda is concentrated around the relations between the British Government and the Baganda.

The crisis of 1953, which resulted in the exile of the Kabaka of Buganda, not only brought this territory to the notice of the British people, but, at the same time, illustrated another of the knotty problems which attend the development of self-government in tropical Africa. There had been riots and disturbances in 1945 and again in 1949, but these were connected rather with the internal politics of the Buganda nation than with the relationship between Buganda and Britain. In 1953 it was the Imperial connexion which was at issue and which created the problems. The exile of the Kabaka was the act of the Governor approved by the British Government. It created such consternation in Buganda that many people simply took to their beds, prostrate from the shock occasioned by the removal of their mystically worshipped Kabaka. Such a catastrophe inevitably deeply affected the relations between the Baganda and the British.

The problems from which the crisis arose really stem from the 1900 Agreement between Britain and Buganda. According to this Agreement, the Kabaka was to be recognized by Britain as the constitutional authority in his country and, on his side, undertook to co-operate loyally with the British Government in the administration of Buganda. This arrangement worked reasonably well for fifty years because the Kabaka was an autocratic, if not an absolute ruler, and could direct his policy to conform with that of Britain. By 1953, however, the position was swiftly changing. His people were now taking a greater share in the direction of policy and he was rapidly being placed in the impossible position of owing allegiance to two masters. In this very year, for instance, the composition of the Great Lukiko of Buganda, the main legislative assembly of that province, had been reformed to admit sixty elected members out of a total of eighty-nine. This was the crux of the situation which was clearly leading to an impossible position.

It was bedevilled by the conflicting personalities of the Governor, Sir Andrew Cohen, on the one side, and the Kabaka, Frederick Mutesa II, on the other. Two relaxed, co-operative personalities could have faced the situation and found a solution. In the event, a tense, pent-up Governor, with an abundance of nervous energy straining his burly frame, faced an equally intense but slight young Kabaka, determined to preserve his pride. The electricity in the relation was fore-doomed eventually to detonate an explosion.

The basic problem from which the situation arose illustrates the great difficulty of grafting a democratic system on to a feudal society. The Kabaka was accustomed to having his people literally prostrate themselves before him, yet he was their leader as well as their ruler. If a clash of policy occurred between his people and British wishes, which side was he to take? Could Britain recognize his changing function from that of a feudal despot to the status of a representative of his people?

The issue on which the clash actually occurred provides another illustration of the tension felt amongst the politically-conscious Africans towards every action of the British Government in colonial affairs. With considerable apprehension Africans in East Africa had seen in 1953 the imposition of federation on their fellow Africans in Central Africa. They had seen the unanimous opposition of local Africans in the Rhodesias and Nyasaland brushed aside. When, therefore, the Colonial Secretary made a casual reference to the future possibility of East African federation in July 1953, the Africans in East Africa immediately bridled. Fears were felt most strongly in Uganda, which was developing towards an African-controlled state. They were felt particularly keenly in Buganda, because of its historical traditions as an independent and then semi-autonomous kingdom. The belief spread that Uganda was to be placed under the control of the dominant white settlers of Kenya.

The reaction was swift. It was decided that Buganda should demand independence, and as they had seen their northern neighbours in the Sudan attaining this status through the Foreign Office, that they should claim to be transferred from Colonial Office to Foreign Office control.

Buganda separatism, by dividing the wealthiest province and commercial centre of Uganda from the rest of the Protectorate, would have vitally crippled the development of that territory as a whole. The Governor therefore resisted this demand when it was submitted both by the Kabaka and the Lukiko. Under the 1900 Agreement the Kabaka was bound to co-operate with H.M. Government which, in this instance, meant with the Governor. This he refused to do unless the Buganda claims were accepted. In spite of the fact that in March of the same year he had agreed that Buganda would share fully in the development of the new

Legislative Council of the Protectorate, he now refused to nominate any representatives from Buganda to it. After a series of meetings, highly charged with tension, between himself and the Kabaka,
the Governor eventually signed an order for the exile on 30
November.

This incident opens one more window to the complex relations
between Britain on the one side and democratically developing
colonial peoples on the other. The events which followed equally
illustrate the flexibility which is still possible in British Colonial
policy. All the incidents leading up to the exile of the Kabaka were
indicative of misunderstanding and divergent outlooks between
the two sides. During the following twelve months means
were found to breach this misunderstanding and bridge the
differences.

In the spring of 1954 the British Government asked Sir Keith
Hancock, Director of the Institute of Commonwealth Relations at
the University of London, to go out to Uganda to try and find a
solution to the constitutional deadlock. The Great Lukiko of
Buganda elected a committee to work with him in this effort. In
November of 1954, just short of twelve months after the Kabaka's
exile, Sir Keith Hancock and his committee, in association with the
Governor, published their proposals. Once again, the reactions to
these proposals illustrate the difficulties of relationship between
Britain and colonial peoples. The proposals themselves provided
for a radical increase in the democratization of both the Uganda
Protectorate and Buganda itself. The Kabaka's position was to be
regularized in Buganda by providing for him to become a constitutional monarch, with elected ministers and assembly. The
Lukiko was to be empowered to decide who they wanted as
Kabaka, even if it should be the present one, and he was to be
installed within nine months of the new constitution coming into
operation. The Legislative Council of the Protectorate, then
consisting of the Governor, fourteen African, seven European and
seven Asian representative members, together with twenty-eight
Government members, was to be expanded so as to increase the
African representation to eighteen members, together with only
six Europeans and six Asians. A ministerial system was to be

introduced with some ministers in charge of government departments. In short, Buganda was to develop towards a representative state with a constitutional monarch, and the Protectorate was to take several steps forward towards becoming a self-governing state under the majority control of Africans. Since then, and after some considerable argument, it was decided to hold national elections in 1958.

One would have expected that this advance would have been warmly welcomed by Africans throughout Uganda. This did not occur. First there were suspicions in Buganda that the status and dignity of the Kabaka were being undermined, and the hope that he would immediately return was shattered. Even when they had overcome these fears, the Lukiko, under the influence of Dr Kalibala, a Baganda who has lived in America for the past twenty-five years and who was a member himself of the Hancock Committee, decided to set up yet another committee to examine the Hancock proposals. This not only undermined the work of Sir Keith Hancock and the Lukiko's own former committee, but inevitably directly postponed the Kabaka's return. The opportunity to develop towards democratic control would probably have been welcomed more if there had been anything approaching a recognized party system in Uganda. Not only was there no such system, but no single party was organized on modern political lines. Probably the organization with the widest support at the time was the Uganda National Congress, the only organization with any claim to nation-wide membership. The Congress, however, has a history of poor and personalized leadership which did nothing to enhance its status in the political scene. Later Congress itself split partly over the immediate issue of demanding that Governor Cohen remained for a second term of office. It may be that this division in Congress ranks represents the beginning of a polarization of African politics according to conflicting policies. It is equally possible that it reflects nothing more than a clash of personalities. In the Kabaka case Congress tried to make capital for itself by cashing in on the Buganda concern at the deportation. It thus flirted with traditional tribalism and has since made little attempt to offer a constructive modern approach to the political problems of Uganda. It may be that with the coming of national elections the National Congress will assume more of the character of a political party.

It is significant that after the return of the Kabaka the division between traditionalism and modern politics became progressively sharp. The traditionalists openly victimized members of the political parties, even excluding some of them from the Lukiko. They succeeded in persuading the Protectorate Government against holding direct elections to the Legislative Council from Buganda in 1958. They tried to get the Kabaka accepted as King of Uganda with a federal state in which Buganda would be dominant. These tactics drove members of the political parties together so that for the first time they came out in the open against the traditional authorities and publicly declared their intention of fighting them. The outcome of this struggle will be important not only to Uganda but to the whole of the African world in East Africa.

There are one or two other small groups in addition to Congress, none of which has secured any mass support. Mr Mulira's Progressive Party has said some sensible things and on occasion showed courage, particularly when it challenged some of the leading members in the Lukiko in 1956 on the question of land allocation. It has been largely confined to the intelligentsia and has made no mass impact as yet. A new party was born in 1956 with some claim to modern democratic outlook, but it is too early yet to judge whether it is likely to have any success.

The elections of 1958 demonstrated the keen interest of large sections of the African population in the process of representation. Although Buganda refused to participate in them, in the other areas over 80 per cent of those qualified registered for the franchise, and of this electorate over 80 per cent actually voted. This was a remarkable demonstration of African interest in the electoral system and gives the direct lie to those who claim that Africans are uninterested in politics and not yet ready for the franchise.

Members of Congress were most successful in these elections, although the Democratic Party, largely based on Roman Catholicism, made a strong fight. After the elections various political manoeuvres took place with the object of uniting parties and forming stronger political organizations. Other forces began to deepen divisions within the existing parties. This may continue for some time, for the political situation in Uganda has not yet hardened into anything like a two-party system, or indeed into opposing policies. The real political battle is between the more modern political thinkers and the traditionalists, strongly entrenched particularly in Buganda around the Kabaka and his court. Some from outside Buganda have even begun to think that the intransigence of the Baganda can only be countered by accepting a federal system. It is likely that for some years the political situation will remain fluid, with the conflict between traditionalists and politicians becoming ever sharper and with Buganda trying every move to break away from a centralized, democratic Uganda state.

This hesitance to accept the responsibilities of democratic progress is further emphasized by fears which are less clearly defined towards the economic progress of the country. Uganda has depended largely upon its cotton and coffee exports. In the production of both these commodities Africans have been encouraged, particularly through the formation of co-operative farms, to increase their output. Consequently there has been rapid development in this field, the value of cotton exports increasing from £3,427,948 in 1938 to £29,942,764 in 1952, whilst the value of coffee exports showed an even steeper rise from £327,636 to £12,345,092 during the same period.

It has been felt, not least by Governor Cohen, that the economic development of the country requires the introduction of industry to lessen the dependence upon these two crops, which rely so much upon the movement of the world market. In 1954, for instance, The Queen, towards the end of her Commonwealth Tour, opened the great Owen Falls Dam, one of the greatest hydro-electric schemes in the African continent which can provide a foundation for industrial expansion. Meanwhile, copper mining has been established at Jinja. This opens the prospect to the Uganda people of widespread industrial development which could increase the income of the nation and provide funds for more roads, education, housing schemes and social services.

Again it might be expected that this development would be welcomed by Africans. Once more, however, African fears sometimes outweigh their hopes. They fear that the coming of industry will bring increased white migration, which may lead to white settlers taking their land. They fear that industrialization may produce a second Copper Belt, with all its industrial and racial tensions. Perhaps, above all they fear the disappearance of their traditional tribal life and customs.

There can be little doubt that Uganda has a great future and a most significant part to play in the historic development of Africa. What we and leading Africans are having to learn is that the introduction of democracy as a new constitutional system and way of life necessitates progressing at a pace only slightly faster than that of African public opinion. Once the pace becomes too fast, public opinion not only stops advancing but turns back upon itself, creating tensions and conflicts which throw all progress out of line and bedevil every relationship.

Kenya

To the ordinary person in Britain during the past few years, Kenya has meant Mau Mau. Before the outbreak of emergency in October of 1952 very few people had any clear knowledge of the country or people of Kenya, and, as is so common, it has required a civil war to give the general public an interest in this African colony. Even after years of conflict most people have, of course, only a hazy idea of what it is all about. These colonial Africans tend to appear to most newspaper readers as something like cowboys and Indians, in a fight between good men and bad men, with very little conception of the reasons for the warfare or the character of the people engaged in it.

All the major problems of Kenya arise from the fact that it is *par excellence* the multi-racial or plural society. Amongst its inhabitants are to be found Africans, Asians, Europeans and Arabs, and each community plays a distinctive part in the life of the nation. It is easy to say—and most British people would superficially say—that the people who live in a country should accept a primary loyalty to it. What is much more difficult is for the

Europeans, who have brought their technical, medical and educational knowledge from a modern, sophisticated continent, to accept a minority position. Should the vastly superior numbers of a largely primitive people entitle them to control enterprises which have resulted from European initiative? It is equally difficult for the Africans, backward in knowledge and skills though most of them may be, to accept the political, economic and social domination of an alien minority whom they believe to be primarily inspired by the desire to seize their hereditary lands; or for the Asians and Arabs to accept with complacency the hostility of both Europeans and Africans, which may lead to the destruction of the great commercial businesses they have created. In short, the main difficulty in Kenya is that each race is separate and apart and thinks first of itself as 'African', 'European', 'Asian' or 'Arab', and hardly at all of being 'Kenyan'.

It is, of course, a gross over-simplification to regard any of these communities as homogeneous. The 5,644,000 Africans are divided between ten major tribes. The Kikuyu are the largest, consisting of nearly one-fifth of the total African population, but a very large number of Africans, over 16 per cent of the total, is unclassified in any tribal category. As in most other African territories, there has also developed amongst the Africans considerable tension between those who still live the old African life in tribal society, and those who have become detribalized, either in the towns or as squatters on Europeans' farms. Amongst these also one should remember that minority, tiny but consisting of very important people, which has adopted European life and has become highly educated in the western tradition. There are Africans indeed better educated and more highly skilled than the average European in the colony.

Amongst the Asians, too, there are considerable divisions. There is, first of all, that separation which is developing amongst the Asian communities all over Africa between the Hindu and Moslem, with loyalties generally directed towards India and Pakistan respectively. This division has become particularly noticeable since the separation of India and Pakistan in 1947. Then again, the Moslems are divided between those who follow the more orthodox Mohammedan customs and those who are followers of westernized trends under the Aga Khan. There is also a distinctive Asian community from Goa, the Portuguese colony in India.

The European and Arab communities are perhaps more homogeneous, although there has inevitably developed amongst the Europeans some considerable differences between the rural farming community and later immigrants into town life. One might also notice a very important distinction between the white settler community and the European administrators, who have never had the same ideas for the future of the country.

To blend all these complex communities into a nation would, in any circumstances, present a major problem. To do so in a country with the hot winds of racial tensions blowing from all parts of the continent presents a task which many consider insuperable.

In every African colony there is a multitude of discontents, feelings of resentment and frustration, sometimes vague, often now becoming vocal, and a confused stirring of hopes, suspicions and fears. In Kenya this welter of emotions has become active in the Mau Mau movement, and since 1952 has resulted in open civil conflict. During the first two and a half years of the emergency 7,811 members of Mau Mau and 510 of the security forces lost their lives. During the same period 1,365 civilians were murdered. In a total Kenyan population of under six million inhabitants these figures represent a wide scale of conflict. When it is recalled that the warfare itself is largely confined to Kikuyu-land, with a population of only just over a million, the full extent of the terror becomes even more apparent.

Yet it should be recognized that the rival camps are not simply composed of Africans on the one side and Europeans on the other. Although all the adherents of Mau Mau have been African, it is from the African community also that most of the anti-Mau Mau forces have been drawn. Of the 510 security forces who have lost their lives, 470 were Africans, whilst of the 1,365 civilian fatal casualties, 1,316 were Africans, thirty Europeans and nineteen Asians. The battle is, therefore, more clearly seen as one between the Mau Mau movement and the united forces of Europeans, Asians and Africans, than between white and black. In this battle, amongst the anti-Mau Mau adherents it has been the Africans who have suffered the most severe losses from Mau Mau attacks.

Yet while this picture should be clearly seen and recognized, to understand the development of Mau Mau and its significance in the total Kenyan situation, one should begin by examining the specifically African grievances which have played a major part in the growth of this organization.

The development of the Mau Mau movement can really be divided into two phases. There was first the rational political stage, in which African leaders were formulating and expressing the general African demand for reform. The second stage is that dominated by witchcraft and superstition, which is largely un-intelligible to modern Europeans.

Africans in Kenya over the past thirty years have been demand-ing more land, better wages, the abolition of the colour bar in all its aspects, and equal status for all citizens. This is a general African demand, not confined either to the Mau Mau movement or to the Kikuyu tribe. It was, indeed, clearly analysed as long ago as 1925 by Norman Leys in his book *Kenya*, when he forecast that unless policies were changed a violent reaction was inevitable.

These demands correspond in part to the normal claims of the under-privileged in any nation as it develops political conscious-ness, but they are also more than this. They represent one side of the racial argument which is conducted everywhere in Africa where white settlement has been established.

In Kenya, as in other white-settled areas of the African con-tinent, the Europeans claim that when they discovered the country the Africans were primitive, barbarous, and waged internecine warfare amongst themselves. They accuse the Africans of destroy-ing the properties of the soil by bad agricultural methods, of being incapable of the efforts required to raise themselves out of their backwardness, of being inefficient workmen, untrustworthy, exploiting their women, and unable to control any kind of modern society without European direction. For their part, the Africans assert that the Europeans have stolen their land, have exploited African labour on the land and in industry to build the foundations of a luxurious white society, believe in and practise the racial theories of a *herrenvolk*, and teach the Christian religion, without either believing in or practising its principles.

Between these two racial extremes are placed the unfortunate Asians, who are disliked and suspected by both European and African. The European considers that the Asian is an imperialist agent of India, capturing the main commercial advantages of the territory and importing an alien culture; whilst the African suspects that he is exploited by the Asian trader and deeply resents the superior status which the Asian community was granted in the economic and political life of the colony.

Where then is the truth to be found amongst such conflicting emotions ? Perhaps we should first look at the early colonization of Kenya by Europeans. It began almost accidentally, for, although the British East African Association, a commercial company, obtained the original concession over most of what is Kenya today from the Sultan of Zanzibar in 1887, it was not until much later that any significant development took place in the territory. This arose, not out of interest in Kenya itself, but over the project to build a railway from Mombasa to Uganda where, in Buganda in particular, there was a well-knit society attractive to the traders. The construction of this line was begun in 1895 and by 1899 had reached the last stretch of open country before the climb over the Kikuyu Escarpment had to be attempted. It was here that the railway headquarters' workshops were established and it is here that the town of Nairobi has developed.

Meanwhile, in 1897, Lord Delamere had imagined the possibilities of white settlement in the highlands of Kenya, and his example of extensive farming attracted numbers of new settlers from 1905 onwards. At the same time the first Indians came into the country, principally in order to provide the labour for the building of the railway.

Now the central argument between European and African is concentrated upon the European possession of land. The European says that the land was unoccupied when he took it; the African believes that it was actually tribal land. The truth seems to be that this land was mainly unoccupied at this time through the effects of rinderpest on the cattle and smallpox upon the human beings.

But there can be little doubt that most of the land occupied by the Europeans was, in fact, considered to belong to the tribes.

Then again, where bargains were made, the European and African conceptions of the character of such transactions are quite contrary. The European believes that he bought the land. The African cannot conceive of tribal land being bought, but only that the European paid for the temporary use of the land, which nevertheless remained as the possession of the tribe.

The fact is that all these misunderstandings have been exacerbated because the Kikuyu areas in particular have become grossly overcrowded, whilst they have been prevented from spreading to the White Highlands.

Much of the friction over the land issue centres round these White Highlands, which consist of about 16,000 square miles. The boundaries of the Highlands with those of the African reserves are defined by an Ordinance and an Order in Council. Any change in the Highlands' boundaries requires the permission of the Highlands Board. The land within this area is let out to the Europeans on leases up to 999 years. According to the Crown Lands Ordinance, 1938, each of these leases 'implied a covenant that he shall not without the consent of the Governor-in-Council appoint or allow a non-European to be manager, or otherwise to occupy or to be in control of the land leased'.

It is easy to see from these circumstances why Africans who find themselves short of land, or living on poor land, believe that their whole land hunger is due to this European monopoly. Whilst it is obvious that, even if these 16,000 square miles of the White Highlands were handed over to the Africans, their land problem would not be solved, it is equally clear that there is no moral justification for the preservation of such a monopoly. Indeed, at least a part of the Highlands is definitely underfarmed and comparatively wasted. The European, of course, argues that it is not only his land which is protected on a racial basis, but also that of the Africans, in their reserves. Here he points out that if the white monopoly is to go there can be no reason for preserving the present system in which Europeans are prevented from buying land in African reserves.

This argument is quite spurious. The one legitimate reason for reserving any land for the occupation of a particular race is obviously that this race at the moment is too weak to protect itself and needs Government protection if it is not to lose its land to a stronger community. The simple fact is that this applies to the Africans at present, but has never applied to the Europeans. There is thus a case to be made out for temporarily reserving certain land for African use but none for protecting that of the Europeans.

Moreover, it should also be noted that land has far more than an economic value to the African. Land has a deeply spiritual significance to the African tribe. The whole of his social and cultural outlook, all his tribal customs and practices, are derived from the land. It is the primeval right of his whole existence and when deprived of it he becomes rudderless and lost.

This fact, of course, raises tremendous difficulties as African society becomes urbanized and economic progress demands some method by which the universal attachment of the African to the land can be modified. Nevertheless, at present, without an understanding of these deeply rooted bonds, the African attitude to the present land division in Kenya is meaningless.

We should look at the significant effect upon African social and economic life of the coming of the European. The processes are seen most clearly in Kenya and in the Union of South Africa, but they affect most parts of the African continent to some degree, and will certainly have an effect in the future upon many other African countries.

Before the coming of the European to the continent most African tribes were nomadic; they grazed their cattle and grew their crops in one area for several seasons until they found its yield rapidly diminishing. Then they moved on elsewhere and repeated the process. This was possible in a large continent with a very small population.

The European, however, stopped the whole process. He raised frontiers, took land for himself, and stipulated boundaries beyond which the tribes should not move. At the same time, the European brought his medicine and his veterinary science. He also brought law and gradually prohibited intertribal warfare. Disease and death took a lower toll; the population of the tribes increased in both human beings and cattle.

The consequence was that more people and more cattle had to live on a restricted area of land. But medicine and law were offered and accepted earlier than the processes of modern agricultural techniques. Most of the Africans continued to use their land and to herd their cattle in the traditional way. The inevitable consequence was endemic over-population of both people and animals, and widespread soil erosion. The cattle were even driven up on to the hillsides in search of new pastures, thus greatly increasing the pace of erosion.

Meanwhile an increasing number of the able-bodied African men were driven by economic pressures to seek wages in the towns. Most of them were only either able or willing to become townsmen temporarily as migrant labourers. The lack of their labour increased agricultural depression, whilst the fact that their families were still dependent on the land increased the whole pressure upon the tribe. As they only stayed for short periods in industry, they did not become efficient industrial workers either, and usually they had to continue to rely upon the tribe for support in sickness, accident, and old age.

The social and economic consequences of these processes form the most important roots of African discontent and unrest. They have been studied by a Royal Commission on Population and Land in East Africa. The recommendations of the Commission are controversial, being based mainly on an assumption of the value of economic competition. Its exposure of the problems which have arisen in this area, however, is very worth while studying.

Although it is the land issue which forms the heart of the European-African relationship in Kenya, it is, in fact, only one of many issues which today are agitating the racial scene. The land issue is itself really only a symptom of the basic long-term conundrum which has to be faced.

The European considers that he has brought to Kenya all that is modern and progressive in that colony. He points to the development of agriculture, the growth of industry, the spread of education and modern health provisions, the introduction of railways, roads, air-services and sea transport. His claim to have brought these modern amenities to Kenya is legitimate.

On the other hand, the African considers the European to be an alien. It is true, of course, that the movement of peoples in all parts of the world ultimately invalidates any claim to original possession of the land. Nevertheless, it is certainly true that the European came to Kenya after the Kenyan African tribes. The African also accuses the European of being a hypocrite. He claims that the European charges him with being backward and primitive, but that when he has acquired the educational standard to compete with the European he is then denied that opportunity because of the white man's fear of losing his privilege. The accusation is particularly made against European pretensions to Christianity. The African who has accepted Christian teachings in his own society finds, when he encounters white society, to him identified with Christianity, that Christian principles are by no means generally practised. There is, therefore, a tendency amongst Africans to consider Christianity as nothing more than a group-religion of white people, similar to the tribal religion which he knew himself.

Above all, the African, and particularly the educated, or partially-educated minority within African society, asks how western democratic principles are to be applied to the 50,000 Europeans and $5\frac{1}{2}$ million Africans. He asks whether the Kenyan view of democracy visualizes the permanent domination of this tiny minority of whites over the vast majority of blacks.

It is these questions and the conflict of outlook between European and African which underlie the whole of the Mau Mau trouble. The Kikuyu tribe was in many ways more advanced and had come closer to the European mental outlook than other African tribes. It therefore provided the most fertile soil in which these feelings of frustration and discontent could flourish. The Kikuyu, because of their higher stage of advance, had felt the frustrations of the colour-bar more keenly, expecting a more rapid fulfilment of the western promise than had their brother tribes. They also had a longer history of contact with European missionaries and farmers, whilst many of them, through a little education, seemed to have gained new powers over their more ignorant tribesmen.

It has thus been possible within the Kikuyu tribe, as distinct from other Kenyan tribes, to develop this primarily racialistic movement. The Kikuyu who, in the early days of European contact, were described as friendly and co-operative people, have become embittered and frustrated through the pressure on their land, their slight acceptance of western ways, and their rejection by westernized society when they attempted to enter it. In short, they have entered fully that transition stage from the stable, disciplined and static life of the tribe towards the more complex, insecure and questioning life of modern society. Like the Europeans of the sixteenth and seventeenth centuries, who underwent a similar process, they have turned, in their frustration, doubts and fears, to witchcraft. The first object of the Mau Mau oaths was to bind the tribe together in a nationalist emotion in order to assert itself. The later oaths deliberately flouted all the traditions of the Kikuyu in order to cut off the oath-takers from any future acceptance within the tribal community, and to bind them permanently, in this world and the next, to their leaders. The primary accusation against Jomo Kenyatta, whether he was responsible for the organization of Mau Mau or not, is that he, with a western experience, lent himself to this nihilistic reversion to psychopathic superstition.

It is obvious that only when this background of Mau Mau is comprehended is it possible to discover realistic solutions to what is primarily a social revolt, employing military and psychological weapons.

The most remarkable feature of the emergency in Kenya since 1952 is the fact that, in spite of it, and, indeed, perhaps partly because of it, progress has developed even more rapidly than previously towards inter-racial co-operation. It was not until 1951 that the first African was appointed to the Executive Council, yet, by 1954, a new constitution had been introduced, based upon the participation of all the races. In the new constitution the Legislative Council remained as previously, with the Governor as President, a Vice-President and Speaker, eight ex-officio members, eighteen nominated members, twenty-one elected members and seven representative members. Of the twenty-one members who were elected, fourteen were Europeans, six Indians and one an Arab. The seven representative members consisted of six Africans and one Arab, nominated by the Governor with the approval of each race.

Three facts emerge from the constitution of this Council. The first is that in Kenya representation was based on equality between European and non-European, there being sixteen European members, six Indians, eight Africans and two Arabs. The second important point is that no African elections were allowed until 1957 and that, therefore, no one could speak with confidence as to the legitimacy of African leadership. This caused considerable resentment amongst the Africans, and resulted in political confusion amongst them.

Thirdly, a new form of government was introduced within this constitution. This was named the Council of Ministers and was composed of the Governor, the Deputy Governor, six official members, six unofficial members and two nominated members. Of the six unofficials three were Europeans, two Asians and one African. At the time of the introduction of the constitution the Africans pressed very strongly for equality of membership with the Asians and were prepared to see European representation increased to four in order to maintain the balance. However, this claim was rejected at the time and representation in these proportions was to be frozen until 1960 unless amended by general agreement before that date. In October 1956, agreement to alter the numbers was reached. An extra African and an additional European were added to the Council of Ministers, leaving the ratio of elected Ministers as four Europeans, two Africans and two Asians. As part of this bargain an elected European Minister, Mr Michael Blundell, was given the portfolio of Agriculture, considered in Kenya as a key post, and one which the Africans considered should be retained by an official member because of the conflict between European settlers and Africans over the land issue. The Executive Council remained in being, consisting of all the members of the Council of Ministers, plus one Arab and two Africans.

This form of multi-racial government did not, of course, go far to satisfy the demands of the Africans. Yet it created widespread discontent amongst the European community. Along with the furore created by the offer in January 1955 of an amnesty from capital punishment to Mau Mau and security forces offenders, it deeply divided the European community. In place of the past practice of maintaining a single European political organization, known as the Electors' Union, two parties came into being. The United Country Party, led by Mr Michael Blundell, supported the new multi-racial Government. The die-hard element amongst the Europeans established a Federal Independence Party, which not only opposed multi-racial government, but believed in a form of racial segregation or apartheid as the future pattern of Kenyan society. Another group of independent European members followed Group-Captain Briggs, and opposed the racial quota system in the ministerial appointments. In the 1956 elections six Blundellites and eight Briggites were elected, but later agreed to act together once more. These divisions were aggravated by the raised tensions caused by the fears brought about by Mau Mau practices and by resentment against the Government's action in prosecuting members of the security forces who committed crimes against captured Mau Mau. In a civil war of this kind brutality is inevitable on both sides, but it is felt by the intelligent that unless the strict principles of British justice can be seen to apply, no genuine alternative example to Mau Mau can be held up to the disaffected Kikuyu.

After this new form of multi-racial government came into operation bitterness in Kenya considerably increased. The Africans complained that only a façade of democracy was offered to them and that the continued detention of thousands of their people was based on victimization. They were infuriated by the exposure of brutalities committed by security forces and officials on African prisoners and the insultingly light sentences passed on such offenders. The Europeans saw their domination weakening and extremists came very near to preaching sedition against the Government based on mob-rule.

Early in 1957 the first African elections were held. These were organized on a restricted franchise in which wealth and education were regarded as basic qualifications, some voters being given as many as three votes, whilst many Africans who were held to be incapable of proving their loyalty against the Mau Mau movement were denied votes altogether.

In the elections themselves various issues emerged. In Nairobi Tom Mboya, who had made a name for himself as a trade unionist and had had the opportunity of experience in Europe and America, competed with Clem Argwings-Kodhek, also European educated and a lawyer. The election was largely fought on personalities, these two candidates being rivals for leadership of the nationalist movement. In the Central Province rival tribalism was the most important factor. This constituency included a large number of both Kikuyu and Meru, who would clearly have been better divided into at least two constituencies. In the event, Eliud Mathu, the leading Kikuyu, first African member of the Executive Council, and for many years a member of the Legislative Council, was defeated by Bernard Mate, largely because a higher proportion of the Meru tribe registered as voters.

Inevitably the eight communally elected African members immediately made fresh political demands. The object of the restricted franchise was said to be an attempt to ensure that moderates rather than extremists were elected. This supposition revealed sheer blindness to the real facts. Whether there was restricted or universal suffrage, the result of the elections would almost certainly have been the same. The Africans, like the Europeans, were being forced by the nature of their representation to organize on a racial basis, and the first political fact that they saw in front of their faces was that five million African citizens were being asked to accept representation by only eight members, whereas the European community, only 1 per cent of the African, was given fourteen seats. The logic of communal representation immediately revealed itself. The communally elected Africans demanded that their number be increased from eight to twenty-three, and to enforce their claim rejected the Lyttelton Constitution by refusing to accept office in the Government.

In an attempt to break this constitutional deadlock, the Secretary of State for the Colonies, Mr Lennox-Boyd, visited

Kenya in the second half of 1957. He first attempted to secure agreement between the different racial groups as to the next steps in constitutional advance. This effort failed, however, for whilst the Africans refused to discuss constitutional reform until their demand for increased representation was met, the Europeans took the opposite view, insisting that increased African representation should only be granted if the African members were prepared to accept office in the Government.

Faced with intransigence on both sides, the Colonial Secretary made his own award. He offered the Africans six extra seats, bringing their numbers in the Legislative Council up to fourteen and thus equal to the numbers of elected Europeans. Secondly, he proposed that twelve new members should be elected, using the Legislative Council itself as an electoral college. These twelve should be equally divided between the three races, four from each. The object of this proposal was to secure for the first time the principle of cross-racial voting with the elected members responsible to an electorate composed of all three races. It was hoped that this would form the first step towards an introduction of common roll elections throughout the country, and it was expressly laid down that no further increase would be made to the communally elected members of any race. Thirdly, a new body was to be set up called the Council of State, to be composed of nominated independent persons charged with the task of examining all legislation and ensuring that any form of discrimination should be reported to the Secretary of State. The basis of this constitution was to remain unaltered for a period of ten years and in announcing it the Secretary of State expressly said that for the foreseeable future the ultimate authority of Government in Kenya must rest with the British Government.

Reactions to this new constitution varied considerably. The Europeans tentatively accepted it, recognizing African political progress as inevitable and in the main reconciling themselves to it provided that the pace was not too fast. They also believed that the constitution guaranteed to them some degree of permanent political influence. Somewhat surprisingly the Africans bluntly rejected the proposals and instead of claiming them as a victory characterized them as a step towards the Central or South African pattern. In the elections for the six new African seats held in March 1958, all the candidates returned were pledged to refuse office in the Government and to oppose the constitution. In these elections Mr Eliud Mathu was again defeated, this time by another Kikuyu, Dr Julius Kiano, a lecturer in government at the Royal Technical College. The African elected members maintained their demand for twenty-three instead of fourteen seats, which would give them an absolute majority over the elected members of the other two races. In addition they demanded an official British Government statement that the ultimate objective was a completely democratic Kenyan state with full adult suffrage; that a constitutional commission should be appointed to work out a new constitution in consultation with all the races; that the new scheme for inter-racially elected members and the Council of State should be dropped; that the racial proportions in the Council of Ministers should be changed; and that the ten-year stand-still be abolished.

The Asians tended to be critical of the new constitution, mainly because of African opposition, but most of their elected members agreed to work it temporarily.

In spite of the opposition of the African Elected Members and of some Asians, elections to the new crossbench within the Legislative Council were held in April 1958. A welter of manoeuvres preceded them. The African Elected Members issued a statement declaring that all Africans agreeing to stand for these seats should be regarded 'as traitors to the African cause', and calling on the African community to boycott them economically, socially and politically. Nevertheless, a number of African candidates stood for election and the stipulated four African members were returned. Meanwhile, the European Elected Members had got together with some of the nominated Europeans to form a caucus. The principal object of this tactic was to secure the defeat of Mr E. A. Vasey, the Minister of Finance and the leading European liberal, who had decided to put his political future at stake by standing for one of the crossbench seats. The European caucus tried to do a deal with both the Africans and the Asians, submitting to them a list of European candidates and agreeing that if the other races supported their list they would reciprocate by voting for agreed Asian and African candidates. This proposal was not accepted by either Asians or Africans, but, as the Africans boycotted the election, the combined numbers of elected and nominated European members in the Legislative Council were sufficient to secure the defeat of Mr Vasey. In fact he tied with the fourth listed European candidate, Mr Slade, and lost after drawing lots with him. Many people felt that by employing such tactics, the Europeans had in fact frustrated the object of these elections, which was to get away from racial blocs and elect members who would represent national instead of racial interests. By employing these tactics, too, the European members went far to justify the accusation of the Africans that the inter-racial character of the elections was a sham because the Europeans could control them through their weight of numbers. On the other hand the result made it apparent that if the Africans had not boycotted the elections but had simply voted for Mr Vasey, his return would have been assured. Their confidence in him was seen when, immediately after his defeat, they moved a resolution in the Council asking that he remain Minister of Finance, and calling on the Governor to renominate him.

After the elections the African Elected Members still refused to take Government office, and maintained their opposition to the constitution. African participation in the Government was now secured by appointing Ministers and Assistant Ministers from those elected to the crossbench. These crossbench members, from each race, also formed a new association to compete with the communal organizations.

At the end of November 1958 the Colonial Secretary replied to the demands of the African elected members. He rejected their claim for a new constitutional conference, pointing out that his constitution had been in operation for less than a year. At the same time he suggested that, provided the principles which he had laid down, namely, no further communal representation, the maintenance of a Government in which all races participate, the creation of opportunities for representation in the Legislative Council based on the non-communal principle, and the institution of a body of local people to prevent unfair discrimination detrimental to any community, were accepted, it should be possible for the Africans to begin discussions with the Governor and other races to see if some agreement on constitutional development were possible. The Africans took this as a flat refusal to accept their basic demand for further discussions, as they considered that the right authority with whom to discuss constitutional progress was the British Government, as the final authority. At the end of 1958, therefore, the African elected members were boycotting the Legislative Council, the Asians, albeit half-heartedly, were supporting them and pledged to withdraw from the legislature and government at the end of the year, and deadlock appeared complete. There was even talk amongst the Africans of 'direct action'—a phrase taken from the history of Ghana, indicating boycott and civil disobedience. It appeared inevitable that constitutional and political conflict would continue for a long time. On the one hand the Europeans have been accustomed to political power and a position of domination; on the other, the Africans, with the weight of numbers behind them, are impatient to gain political dominance in the immediate future.

The prospect for Kenya thus seems pretty dark, and it is difficult to visualize how a period of intense political conflict can be avoided. On the other hand, there is a deep undercurrent of more dangerous significance. The cry of 'Africa for the Africans' is sometimes heard. It is perhaps the natural reaction to white efforts for domination and to the period in which the whites have imposed their will on the vast black majority. If the African politicians lend themselves to this idea, however, and it might even be that their personal rivalries will drive them to do so lest anyone of them be outbid by his fellows, the political conflict could be distorted into a racial battle. Such an outcome would inevitably ignite such passions and bitterness as to sour and possibly destroy any attempt to build a new nation.

From this very fluid position a number of basic lessons have emerged. In the first place, no matter how franchise qualifications may be devised it is quite clear that so long as representation is by racial community instead of according to political policy the public stage will be dominated by inter-racial conflict. Whilst both African and European members have to appeal to communal electorates this involves them in competing with their rivals in extreme racialism. The European candidate who wishes to be elected must be able to satisfy his European electorate that he will think first of safeguarding white interests against the menace of being engulfed by the black man. The African candidate has to rival his competitors in assuring the African electorate that he will be completely intransigent towards any scheme which does not immediately produce a black majority. Compromise which could lead to the evolution of confidence between white and black is therefore impossible, and any policies which could cut across the racial division are completely ruled out. Politics, in fact, is forced into racial strait-jackets, with scant thought being given to political parties or policies which could be supported by members of each race.

This preoccupation with race has frustrated the first tentative attempt to introduce inter-racial elections. The solid boycott of the Africans and the European caucus tactic have largely destroyed its value. It is also significant that in these crossbench elections the Government side, through its officials and nominees, were in a position to determine who should be elected. They could, indeed, have secured the election of Mr Vasey even without the support of the African Elected Members. Those who have been elected by this method, therefore, are unlikely to be critics of Government policy since they owe their seats to Government support. It might well have been better to secure genuine cross-racial voting by confining the election to elected members. In these circumstances it seems extremely doubtful whether the new crossbenchers' association or the new inter-racial organization associated with Mr Vasey are likely to attract African support away from the communal bodies. Theirs is a long-term and unpopular task.

Other schemes aimed at the same purpose have been proposed, including one put forward by Mr A. B. Patel, a former Hindu member of the Council of Ministers. He suggested that alongside communal representation there should be a common electoral roll with franchise qualifications applying equally to all races to elect additional members of the Legislative Council who should sit on a crossbench and represent national as distinct from racial interests. It might be that as a transitional stage to encourage feelings of confidence between the races in such constituencies each elector would have three votes and a member of each race be elected, as is being tried in Tanganyika.

Whatever transitional methods are used, therefore, two principles have now become quite clear. The first is that a clear ultimate objective of complete democracy with full adult suffrage must be categorically stated. The second is that all methods of 'fancy franchise' have failed and will continue to fail because the Africans are now seized with the idea of universal suffrage. Any transitional plan must take account of these two implacable demands.

Meanwhile, both the European and African communities are in some confusion. The foolish tactics of the Europeans over a number of years have left them particularly exposed to African hostility. They first of all condemned the common roll, even though it was obvious that this alone could save their influence and allow them the opportunity of convincing African opinion of their good will. Now, when they have felt the first breath of the hot winds of African political racialism, they have scuttled towards the common roll escape hatch, but have so misused it as to destroy any African confidence in its justice. Similarly one can see their stupidity in the treatment they have accorded to the most distinguished African public figure, Mr Eliud Mathu. Whilst he was the sole African to distinguish himself in the Legislative and Executive Councils they resented his ability to debate on equal terms with them and consistently vetoed his appointment to high office. He was the obvious nominee as first African Minister under the Lyttelton constitution, but European opposition prevented his appointment. In the first African elections of 1957 the Europeans and the Administration so manipulated constituency boundaries and registration of electors that Mr Mathu's defeat was assured. The Europeans thus ensured that the first African Elected Members should be both inexperienced and intransigent. They began to yearn for the moderation and statesmanship of the man they had driven from the public scene. Characteristically their unimaginative reaction was to drive the last nail in his political coffin by openly supporting him in the second set of African elections in 1958. This in itself was enough to secure his defeat and moreover to discredit him with his own people. European lack of understanding of Kenyan realities could hardly be more blatantly exposed.

On the other hand the African leaders have got themselves into a completely negative position. The increase in their representation from eight to fourteen under the Lennox-Boyd constitution, although not satisfying their demands, was in fact a triumph for their tactics. They completely failed to represent it as such, but rather attempted to persuade their people that it constituted a defeat for their demands. Fearful of being outbid by their rivals they took up a posture of intransigent opposition to every part of the constitution. This represented a sharp contrast to the political wisdom shown by their idol Dr Nkrumah, who, when he was faced in 1951 by a similar choice of taking modified powers or refusing to accept other than his complete demands, accepted the former alternative. He saw that if he took even the partial opportunities of responsibility offered to him and used them skilfully he could attain a position in which his full demands could not be withheld. This negative attitude of the Kenya Africans inevitably led to some dissension amongst them. Messrs Odinga, Mboya, Argwings-Kodhek, and Kiano were all rivals for leadership. The true test of leadership character might well be the courage to see farther than the immediate emotions of the masses, and to accept the risk of unpopularity by facing realities and plotting a course which could lead to a constructive future. These leaders, all of whom are looking towards a westernized future for Kenya, should beware of the racial threat from within their own community. Since Mau Mau, a new, similar organization known as Kiama Kia Muingi, has emerged and was proscribed in 1958.

Realistic and intelligent Africans recognize that both Europeans and Asians have an important part to play in the development of a prosperous Kenyan nation. What they legitimately object to is the privileged position of the immigrant communities, but their skill and wisdom should surely embrace constant attempts to secure the adherence of both Europeans and Asians as they advance forwards towards a democratic state. However this is achieved it will have to be based on a sense of loyalty to Kenya itself rather than to racial communities. This will necessitate breaking down segregation in education, social life, and land tenure. Such an attack on the long-established social customs of the Kenyan peoples is more likely to succeed if it is done gradually though progressively, than if it emerges from racial conflict. If it is to be achieved without intensifying racial hostility it will necessitate the formation of political parties composed of members of all races, with divisions fixed on policy instead of on race. It may well be that the arrogant intransigence of reactionary Europeans will have to be broken in the process, but it is equally certain that it is now the Africans who are also called to find wisdom and tolerance. In the long run the Africans know that the weight of their numbers is bound to prevail. The choice before them is whether it shall prevail destructively, by alienating the immigrant communities, or constructively, by taking them along with them in the march towards a democracy which will include members of different races with equal individual rights of citizenship, but with race and colour relegated to insignificance in national life.

Tanganyika

Tanganyika is the largest of all British dependencies, covering 362,688 thousand square miles, 20,000 of which is composed of lakeland. Like the other East African territories, it forms a plural society composed of Africans, Europeans and Asians. In this respect it lies somewhere between Kenya and Uganda models, its non-African population being larger than Uganda's, but smaller than that of Kenya. In the middle of 1954 the total estimated population was 8,196,000, of whom 8,084,000 were Africans, 22,500 Europeans and 89,200 other non-Africans, mainly Asians.

Tanganyika is different from most of the other British African territories as, though it is administered by Britain, it is actually under the authority of the United Nations. It was Dr Karl Peters, the German explorer, who originally negotiated treaties with the chiefs and brought European companies into the country. The land of these chiefs was declared German after the negotiation of treaties, and it was Germany which acquired the important coastal stretch from the Sultan of Zanzibar in 1890. During the First World War the British and German armies and navies engaged each other in the territory, the Germans eventually being expelled towards the end of 1917. Sunken German gunboats can still be seen in the harbour and creek of Dar-es-Salaam.

By the Peace Treaty of 1919 the Germans were forced to surrender all their colonies and the League of Nations took authority over them through its Mandates Commission. Britain was mandated to administer Tanganyika and report upon its administration to the League of Nations. When the League collapsed during the Second World War and was replaced by the United Nations, the Mandates Commission was succeeded by the Trusteeship Council of the new body. Those powers holding mandates were invited to negotiate trust agreements with the new authority. Under this arrangement in 1946 Tanganyika was placed under the Trusteeship Council as a Trust Territory, with Britain still responsible for its administration.

This is a curious kind of arrangement, originally introduced after the First World War as a compromise expedient designed to satisfy both those who believed that imperial control of colonies should pass into the hands of the new international authority, and the imperial powers themselves, anxious to divide up the spoils of the German Empire. It has opened the colonial administration of the imperial powers to international debate and criticism, first under the Mandates Commission and now before the Trusteeship Council. Every three years a delegation from the Trusteeship Council visits the Trust Territory and reports back on its administration. Although real power still remains in the hands of the imperial authority, international discussion on colonial policy and administration can be of benefit. On the other hand, this opportunity is often used by states without experience in the responsibility of colonial administration to make destructive and ill-informed criticisms. As a result, many of the former supporters of the conception of direct international colonial administration have now been converted to the belief that only those powers with the experience and the machinery can provide good government in these dependent territories. So far no considerable clash has occurred between the international authority and the mandatory or trusteeship power, though criticism has often been sharp. The final destiny of trust countries is yet to be decided. In the case of Tanganyika it is undoubtedly self-government and independence. When this becomes a more practical objective of the foreseeable future it may well be that dispute will arise with the United Nations over a time-table for independence, as foreshadowed in the debate at the Trusteeship Council in 1955.

At the moment, however, a tremendous task of development in economic, political and social life is presented to the Tanganyikan administration. The coastline, like that of the rest of East Africa, has an ancient history of contact with the outside world. The Arabs were here certainly in the eighth century, and it is almost certain that contact with the outside world began long before their arrival. Traces have been found of both Persian and Chinese contact with the coastal strip. The Turks and the Portuguese settled for short periods in the sixteenth and seventeenth centuries. So far as is known, however, none of these outsiders ventured much beyond the coastline, which, like that farther north, provided in modern times suitable harbours both for East African Arab trading and for the organization of the slave trade.

The interior, as well as being continually harassed by slave raiding during the nineteenth century, was also undoubtedly affected by the movements of the Bantu tribes over the past four or five hundred years. These disturbances of social progress, along with the lack of external contact, has left most of the African peoples of this large country in a backward and often semi-primitive state. The only considerable town in the whole territory is Dar-es-Salaam, with a population of about 100,000 and large port facilities. There are few railways and most of the roads are still little more than tracks.

On the other hand, although industry has not yet developed to any appreciable extent, considerable progress has been made in recent years in the growing of important crops. The export of sisal and coffee has increased rapidly since the Second World War and the two now bring in over £20,000,000 a year in export payments. In this productive enterprise the development of co-operative farming has been of particular importance in Tanganyika, especially amongst the Chagga tribe around Moshi on the slopes of Mount Kilimanjaro. Here a remarkably successful experiment in co-operation has developed since the war, bringing very considerable wealth to this particular tribe.

Each of the East African territories—Uganda, Kenya, and Tanganyika—has a multi-racial population, but the development of political institutions in the three territories has been quite different, showing little sign of common thought. The only exception is the existence of the East Africa High Commission, which organizes joint railway, postal, currency services and the like. Because Britain is the administering power in each case the final aim of policy has been the same, at least in recent years. Generally speaking the British colonial objective now is the creation of self-governing states out of the dependencies or, in some cases, from a collection of dependencies joined in a federation. There are certain influences in Britain which would still resist this objective, but gradually it has come to be accepted as a common political aim of the main British parties.

The statement of this aim in the case of Tanganyika was made on 25 June 1952 by the Secretary of State for the Colonies in the House of Commons in these words:

'First, it is the intention to continue to administer the territory in accordance with the terms of the Trusteeship Agreement until the ultimate goal of self-government has been reached. Her Majesty's Government confidently hope that when that goal has been attained Tanganyika will be within the British Commonwealth. Her Majesty's Government attach importance, for the interests of the inhabitants of Tanganyika, to the maintenance and promotion of British traditions and the British connexion with the territory. Secondly, Her Majesty's Government interpret the Trusteeship Agreement and Article 76 of the United Nations Charter as imposing on the Administering Party an obligation to provide for the full participation of all sections of the population, irrespective of racial origin, in the progressive development of

political institutions and in the economic and social advancement
of the territory. Each section of the population must be enabled
and encouraged to play its full part in the development of the
territory and its institutions, in complete confidence that the rights
and interests of all communities, both indigenous and immigrant,
will be secured and preserved.'

This aim of developing towards self-government is held in
common towards the three East African territories and, in this
respect, the main argument now rests upon the pace of that
advance and the degree of influence accorded to the different races.
Yet practice in each of the East African territories shows sharp
contrasts. Uganda is to become 'primarily an African state'; Kenya
remains mainly under the control of Europeans and its future is
clearly seen by no one; Tanganyika lies somewhere between these
two models.

This situation is reflected by the curious use of the term 'parity'.
This word is used to describe racial representation in each of the
three territories. Yet, though the word is used in common, it is
interpreted in three different ways. In Uganda 'parity' has meant
equal representation between African and non-African; in Kenya
it has been used to describe equal representation between European and non-European; in Tanganyika it reflects equal representation for African, Asian and European communities.

These differences illustrate the varied methods used in the three
East African territories for approaching the complicated problem
of multi-racial politics. In all three cases the population is made
up of a very large majority of Africans and minorities of Asians and
Europeans. It is generally conceded that the immigrant communities have brought with them methods of development which would
otherwise be unavailable to the African people. As the latter part of
the above quotation from the Secretary of State indicates, the
object of the British Government has been to preserve the confidence of these immigrant communities whilst increasingly
allowing for greater participation by the African majorities.

In Tanganyika this has taken the usual British colonial form of
developing first Executive and then Legislative Councils. The
German administration was conducted by a Governor and an

advisory council. This system was continued under British rule until 1926, when the Governor formed the first Legislative Council, consisting of both officials and unofficial members, the latter nominated by himself. It was not until after the Second World War that Africans and Asians were appointed to the Legislative Council, which, from 1948, took the form of the parity known in Kenya. From that year, of the fourteen unofficial and nominated members, seven were Europeans and seven non-Europeans, four being Africans and three Asians. In the same year, the Executive Council was revised to introduce the system in which individuals on the Executive Council assumed responsibility for Government departments.

In 1949 the Governor set up an inter-racial committee to consider the constitutional future of the country. This committee recommended that the Legislative Council should be enlarged; that the form of parity representation should be changed to one in which each race had equal representation; but that the official majority should be retained. The recommendations were accepted by the British Government and a new Legislative Council came into being in April 1955. The new Council consisted of sixty-one members, thirty-one of whom were official and thirty unofficial. Of the latter, Africans, Europeans and Asians were represented by ten members each; one each from the eight provinces, one each from Dar-es-Salaam, and the tenth to represent special interests. All these members were still nominated by the Governor though elections on a qualified franchise were planned for 1958. Meanwhile, the Executive Council was also enlarged and included the Governor, three ex-officio members, five nominated official members, and six unofficial members, two from each race.

One further interesting constitutional experiment in Tanganyika was the appointment of Professor W. O. Mackenzie, Professor of Government at Manchester University, to inquire further into the constitutional problems of the country. Professor Mackenzie's most important recommendations were that an electoral system should be introduced to replace the nomination of unofficial members of the Legislative Council and local government bodies, and, secondly, the suggestion that an experiment should be made in an inter-racial election, probably in Dar-es-Salaam. The advantages of an electoral over a nominated system for the Legislative Council are obvious if the representatives are to represent truly the outlook of the people. The main problem now is to secure a system of election satisfactory for such a mixed population.

The second proposal is much more controversial and, indeed, may be profoundly significant as an attempt to solve the main political problem in multi-racial territories. Professor Mackenzie suggested that, as an experiment, a common electoral roll should be instituted in one constituency. A list of candidates from all three races should then be drawn up and each voter entitled to three votes. The three candidates elected would be the African, Asian, and European gaining most votes. Parity of representation would thus be preserved in order to avoid, at least for the moment, a swamping of immigrant races by the more numerous Africans. Yet, at the same time, all the candidates would be responsible to a multi-racial electorate. In this way it is hoped to develop politics free from racial considerations and to persuade each of the three races that their interests are virtually common.

After a further visit by Professor Mackenzie and study by a commission, the Tanganyika Government in 1956 made a number of constitutional proposals. The principal one was that, as from 1958, some of the representative members of the Legislative Council should be elected instead of nominated. The elections would take place on a common electoral roll and the franchise would be limited according to certain economic and educational qualifications. The proposal was later amended to provide for election of all representative members, a half in 1958 and the rest in 1959.

These proposals represented a recognition by the Tanganyikan Government that political development must take place and a desire of the Government to develop slowly along the multi-racial lines. They clearly demonstrated that the Government intended to keep equal representation of the races whilst introducing the practice of common voting in order to introduce gradually the conception of a common citizenship.

It will be seen from this brief outline that Tanganyika is at present a country of experiment and innovation. An opportunity for the meeting of such lines of thought has been provided by the comparatively peaceful race relations of recent history. One has only to visit Dar-es-Salaam and see members of all three races, with their variety of languages, colours and religions, mixing freely and on good terms with each other, to recognize the fertile soil provided here for inter-racial experiments.

Yet political ideas develop so quickly in present-day Africa that, even before the new Legislative Council had met, awkward questions were being raised by the Africans as to what is to be the future of their country.

The conception of equal representation for each of the three races marks an advance on the past and represents a more liberal constitution than that of Kenya. It is already clear, however, that this cannot be the final arrangement. It is ludicrous to suggest that it is democratic in any sense of the term for eight million Africans, 90,000 Asians and 20,000 Europeans to be represented by the same number of members. Because of this great disparity in numbers and the tiny size of the immigrant minorities, most Africans regard self-government as government by Africans. They have now begun to demand self-government, as opposed to multi-racial government.

The Africans were encouraged in this demand by the report of the United Nations visiting mission which toured the country in 1954. As a Trust Territory Tanganyika is visited every three years by a United Nations delegation of three who report to the Trusteeship Council on the administration of the country. In this report it was suggested that a time limit for independence of twenty years be fixed by the British administration. The British Government and many other observers refused to consider the report seriously, characterizing it as 'wild and extremist'. This was not, however, the reaction of the Africans, who not only gave evidence to the delegation, but sent their leader, Julius Nyerere, to the United Nations in order to represent their case before the Trusteeship Council.

The Africans do not insist on a set time limit for independence at present, but they have a profound desire to be assured that multi-racial government with racial quotas is not a permanent institution in their country; that full, unconditional democracy will be developed; and, ultimately, that they will become an independent state. They therefore ask the British Government for assurances that the present form of constitution is only a transitional step towards democracy. They similarly demand that an electoral system be devised which, during this transitional period, will enable them to elect their own members in place of the Governor's nomination and thus ensure that such members are truly representative of majority ideas. They further believe that the electoral system should be developed in such a way that racial considerations will cease to exist and fully democratic elections with equal rights for all races be fully established.

Some people say that there is no such thing as 'African opinion', and that, in fact, such political ideas as are outlined above represent nothing more than the wishes of a handful of political agitators. It is obviously true of every part of a backward continent like Africa that, in the initial stages, political ideas will be put forward by a small cadre of politically-conscious leaders. Such has been the case in every democratic country in the world. It is equally obvious that much of the future peace and progress of these countries depends upon these early leaders. If they are embittered and frustrated by a colonial administration which refuses their right to speak for their people, nationalist and possibly racialist movements will dominate political thought and make any peaceful development towards democracy impossible. It may even turn the people of these territories against western democratic ideas altogether and replace moderate by extreme leaders.

On the other hand, if such leaders are encouraged, advised and accepted on friendly terms, it will be found, as in West Africa, that the understanding thus established forms a sure foundation for the confidence between British administrator and colonial politician which is essential for the peaceful development of colonial peoples.

In Tanganyika political organization amongst the Africans is young, but extremely virile and making most encouraging progress. The organization known as the Tanganyika African National Union is led by Julius Nyerere, a remarkably quiet, modest, and sincere young man, whose good humour and tolerance contrast sharply with the fanaticism of many other politicians in the continent. The Union itself reflects these same characteristics, yet has secured widespread support in Dar-es-Salaam which is rapidly spreading to other parts of the country. The movement has now become the main social and political focus in Tanganyika. It has taken the lead in opposing the Government's 1956 proposals. Its demands are moderate, being mainly composed of the claim for a guarantee of gradual evolution towards full democratic self-government and independence.

The Tanganyika African National Union is opposed by the United Tanganyikan Party, which consists largely of the previous members of the Legislative Council and their supporters. The U.T.P. has at present one advantage over T.A.N.U. in that it has started its political life as a multi-racial organization, admitting members of all races. Discussions have taken place inside T.A.N.U. on the question of admitting members of other races, and it is likely that they will eventually do so, as soon as they feel a greater political security. They certainly have a greater drive and a more imaginative leadership than the U.T.P., and are backed by the Asian Association which has most intelligent and far-seeing leadership. This friendship and political agreement between Asians and Africans in Tanganyika can be of the highest significance in the political development of the whole of East and Central Africa.

It seems probable that the Tanganyika Government has made the mistake of underestimating the momentum of African political consciousness. Often they have appeared to be openly hostile to Julius Nyerere and his Union. When in this position they seem to be deliberately trying to stem such momentum. Tanganyika Africans test every new proposal according to whether it will bring them closer to a genuine form of political democracy. This they know will give them political power. Inevitably, therefore, as all politics are concerned with gaining power, the main African leaders rejected the 1956 Government proposals on the grounds that, first, they would enfranchise every European, most Asians, but very few Africans; second, that the time had come to increase the number of African representatives to a majority of the unofficial membership of the Legislative Council with full adult suffrage in order to represent more closely the racial proportions of the population: and third, that it made nonsense of democracy to force Africans to use their votes for the election of an equal number of Europeans and Asians as well as Africans, considering the vast preponderance of the African population.

This situation is fraught with the gravest danger for racial peace in Tanganyika. The relations between Africans and the immigrant races have a history happier than that of most multiracial African societies. This can only continue so long as the Africans are able to trust the immigrants to encourage them in developing politically, socially and economically. It demands tolerant and good-humoured sympathy with emerging African organizations from both the immigrant residents and the administration. If this is not shown, and particularly if there is not a continuous movement towards greater political influence for the Africans, moderation will be undermined. If the moderate leadership of Julius Nyerere and his colleagues is not seen to bring results the African masses will be ripe to heed the words of extremists, who will certainly be black racialists. A small movement of this character began in 1958 when a group calling themselves the National Congress hived off from the African National Union, calling for an indigenous African state. Already, because T.A.N.U. has been so frequently resisted by the Government, pressures have appeared within the organization itself forcing the leadership to move somewhat away from their moderation. In 1958, for example, at their Annual Conference, they moved from a demand for half the unofficial seats in the Legislative Council to calling for a majority over the other races, and dropped their support for the maintenance of an official majority. Nyerere's moderate evolutionary policy can only be maintained if it is encouraged by the administration in the form of constant concessions. As in other parts of the continent, the frustration of moderate nationalism must inevitably lead to extreme racialism, tragically destroying the very wide opportunities for racial harmony which still exist in this country. A little sympathetic imagination would show that a man like Julius Nyerere has taken on a gigantic task in establishing a modern political party in a country like Tanganyika. Scarcely one of his colleagues has had his advantages in overseas experience. He has to keep his finger on national control of policy, and at the same time tour this vast country to organize its branches. Small wonder that some of its officials lose their way or that he himself has to guard continually against the pressure of its members to turn him into a legendary hero. What is needed above all in Tanganyika is a repetition of the Arden-Clarke–Nkrumah relationship between the Governor and Nyerere to lead its people into the constantly flowing stream of modern political progress and responsibility.

The first batch of elections in September 1958 showed the strength of T.A.N.U., significantly not only amongst the Africans, but in both European and Asian political circles as well. All the T.A.N.U. candidates were elected and every European and Asian supported by T.A.N.U. was also successful. The United Tanganyika Party was overwhelmingly defeated, as was the African National Congress. The demonstration of support for T.A.N.U., its policies and its leaders could hardly have been more clear cut. The new Governor, Sir Richard Turnbull, was showing common sense in his relations with Julius Nyerere and signs were evident of a happier race relationship. There seems every possibility that Tanganyika will set an example in multi-racial Africa which may well have a tremendous influence in both the east and centre of the continent. If this succeeds, Julius Nyerere will have done more than any other African leader to show the value of moderate, democratic persuasiveness and firm, patient leadership in defeating the evils of racialism.

The second batch of elections in February 1959 were also won by T.A.N.U. and T.A.N.U. supported candidates. It seems likely, therefore, that T.A.N.U. is becoming in Tanganyika, like the C.P.P. in Ghana, the one political party capable of influencing constitutional development.

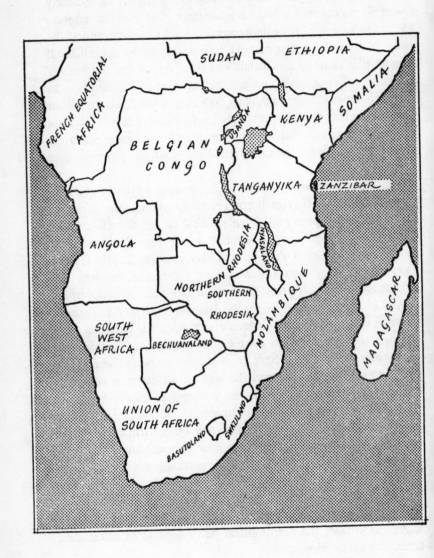

IV: CENTRAL AFRICA

LIKE most of the African continent between the Sahara Desert and the Kalahari, Central Africa was practically unknown to the outside world until the middle of the nineteenth century. The Arab slave traders found this fertile country for their trade and the earliest accounts of the people of the area come from the reports of explorers like David Livingstone who set out to destroy slavery.

It was Livingstone who reached the Zambezi in 1851 and the Victoria Falls four years later. His discoveries awakened interest amongst other Europeans, an interest which was greatly increased when gold was discovered in Mashonaland during the following decade. Livingstone's discovery of Lake Nyasa in 1859 also produced the initial impulse for the growth in that country of the missionary efforts which have been so important to its social development.

Cecil Rhodes was the next important figure to impress his personality upon Central Africa. In 1887 he persuaded the British High Commissioner to send an official into Southern Rhodesia in order to negotiate a treaty with Lobengula, Chief of the Matabele, a tribe which traced its origin to the Zulus. The Chief gave a monopoly of the mineral rights in his kingdom to Rhodes' representatives, and the Rudd Concession, as it came to be known, led eventually to the formation of the British South Africa Company. Under the Royal Charter which this company received in 1889 it was given the responsibility of promoting trade, commerce and government to the north of British Bechuanaland, to the north and west of the South African Republic, and to the west of the Portuguese Dominions. In the following year a pioneer column marched northwards, occupying Mashonaland. In the same year Lewanika, Chief of the Barotse, asked for the protection of Britain against the Matabele and gave a concession over mining and trading to the company. During the following years both the Matabele and the Mashona were crushed by war; and by 1897 the British had obtained control over the whole of their lands.

Meanwhile the British South Africa Company continued to administer Northern as well as Southern Rhodesia, an administration supported by Orders-in-Council in 1889. Barotseland, however, maintained a different constitutional connexion which left power in the hands of the Paramount Chief, but commercial rights with the company. It was in 1911 that the name Northern Rhodesia was given to this territory, though the company continued its administration, under a certain degree of Crown control, until 1924, when it was placed completely under the administration of the British Government.

The missionaries meanwhile had been extending their work in Nyasaland, particularly under the aegis of the Universities Mission, the Free Church Mission, and the Church of Scotland Mission. Tribal wars were gradually suppressed and the slave trade abolished. In 1891 a British protectorate was proclaimed, the Crown becoming responsible for the administration of the country 'with the consent and the desire of the chiefs and people'.

Although these three countries border each other and together form British Central Africa, their history since European settlement was established has shown marked differences. Most of these arise from the different circumstances in which they came under European control. Southern Rhodesia was conquered and its main tribal system destroyed through the defeat of Lobengula and the reduction of the Matabele and Mashona when they rebelled. The Europeans settled here, then, as conquerors, with the Africans subjected through force of arms. It is significant that the Orders-in-Council regulating the administration of the British South Africa Company insisted that special reserves be set aside for the native population, who were to be accorded definite protection.

From the start, therefore, the conception in Southern Rhodesia was that the European immigrants and the native population had separate interests, derived from their original enmity. Consequently it was logical to divide the country between them, the Europeans taking land for their development by right of conquest, the Africans being granted a separate area for their own societies. This division of land in Southern Rhodesia was confirmed by the Land Apportionment Act of 1930, which divided the country into Native areas, European areas, and unassigned, undetermined, and forest areas. Under this division the Africans received 33 per cent of the land, the Europeans 50 per cent, the rest remaining un-allocated.

Northern Rhodesia, however, was not conquered, but peacefully penetrated by the British South Africa Company. In place of conquest, a series of treaties were negotiated, leaving the chiefs and other traditional authorities with their political control almost untouched. Land division did not, therefore, follow the Southern Rhodesian pattern. In Northern Rhodesia land was divided be-tween Crown land, which can be leased to Europeans, Native reserves, including Barotseland, and Native trust land. The re-serves are, as in Southern Rhodesia, for the exclusive use of the Africans, and the trust land is also intended primarily for their use, though on occasion the Governor may grant rights of occupancy to non-Africans. Only 6 per cent of Northern Rhodesia has been allocated to Crown lands, 34 per cent consisting of Native reserves and Barotseland, and 60 per cent as Native trust land.

In Nyasaland force played a part in the penetration of Euro-peans, but rather to suppress tribal warfare and to combat the slave trade than to seize land. The major European influence in the country has been that of the missionaries. No reserves have been set up in Nyasaland, the land being divided between freehold, public land, and African trust land, similar to that of Northern Rhodesia. Europeans and Africans can acquire land on the same terms, though it is laid down in the Order-in-Council that in the trust land African interests shall be paramount. Five per cent of the land area is held as freehold, 8 per cent as public land, and 87 per cent as African trust land.

The difference in this system of land division and land tenure marks the initial cleavage in racial policy between Southern Rhodesia, on the one hand, and the two northern territories on the other. Whereas the Southern Rhodesians started from the con-ception that their country could be developed as two separate areas, white and black, Northern Rhodesia and Nyasaland laid down quite different patterns. In Nyasaland, in particular, European and African land development was to be complementary, and in Northern Rhodesia too, white and black were to be closely associated.

Similarly, the different histories of European penetration have produced sharp contrasts in political development. The Europeans of Southern Rhodesia conquered the African tribes and, therefore, rule them directly. In both Northern Rhodesia and Nyasaland the local authorities, through chiefs and tribal councils, were maintained, European rule operating largely through them. In the former case Africans have become simply subjects of the white man; in the latter they have continued to participate in the government of their localities and, to a lesser degree, of their countries.

These initial divergent trends have been strengthened and emphasized by subsequent developments in all three territories.

From early in its European history Southern Rhodesia was planned as a country for European settlement. Railways were built to link it with South Africa in the south and the sea to the east; mining attracted settlers, whilst tobacco and secondary industries were gradually added. By 1923 the European population had grown to 35,000; by 1939 to 64,000; and by 1950 to 128,000, still increasing at between 10,000 and 12,000 annually, so by 1959 around the 220,000 mark.

Politically Southern Rhodesia followed a similar pattern to that of South Africa. The European settlers considered it to be mainly a white country, and, although some consideration was given to the Africans in the reserves in social and economic affairs, they were never thought of as a part of the political scene. Meanwhile, however, the European settlers, as in most other colonial areas, began to demand from Britain an increasing share of control over their own affairs. By 1923 a strong agitation for self-government had developed and in that year Southern Rhodesia was given the option of either joining the Union of South Africa or of gaining a large measure of self-government. In the proportion of about four to three the settlers voted in favour of self-government. Since then they have built up a parliamentary system based on British practice. Their Parliament has consisted of a single chamber, with thirty members elected on a constituency basis, and with a Cabinet system. A Governor represents the British Monarchy. This is not quite full self-government, for legislation which may discriminate against the Africans is subject to the veto of the Secretary of State, and external affairs are conducted by the British Government. The semi-independent position of the colony, however, has been recognized by placing it under the Commonwealth Relations Office instead of the Colonial Office, and by frequent invitations to its Prime Minister to attend Commonwealth conferences.

Having attained this position of being almost self-governing, the European settlers, almost all British and South African, have followed the South African example of keeping politics almost as their sole monopoly. They have not, however, like their South African neighbours, instituted separate representation for the African community. Rather have they followed the earlier example of the Cape Colony in allowing political rights to a tiny fraction of the African population. Until 1951 the qualification for the vote was to possess property to the annual value of £150 or an annual income of £100, plus a simple educational test in English. These qualifications applied indiscriminately to all races. In 1951 a move was made to provide for separate African representation. This was quickly dropped, largely through British pressure. In its place, however, the financial qualifications were drastically increased to £500 and £240 respectively. In the debate introducing this change, the Minister said bluntly that the object was to prevent any rapid increase in the number of Africans on the electoral roll. Yet, out of an electorate of about 50,000, only around 400 were Africans. It is probable, however, that this number could have been much larger if all those Africans qualified had, in fact, registered. If they did, of course, it might well be the signal for a further increase in franchise qualifications. Significant events occurred in the political scene of Southern Rhodesia in 1957 and 1958. A new franchise was introduced on somewhat similar lines to the new Federal franchise (see Appendix 2). Two electoral rolls were created, the one with high financial and educational qualifications applying almost solely to Europeans, and the second, on lower qualifications, applying mainly to Africans. At no time can the number of special votes registered exceed one-fifth of the ordinary electors enrolled.

Although this provision appeared to guarantee European political control for the foreseeable future, it soon became clear that even this moderate introduction of Africans to the political scene aroused widespread fears amongst the European community. At the beginning of 1958 a split in Mr Garfield Todd's Cabinet provoked a political crisis. Mr Todd eventually resigned as Prime Minister and was replaced by Sir Edgar Whitehead, who had been the Southern Rhodesian representative in New York. A general election followed at the beginning of June, by which time Mr Todd and his moderately liberal supporters had left the United Federal Party and revived the United Rhodesia Party, which had previously merged with Roy Welensky's federal organization. The third party to fight the election was the Dominion Party, which had emerged from a variety of opposition movements, and which, though not expressly a party supporting apartheid, nevertheless included the apartheid supporters in Southern Rhodesia and all those who were opposed to the pace of African political advance. In the general election Sir Edgar Whitehead's United Federal Party was returned with seventeen seats. The Dominion Party gained thirteen, and Mr Todd and his friends were heavily defeated in all the seats in which they put up candidates.

It seemed likely after the election that Sir Edgar Whitehead's party and government would try to walk the narrow tightrope of compromise in much the same way as had the United Party in South Africa. At the same time, the Dominion Party was obviously gaining rapidly in strength, representing not the extreme racialism of the South African Nationalists, but certainly the determination of the majority of Rhodesian Europeans to maintain their control of government. Liberalism even in its moderate form had been wiped out from parliamentary representation and left to plough the long furrow of a small minority. It was clear that there were thunder clouds ahead, and that the pretence of basing Federation on an undefined 'partnership' had been baldly exposed. It is hardly surprising that in these circumstances African opposition to

Federation became even stronger in the northern territories, whilst the Africans in Southern Rhodesia, organized in the young but growing African National Congress, began to awaken to the fact that they would have to organize themselves politically if they were ever to gain any kind of political influence.

During the course of this rapid European development Southern Rhodesia experienced the same kind of problems as have beset the Union of South Africa since the beginning of the century. Mining and industrial progress demanded labour, and labour in any quantity was only available through the use of Africans. The conception of two completely separate societies has, therefore, been breaking down under economic pressure. On the one hand, the needs of industry and of European services have demanded the presence of Africans in the towns. On the other, the pressure of the African population upon their limited land has increased the same tendency by forcing many Africans to leave their tribal areas. From these two pressures African urbanization has grown.

The reaction of Southern Rhodesia to this phenomenon is best seen in the Industrial Conciliation Act of 1934. Under this legislation, in any industry where a wage agreement has been reached between European employers and workers, employers may be prevented from employing skilled labour at lower wage rates than those in the agreement. On the surface this appears to be a maintenance of the trade union principle of 'the rate for the job'. In practice it is the application of an industrial colour bar preventing Africans from entering the skilled trades.

And, in addition to this legislation, no provision is made in Southern Rhodesia for the recognition of African trade unions, whilst Africans in the towns must carry passes. It can therefore be seen that the segregation attitude has been strongly entrenched in this colony.

In contrast to the history of Southern Rhodesia, European settlement in Northern Rhodesia and Nyasaland has been on a much lower scale. It seemed for a long time that there was little attraction for white settlers in Northern Rhodesia. As late as 1920 the European population was only just over 3,000. It was the development of the copper mines in the country which produced the increase in European settlement, reaching a figure of 36,000 in 1950, increasing at the rate of over 6,000 annually.

The European settlement of Nyasaland was on an even smaller scale and, although it doubled in the five years after the Second World War, it had only reached 4,000 in 1950. There seems little reason to suppose that European settlement in Nyasaland will ever reach considerable proportions, for there is no known important deposit of minerals, the country's wealth depending almost entirely on agriculture, mainly the production of tobacco, tea and cotton. In Nyasaland, however, the Asian population has grown rapidly, now surpassing that of the Europeans.

Both these two northern territories are protectorates, under the supervision of the Colonial Office. In each of them local government has encouraged African responsibility, whilst at the centre Executive and Legislative Councils have been established on the usual principles of British colonial policy. A general attitude in both territories is that Africans shall learn political administration in their own areas and then increasingly extend their influence at the centre. In both countries officials retain a majority in both the Executive and the Legislative Councils, but since the war Africans have been introduced into both the Legislative Councils. In Northern Rhodesia there were four Africans nominated by the Governor, two of them selected by the African Representative Council, compared with twelve European elected members. In Nyasaland, under the 1956 constitution, six members are elected by Europeans and Asians and five Africans are nominated by the Governor after election of the African Provincial Councils.

In both these northern territories the Africans believe that they are already junior partners in the political development of the country, and that Britain is the trustee for the continuation of their developing political influence, which must eventually give them a majority control. They would like to see this political progress speeded up and there has been a strong agitation in both countries to increase their proportions compared with that of the Europeans. They are also anxious to secure direct African elections in place of nomination. Nevertheless, in both cases they contrast their position favourably with that of the African in Southern Rhodesia. The

constitutions of both were under discussion during 1958; Northern
Rhodesia's was revised in 1958 and Nyasaland's will probably be
some time in 1959. In March 1958 the Government of Northern
Rhodesia published a White Paper with its proposals for constitutional change. These may be summarized thus: the Legislative
Council to consist of a Speaker and thirty members; twenty-two
of the thirty to be elected, twelve of them from the areas along the
railway line where most of the Europeans live, six in the other
areas mainly inhabited by the Africans, two reserved for Europeans
in the African areas, and two reserved for Africans in the European areas. In addition there would be six official and two nominated members. The Executive Council to consist of the Governor
and nine Ministers, four of them officials and of the other five, four
would be taken from the European Elected Members of the
Legislative Council, leaving a maximum of one African. Franchise
would be qualified with two rolls. Financial qualifications for the
higher or 'ordinary' one would limit it almost entirely to Europeans, the lower or 'special' including mainly Africans. Special
provision to be made that in the twelve European constituencies
'special' votes, which will be almost entirely cast by Africans, must
not count for more than one-third of the total 'ordinary' votes, and
similarly for the six African seats the 'ordinary' or higher qualified
voters not to count for more than one-third of the total 'special'
votes. For the four extra constituencies reserved for two Europeans
and two Africans the same limitation applied.

Candidates were to be qualified corresponding to their constituencies, in the European seats on the higher roll, in the African
on either, and in the reserved seats on the higher roll. A further
provision demanded that any candidate who qualified only on the
lower roll would have to obtain permission to stand from two-
thirds of the chiefs in his constituency.

These proposals were extremely complicated and on that ground
alone were unlikely to appeal to the majority of Africans in the
territory. On the other hand, they represented an attempt to bring
Africans and Europeans together as an electorate without the
suspicion that the African candidates would in fact be elected by a
mainly European electorate, as in the Federation, thus becoming

'European stooges'. However, even the most moderate African demands included equal representation in the Legislative Council, whereas in these proposals they would have obtained only eight seats compared with fourteen European, and two ministerial portfolios in place of the one offered here. Nor could the Africans be expected to be content with only one of their constituencies, and that one of the extra ones, being allocated to the densely populated, urbanized Copper Belt. What is more, the Government planned to raise the level of qualifications for the lower roll over a period of ten years, until they reached the level of the higher roll. Their argument was that, as economic conditions improve, so Africans would be qualified on the upper limit. This presupposed further that a high income should remain a permanent qualification for the franchise, an assumption which is certainly rejected by the African community. The principle of adult suffrage, of 'one man one vote', and of political equality is spreading far too fast for these Government proposals or any similar ones to satisfy African ambitions. If Europeans have any desire to retain the slightest political influence they will have to recognize these ambitions, which are based on European teaching, work sympathetically with the Africans to achieve a genuine democratic society, attempt to remove race from politics, and then rely on their ability instead of their race to attract political support. Any other policy is bound to increase the racial content of politics, inevitably resulting in the eventual political submersion of Europeans.

In September 1958 the Colonial Secretary published his proposals on the Northern Rhodesian constitution, based on the Governor's proposals referred to above. He made some slight but significant amendments. The number of African Ministers in the Executive Council were to be increased from one to two, with the idea of Assistant Ministers being dropped. Electors on the General, i.e. mainly European, Roll were not to have their votes devalued in the eight African constituencies, but the special voters, almost entirely African, were to be devalued in European seats. All African candidates, whether ordinary or special electors, were to be compelled to secure the approval of two-thirds of the chiefs in their area in order to be allowed to stand.

These proposals aroused hostility from both European and African. The Europeans, led by Sir Roy Welensky, the Federal Prime Minister, strongly criticized the increase in African Ministerial appointments, claiming that such Ministers would be appointed according to race instead of on merit. They had not criticized the appointment of the single African Minister, however, and consequently were self-exposed as being concerned with the numbers of Africans rather than with the racial consideration. What they obviously feared was that once the two African Ministers were appointed an irresistible demand would develop for their numbers to be increased. The Africans criticized the introduction of the chiefs into the political field as a clear determination on the part of the Government to exclude African politicians. They pointed out that all the chiefs are appointed and removable by the Government, which would clearly be able to influence their decisions. They were also strongly opposed to the African vote being devalued whilst that of the Europeans could be cast in full. This would mean that the Europeans could control the election of the two special African members in the European areas, thus gaining a representation of sixteen nominees as against only six direct African representatives. Above all, they saw in the decision to raise the qualifications of the special voters periodically as their numbers equalled those on the Ordinary Roll the backing of the Colonial Office for the determination of Europeans to maintain permanent political control over their country.

To all in Northern Rhodesia this Constitution has a special significance, as it will determine the character of the Northern Rhodesian delegation to attend the 1960 conference on the constitutional development of the Federal State. Africans are more determined now than ever before to resist the claims of Sir Roy Welensky, his supporters and his Dominion Party opponents for independence in 1960. They see this as a repetition of the South African tragedy whereby a British Government is being asked to hand over its protection of the African majority to a European minority. They have already discussed whether in view of their under-representation in the constitution and the manoeuvres to minimize their political influence they should boycott the territorial elections in the same way as they boycotted those for the Federation. It is probable that they will decide to persuade those qualified to register and fight the elections, but even so it is quite clear that these will be fought on opposition to the constitution and to Federation, and that after the elections a bitter political struggle is certain to develop.

Similarly in Nyasaland the Africans, who have not yet been allowed to elect their own members directly, demand adult suffrage with an African majority in the Legislative Council and in the Executive Council. Their opposition to Federation has gone so far that they have firmly made up their minds to secede from the Federation and to set up an independent Nyasaland state under African control. In the circumstances of Nyasaland, particularly with its scanty economic resources and lack of a coastline, this may seem unreal. Nevertheless, nationalist movements have often aimed at unreal objectives and secured mass support for them. Certainly Nyasaland Africans have become completely intransigent against Federation, with the consequence that their previously happy relations with their own Europeans, and particularly with officials, have been destroyed, leaving the inevitable ugly signs of racialism. They sometimes toy with the idea of linking up with either Tanganyika or Northern Rhodesia. Tanganyika, however, is almost as poor as Nyasaland, whilst the copper wealth of Northern Rhodesia would certainly provoke the Europeans to a determined effort to preserve the territory from African control. The whole situation is desperately unhappy, stemming largely from the folly of trying to impose Federation against the will of the vast majority of the inhabitants, and future prospects are not enhanced by the very low development of African organization in every part of the area. The Africans in their National Congresses in both territories have never developed strong, coherent organizations. Nevertheless, both Congresses represent a general mood much wider than their actual membership. They have demanded increased representation in both Legislative and Executive Councils with the objective of controlling both in the near future. They are vigorously opposed to Federation and would like to take their countries out of it, setting them up as separate states or joining together perhaps with

Tanganyika under African control. Their biggest need if they are to become a serious political influence is much stronger organization throughout their territories.

A new sense of leadership and strength in organization may come to the Nyasaland Congress through the return to his homeland of Dr Hastings Banda, who has had long experience in Britain and Ghana. Throughout his long absence from Nyasaland Hastings Banda became almost a legend to his own people, who constantly looked to him to return and lead them from their plight when the time was ripe. On his return in 1958 he was greeted as a Messiah, and quickly drew the threads of the organization together in a new effort for increased African political power in Nyasaland and still more determined opposition to Federation. He was unable, however, to heal the split which had developed over the refusal of Wellington Chirwa and his colleague Kumbikano to resign from the Federal Assembly. These two experienced Nyasaland leaders, no less fervent opponents of Federation than their Congress critics, gathered their supporters around them in a separate organization, though all are badly needed by Congress in the national struggle. All their strength will be needed when the details of the new Nyasaland constitution are published. Similarly, in Northern Rhodesia two of the leading Congress officials, Kenneth Kaunda and Simon Kapwepwe, broke away from the main Congress body and its leader, Harry Nkumbula, to form their own organization. Both examples show the weakness of organization, discipline and sense of public service in these African organizations. As in other countries at this early stage of development, it will take time for leaders to learn that as public figures their first duty is to those whom they lead and represent. The danger is here even graver than anywhere else in Africa that the continued hostility and pressure of White politicians will drive the African masses to reject moderate leadership and turn towards sheer racialism. If this happens, as is inevitable if the political scene remains based on a torrent of racial emotions, Central Africa will become a battleground between White and Black more dangerous than anything seen before in any part of the continent.

Economically and socially also the northern Africans feel they are better off than their brothers in the south. There may seem to be some little confusion here. The industrial colour bar has been as deeply rooted on the Copper Belt in Northern Rhodesia as anywhere in the world. It is only as a result of twenty years' struggle that the monopoly of the European copper miners in skilled work has eventually been broken. This was only accomplished in 1955 and accompanied by wide guarantees to the European miners. Meanwhile, the European Miners Union has waged a bitter warfare against the establishment of an African Union and at one time, early in 1955, appeared to be on the verge of breaking it completely.

In spite of this bitter struggle, however, the Africans in Northern Rhodesia feel that they have had a far better deal than those in the south. African trade unionism has never been illegal in the north and, indeed, has had very considerable encouragement from the Government. In addition, both Government and copper employers have continually exerted pressure on the European miners to break their colour bar. As a result, and with the infinitely important assistance of international trade unionism, a union has been built in Northern Rhodesia which is probably the strongest African union in history. The fact that many, though not all, African miners on the copper belt are immigrant labourers, coming and going between their villages and the mines, has, in itself, spread a knowledge and experience of democratic trade union organization far wider than the actual numbers of union membership would indicate.

In Nyasaland conditions are different. There is no considerable industry and on the plantations feudal relations are still widely prevalent. As in any such society the good feudal employers provide excellent social conditions for their workers, which contrast sharply with the conditions under bad employers. Yet, in spite of growing discontent with this feudal relationship, the influence of the missions and the absence of any obvious threat to their land from the few European settlers have laid the basis of comparatively happy race relations. Nyasas often have to leave their country to find a reasonable living and are to be found all over Southern

Africa, where they have the reputation of intelligent and dependable workers. As in Northern Rhodesia, their freedom from pass laws and discriminatory restrictions has given them a feeling of opportunity and a hope of progress largely absent in Southern Rhodesia.

It is from this background that we should consider the establishment of the Federal State of Central Africa. Federation became a major political issue between 1951 and 1953, not only in these three countries, but in Britain itself, and indeed throughout the rest of Africa. In spite of the many different facets of the question, in reality the focal issue was whether the six million African inhabitants of the three territories should be brought under the control of the 200,000 white settlers. After continuous bitter political struggles the Federal State was eventually established by the British Parliament in July 1953.

The history of Central African Federation goes back over nearly thirty years. At various times during this period efforts have been made by the European inhabitants of these three countries to find a formula through which the three territories could be brought close together. There are many reasons for this desire. Some felt that only by creating a single Central African state could the British influence in this area be firmly established and enabled to resist the efforts of South African Afrikaners, and possibly other alien influences. Others feared the development of African influence in other parts of the Continent and felt that colonial policy in Northern Rhodesia and Nyasaland was following too closely along similar lines. They desired to establish European authority before the Africans could advance too far. Still others considered that any genuine economic progress required a single co-ordinated economy for the whole area. Some even believed that a single state controlled by Europeans would eventually turn southwards and join up with the Union.

The various efforts for closer association apparently came to a halt when, in 1938, the Bledisloe Commission was appointed to study and report on the question of closer association between the three territories. It firmly turned down any question of amalgamation, largely on the grounds of African opposition to it.

Nevertheless, the issue was revived after the war, and, in 1949, an unofficial conference was held at Victoria Falls between representatives of the three European populations. The agitation continued and pressure on the British Government increased even though a Central African Council was already co-ordinating many services. Eventually, in 1950, a committee of officials was set up to study the whole issue afresh. It was generally believed at the time that the officials would report against closer association and thus kill the idea. Instead they reported in 1951 and produced a draft scheme for the establishment of a Federal State.

The publication of this Federal proposal provoked a debate which shook not only Africa, but the British political scene. When it was first published in 1951 a Labour Government was in office in Britain, the Secretary of State for the Colonies being Mr James Griffiths and for Commonwealth Relations Mr Patrick Gordon Walker. The Government decided that before making up its mind on the scheme these two ministers should visit the territories concerned in order to discuss the proposal with all sections of the people and discover their reactions.

Meanwhile, in Central Africa itself, considerable emotion was engendered as to the merits, motives and effects of Federation. The leading European politicians in each of the three territories were in favour of Federation and had, in fact, been largely instrumental in persuading the British Government to appoint the official committee. Sir Godfrey Huggins in Southern Rhodesia and Sir Roy Welensky in Northern Rhodesia were the two men consistently leading the pressure for closer association. They did not approve of all the details of the scheme produced, but were certain that some form of association was necessary.

It was frequently said during the many debates which followed that it was impossible to gauge accurately the opinion of Africans. This may have been largely true in Southern Rhodesia, where African political organization was negligible, as it had always been strongly discouraged by the Government. Yet in the two northern territories some degree of opinion could be expressed. In both countries African Congresses existed—the usual title for early African political organizations. In both territories African consultative councils were established; in Northern Rhodesia it was known as the African Representative Council and in Nyasaland as the African Protectorate Council. In both territories also Africans were nominated to the Legislative Councils.

Though no one would claim that these African politicians could represent their entire populations, it is certainly true that they represented the growing political consciousness of considerable numbers of their people. It is equally significant that every recognized African spokesman in both these two territories consistently opposed and condemned the Federal scheme from the start. There may have been some degree of simple conservatism in this opposition, but its central feature was undoubtedly a hostility to the idea of placing the six million Africans of the three territories under the political control of the 200,000 white inhabitants. They saw in it a repetition of the mistake made by Britain in 1910, when the white inhabitants of South Africa were given power over the Non-European majority of the population. They feared that the Colonial Office was giving up much of its control to the local European residents. It is highly significant from the standpoint of British policy to note that in this plural society of Central Africa the African majority of the population opposed any reduction in British control before the African community had developed to a point at which they could hold their own with the local Europeans. In short, the Africans regarded the British Colonial Office and the British as their protector against local white rule.

Amongst the Europeans of the territories the views of Huggins and Welensky were by no means unanimously supported. Some Europeans saw the Federal scheme as an invasion of their predominantly white control. In Southern Rhodesia there were those who feared the influence of the Colonial Office policy in the north, whilst in all three territories some of the white inhabitants were shocked at the suggestion that African representatives should appear in a Federal Chamber along with the whites. There were undoubtedly some people also among the white community who saw Federation as a step away from the Union and would have preferred to turn southwards.

In Britain the consideration of Federation was at first confused.

After the visits of the Secretaries of State, the Labour Government realized that African opposition was so widespread that no further immediate steps should be taken. A few weeks later they were defeated in the 1951 General Election and a Conservative Government took office. One of its first acts was to announce its support of Federation and plans to speed up the measures necessary to bring it into effect.

Within the Labour Party there were voices both against and in favour of the Federal scheme, but gradually it became apparent that the vast majority of the Party opposed Federation, if only because the Africans expressed their firm and united opposition to it. A widespread campaign, in which certain churches were particularly prominent, especially in Scotland, was now organized. Meetings of protest were held in various parts of the country and a variety of African politicians came to Britain from Central Africa. On the other side, Huggins, Welensky and their supporters were also strongly represented from time to time in Britain and conducted a powerful lobbying campaign in political circles.

A number of important debates were held in the British Parliament and by now the Labour Opposition spoke officially against Federation, though a handful of members who supported it abstained when divisions were held. In Southern Rhodesia a plebiscite was organized on the issue. It was conducted amongst the electorate, of whom only about 400 were Africans. The plebiscite showed a majority in favour of Federation, with a substantial minority opposed to it.

Eventually this maelstrom of debate, discussion and political conflict came to an end in the summer of 1953, when the British Parliament approved the measure. The new federal State of Central Africa was established, political responsibility was to be divided between the Federal Government and Parliament, on the one hand, and the three territorial governments on the other. The Federal Assembly was to consist of thirty-five members, twenty-six of whom were to represent the 200,000 Europeans, whilst the remaining nine, six Africans and three Europeans, were to represent the six million Africans. Perhaps the most significant aspect of this new constitution was the provision that a two-thirds majority of the Assembly was required to effect constitutional change. There seemed little chance in these circumstances for an increase in the proportion of African representation. On the other hand, an African Affairs Board was established within the Assembly to prevent the passage of any acts of discrimination. The whole of this constitution is to remain as it is until some time between 1960 and 1962 when a conference will be convened to review it. The four governments and the British government will take part. It is far too early to judge the fate of this new and curious State. Nominally it is based upon the principle of 'racial partnership', but no one has yet defined the practical meaning of this phrase. It is already clear, though, that Central Africa is one of the most important crucibles of race relations in the African continent. The European politicans in this area are divided broadly into those who support some form of association with the newly developing representatives of African political consciousness, and those who prefer as great a degree of racial separation as can be attained. These two views were represented by the two main political parties, the Federal Party and the Confederate Party, though the latter has changed its name and personnel several times. In the first elections, held in 1953, the Federals, led by Huggins and Welensky, secured a sweeping victory, yet about a third of the electorate voted against them. Sir Godfrey Huggins, now Lord Malvern, became the first Prime Minister, with Sir Roy Welensky as his deputy. Huggins, who once believed in racial separation, is now convinced that if European settlement in Central Africa is to be maintained the Europeans must take the Africans along with them. He frequently tells the white population of Central Africa clearly that the doctrine of racial superiority is indefensible and dangerous, and that the future of their children depends upon developing racial harmony. Yet, at the same time, his opposition to a closer definition of a detailed pattern of race relations and his occasional slights upon African leaders prevented him from securing any widespread trust from the Africans. In 1956 Lord Malvern retired, and Sir Roy Welensky succeeded him as Prime Minister.

The African community itself has been somewhat bewildered since its campaign against Federation was defeated. In Southern

Rhodesia, where the election of African representatives was held on the general electoral roll, consisting almost entirely of Europeans, the two African members were sponsored by the Federal Party and tried to co-operate with them. In the two northern territories African representation is much more independent of the Europeans and continually attempts to use the Assembly in order to debate race relations, though as yet without much success. Pressure against any hint of recognition of Federation has even led the African Congress in Nyasaland to expel its two members of Parliament when they refused to resign their seats.

The whole situation is really in the balance. There are at one and the same time both signs of greater awareness of the necessity of racial co-operation and yet evidence of efforts to preserve white domination. As this area of Central Africa stands between the Union, based completely on the principle of permanent domination by the white minority, and the British Colonies of East and West Africa, where Africans are being encouraged to take greater responsibility and ultimately gain full and equal rights, the significance of what happens in the new Federal State is profound. Britain still retains a measure of responsibility, particularly in Northern Rhodesia and Nyasaland, and has the ultimate sanction over the Federation itself.

Two important issues agitated afresh the relations between both the Federation and Britain, and the Europeans and Africans within the Federation. The first is the amendments to the constitution, contained in the Constitution Amendment Act, and the Franchise Act. The former simply increased the number of members in the Federal Assembly from thirty-five to fifty-nine. In doing so it increased those members elected almost entirely by Europeans from twenty-six to forty-four, and African representatives from nine to fifteen. The latter act made new provision for franchise qualifications on two electoral rolls. Both these measures were held by the African Affairs Board to be discriminatory, and in consequence there were debates on them in the British House of Commons. On both occasions they were opposed by the Labour Opposition, but in the divisions the Conservative Government secured a majority.

The main significance of these acts was that the new African representatives, instead of being directly responsible to Africans themselves, were to be elected on mixed rolls in which Europeans will normally predominate. As a sop to democratic opinion the two new voters' rolls were opened to citizens of any race, but wealth qualifications limited the higher roll almost entirely to Europeans, whilst the lower roll included only a small minority of adult Africans. It is significant too that electors on both rolls are now entitled to vote for the six new African members, who will thus become, like the present African representatives in Southern Rhodesia, responsible to a largely European electorate. This fact is also likely to change the character of the African Affairs Board itself, as Africans dependent on European votes are nominated to it. In any case, the African Affairs Board has lost most of what prestige it ever had as a safeguard for African interests through the rejection by the British Parliament of its opinion that these two laws are discriminatory.

The second issue of conflict concerns the status of the Federation itself. Many of its leading politicians always saw the establishment of the Federation as a long step towards independence within the Commonwealth. This desire has been greatly increased as they have watched the Gold Coast rapidly marching towards independent statehood, and have resented Africans being given a position which they, as Europeans, were denied. Lord Malvern put forward proposals for what he called 'technical independence' at the 1956 Conference of the Commonwealth Prime Ministers. His proposals were rejected by the British Government which led to angry reactions amongst the white politicians in the Federation. There was even the braggart, but empty, threat to follow the example of the American colonies in the eighteenth century and fight a war of independence against Britain. Whilst rejecting Lord Malvern's proposals, the British Government, nevertheless, promised to make counter proposals. Sir Roy Welensky followed up Malvern's pressure and is demanding greater power by 1960. The British Government must be aware, however, that any suggestion of weakening the ties between Britain and Northern Rhodesia and Nyasaland would raise an immediate outcry from the Africans of these two territories, who still regard the British connexion as their last defence against the control of their own white settlers.

The whole future of the Federation is now in the melting pot. Sir Roy Welensky and his followers have made no secret of the fact that since the Labour Party published its statement *Plural Society* in 1956, with its emphasis on the ultimate aim of complete democracy based upon adult suffrage and the principle of one person one vote for every territory under British influence, the governing party in the Federation will try to secure the maximum commitments from Britain before the next British general election. In short, they are determined at all costs to preserve white control for the foreseeable future. Welensky secured two commitments from the British Government in April 1957. The first was that the constitutional conference scheduled to take place between 1960 and 1962 would, in fact, be held in 1960. The second was that the British Government would not introduce legislation concerning the Federation except at the request of the Federal Government. Both promises are, in fact, empty. It is virtually certain that there will be a British general election before 1960. Power of legislation still rests with the British Parliament, no matter what any British Government may promise.

At the same time the Africans of Northern Rhodesia and Nyasaland, their fears aggravated by the new pressure of Welensky, have become increasingly hostile to the existence of federation itself. They have tended to expect the next Labour Government to break up the Federation and reconstitute the complete autonomy of Northern Rhodesia and Nyasaland. This is unrealistic, for once a measure of political power is transferred from London it is almost impossible to recover it except in circumstances of crisis. On the other hand, there can be no doubt that a future British Labour Government would use all its powers to insist on genuine democracy being established in the Federation before British authority is withdrawn.

Meanwhile, Welensky and his government have been expanding the federal assembly, suggesting a broadening of the franchise and giving the white dominated electorate increased powers of electing African representatives. They clearly fear the logic of maintaining communual elections as has been done in Kenya; they know that this opens the way to an irresistible pressure from the Africans for steadily increased representation to match the figures of their population. They are trying to avoid this danger by allowing a selected minority of Africans to qualify for an electoral roll, which will be dominated by the Europeans for many years to come. Holding the power of altering franchise qualifications, they foresee a permanent opportunity to maintain their own control.

Yet the Federation has been based from the start on the principle of 'partnership' which is written into the preamble of the federal constitution. Partnership can be defined in one or two ways. It can either be a partnership of two separate communities, which in Central Africa implies the permanent domination of the minority white society; or it can be defined as genuine co-operation between individuals of different races, based not upon race but upon mutual respect for individual worth. It is the latter definition only which can be accepted by Britain as a qualification for a genuinely democratic and eventually independent state. If the Federation is to be established as a state it can only be on this basis.

In November 1958 the second Federal election was held under the constitution amended as described above. Two features of it immediately became apparent. The first was that Sir Roy Welensky and his Federal Party clearly retained the support of the vast majority of the European electors. They won forty-four seats as compared with eight for the Dominion Party. During the election much was made of statements by Winston Field, the Dominion Party leader, to the effect that if returned he was prepared to declare the Federation independent and defy the British Government to oppose him if it dared. Despite his previous similar statements, Sir Roy Welensky attacked this as unconstitutional, though still maintaining his resolution to press for independence in 1960. His experience and that of his colleagues won the day. He is now armed with a mandate from the Europeans to bring every possible pressure on the British Government in 1960 to hand over control of the whole federal state to a government elected almost entirely by the European community.

The second significant feature was the almost complete success of the African National Congresses in boycotting the election. They advised Africans against registering as electors and were so successful that on the day less than 2,000 had done so. Their object in this tactic was to expose the farce of pretending that the constitution gave any considerable voice to the seven million African population.

Twelve Africans were actually elected to the new Federal Assembly, although eight of them owed their election to European voters, seven standing as Federal Party candidates and one for the Dominion Party.

A second and equally important result of this tactical manoeuvre is to deny to Sir Roy Welensky and his colleagues the possibility of claiming that any number of Africans are willing to give up their protected status under the British Crown to a Federal Government. This is vitally important, for in the Preamble to the Federal constitution, it is clearly stated that this protected status will not be infringed unless it is desired by the people and the British Government has already defined 'people' as the whole people, implying a majority of the Africans.

So far, therefore, Sir Roy Welensky and his white politicians have entirely failed to persuade their African populations to lend any support to the Federation, far less to be willing to see the white minority take over political control of Northern Rhodesia and Nyasaland from the British Government. It may be that Sir Roy will try and get round this by suggesting that a treaty be signed between a newly independent Federal Government and the British Government, assuring the protection of the Africans. This will mislead no African. The African population has seen what has happened in South Africa when British control is handed over to the local white population, and they will have none of it. Any attempt to force any form of independence by a white-dominated Federal Government will lead to such revolt amongst the Africans as to shock the whole continent.

In the final resort, it appears inevitable that the continued existence of the Federal State will depend upon its acceptance of those same principles of racial equality which are becoming established farther north. If that happens, South Africa and its policies will be still further isolated. If it does not happen, racial conflict is bound to spread throughout the southern half of the African continent.

V: THE HIGH COMMISSION TERRITORIES

BECHUANALAND, Swaziland and Basutoland are commonly known in this country as 'the Protectorates', but they are more properly termed the High Commission Territories. This title originates from the fact that they are all administered under the British High Commissioner for South Africa, whose office is in Pretoria. A glance at the map shows the close connexion between each of these three countries and the Union of South Africa, and the most important issue common to all three is the desire of South Africans to incorporate them into the Union. This desire has lasted from the first years of this century, when the four South African colonies were discussing uniting into a single state. Indeed, efforts were made during the nineteenth century by the Transvaal Republic to take over Bechuanaland and Swaziland, and by the Orange Free State to annex Basutoland.

Nevertheless, in spite of the very close geographical and economic links between all three countries and South Africa, at the time of Union in 1909 Britain retained her administration, though the Act of Union made provision for their incorporation into the new South African state at some undefined future date. Since then successive South African governments have continually pressed Britain to negotiate their incorporation into the Union. A number of discussions have taken place, but no practical results have yet materialized.

The central issue in this relationship is the contrast between the wishes of the inhabitants themselves and the racial policy pursued by South African governments. A clause in the Act of Union relating to this issue speaks of 'consultation with the inhabitants before incorporation'. This does not of necessity imply 'consent';

it does not necessarily prevent Britain from handing over the territories against the wishes of their inhabitants. Indeed, the South Africans have always submitted an interpretation which would allow Britain to consult with the three populations, but hand over the territories whatever wishes they expressed. They point out almost relevantly that this was the process followed by the British Government in the establishment of the Central African Federation.

Meanwhile, the peoples of these three countries, almost all Africans and numbering something over a million, have consistently shown their strong and united opposition to being placed under South African rule. They recognize that as a part of South Africa they might well expect some improvement in their economic and educational opportunities. They are quite definite, however, that they have no intention of buying these advantages at the price of coming under the racial policy of the Union. No British Government has stated that it will not transfer the three territories to South Africa against the will of their peoples. In present circumstances, however, and in the foreseeable future, it is obvious that any attempt to do so would be met by deep and widespread opposition from the people of Britain and of the territories themselves.

★   ★   ★   ★   ★

Bechuanaland

British protection over Bechuanaland was only granted some years after the first request had been made by some of the tribal chiefs. From early in the nineteenth century South Africa had been influenced from two main sources. In the first place there was the continual friction between Briton and Boer which resulted in a competition for land and later for mineral rights, together with frequent conflicts of policy towards the African tribes. In the second, the power of the Zulus under Chaka and Dingaan led to frequent intertribal warfare, a fragmentation and constant movement of the tribes and their splinters across vaguely defined frontiers.

It was natural in these circumstances for certain tribal chiefs to be anxious that their people, cattle, and land should be taken under the protection of a strong power. This desire was greatly stimulated when the Boer farmers left the Cape and set off to establish new farms and eventually new states in areas which were formerly African domains.

Bechuanaland felt both these influences; it lay athwart the road to the north, a road travelled by both missionaries and gold seekers, and a road constantly surveyed by the eyes of the Transvaal Boers. The Bechuana tribes were also affected by the break-away of the Matebele section of the Zulus, and most of them suffered in some way from their raids. Bechuana chiefs began to ask for British assistance from the 1860s onwards, but it was not until 1885 that the British Government, by Order-in-Council, proclaimed a Protectorate over the country. The Governor of the Cape Colony was appointed to govern also the new Protectorate, which he undertook from Mafeking.

From 1889 onwards, Rhodes, with his British South Africa Company, was looking northwards, hoping for further British development in that direction. To smooth the way he tried to include Bechuanaland within his field of operations in the terms of the company's charter. The leading African chiefs, however, preferred Imperial to company rule, and three of them, Sebele, Khama and Bathoen, made their famous visit to London in 1895 in order to resist this attempt. Finally, a compromise was reached in which they remained under Imperial control but agreed to assist the company to extend the railway from the south alongside the northern road from their country into what is now Southern Rhodesia. This railway remains the only real link between South Africa and the north.

Bechuanaland has remained under British administration. It is largely a flat, dry, dusty country, one of its chief problems being to find an adequate water supply. Much of its large area is covered by the Kalahari Desert and there are some swamps. In the west there are still to be found primitive bushmen living a life untouched by the modern world. In the east, however, where most of the population is to be found, there is good cattle country and, in contrast to the rest of the continent, the Bechuana cattle are very fine healthy beasts. Most of the wealth is measured in cattle, now increasingly transformed into cash through the Union market. Recently the building of an abattoir by the Colonial Development Corporation at Lobatsi has allowed the export of carcase meat to replace the previous method of sending the cattle southwards on the hoof. It is known that minerals are to be found in the Protectorate, for some gold has already been mined and there is certainly copper and coal. Little development has yet taken place in this field and until a thorough geological survey has been made no one can tell the extent of the wealth to be found in the country.

With very few exceptions, the life of the Bechuana people is semi-primitive and very poor. There are some areas farmed by Europeans, but at the last census there were only 2,379 Europeans in the country, compared with 292,755 Africans. Schools and hospitals are scarce, although valiant work is done with little money by both education and health departments. Social amenities and communications are almost non-existent, with the exception of the one main road and railway.

The administration has been based mainly on the principle of indirect rule, in which the chiefs and their tribal organization maintain much of their traditional responsibility under British administrative officers. The pattern inevitably shows wide variations according to the character and capabilities of both chiefs and administrators. In 1920 a European Advisory Council was constituted on an elected basis to advise the Resident Commissioner on matters affecting the European residents. At the same time a Native Advisory Council was set up for a similar purpose in relation to African affairs. Its title was later changed to the African Advisory Council. It consists of thirty-eight representatives from the different tribes. In 1951 both Advisory Councils agreed to set up a Joint Advisory Council, consisting of eight members from each, with four official members, meeting twice a year under the presidency of the Resident Commissioner.

There are distinct signs that a certain restiveness is developing over the maintenance of this old method of indirect rule. It depends essentially on the flexibility of the administrative officers in dealing with different problems and different personalities. It is designed to treat rather with primitive tribal problems than with the issues which continually arise in a modern world. The only hope of its useful continuation is in the gradual adjustment of the administrative officer from the post of ruler to that of adviser, as the chiefs grow in experience and knowledge.

Even in this remote part of the continent progress in other parts of Africa eventually becomes known, and for some time there has been a growing desire by the more progressive chiefs to see the development of a more democratic and responsible constitution, leading to the establishment of a Legislative Council. Few positive steps in this direction have been taken either by the administration or by the chiefs, but the seeds have been planted. In 1958, it was significant that both Europeans and Africans joined together in a joint demand that such a council should be established.

The breakdown of the policy of indirect rule was seen in its most spectacular form in the Khama case, which focused the eyes of the world upon the Bamangwato, the principal tribe of Bechuanaland. In 1948 Seretse Khama, the Chief-designate of the Bamangwato, married a British girl in London. The marriage was opposed by his uncle, Tshekedi, who had been the tribe's Regent since 1926, and who had made himself the strongest and cleverest ruler in southern Africa. After three tribal meetings, or kgotlas as they are called here, had been held in 1948 and 1949 to discuss the issue, the British Government stepped in. The first kgotla had decided against Seretse; the second was indecisive; and the third decided to accept him as Chief and his white wife as Queen. Tshekedi and the dissident faction thereupon withdrew from the tribal reserve and continued their agitation against the decision. The British Government decided in 1950 that, in order to avoid further tribal conflict, Seretse should be exiled from the Protectorate for a period of not less than five years, and that Tshekedi should be forbidden to live within the reserve for a similar period. When the British Government was changed in 1951 the new Conservative administration allowed Tshekedi to return to the reserve as a private individual, but declared that Seretse would never be recognized as Chief and would not be allowed to return to his home until an alternative Chief had been fully established.

In spite of the efforts of Seretse's supporters in the tribe to persuade the British Government to allow their hereditary ruler to return to them, the British Government refused to change this policy. For a time the district officer took over direct rule of the tribe, but in 1953 the third in the line of succession after Seretse and Tshekedi, a man named Rasebolai, was appointed as Native Authority, and the administration tried to persuade the tribe to accept him as Chief. This they refused to do. Meanwhile Tshekedi lived as a private citizen in a new village he built for himself at Pilikwe, though with a continuing influence over his supporter, Rasebolai. Seretse, his wife and two children remained in exile in London.

The result of this situation was that much of the life of the tribe remained at a standstill. They felt that they could take no important decisions, such as the granting of mineral rights or developing educational schemes, in the absence of him whom they considered still to be their rightful ruler. So long as Seretse was alive and had not voluntarily and genuinely renounced the chieftainship, there was no possibility under tribal custom of the acceptance of a new Chief. The situation, therefore, remained in complete deadlock.

The reverberations of the Khama incident were felt throughout Bechuanaland and indeed in all parts of the African Continent. It cast doubts as to the honesty of British pretensions in the minds of many colonial peoples throughout the world. It seemed to them that, whilst Britain was using fair words on the theory of racial equality and the abolition of colour discrimination, on the one occasion in which her pretensions were put to the test, British hypocrisy was again revealed. The coloured peoples of the world could not be expected to appreciate all the diplomatic and constitutional issues involved. They saw two simple facts: one that a black chief had married a white girl; two, that the South Africans fanatically abhor all mixed marriages. They put the two together and universally concluded that Britain was supporting South African racial attitudes by victimizing the unhappy couple. So long as this smear remained across the page of British colonial history, the other words written into Britain's colonial policy went unheeded.

Final settlement of this significant issue came suddenly, but as a result of two years' carefully planned effort. In September 1954 the National Executive Committee of the Labour Party began a detailed study of the whole problem. The five years' exile originally announced for Seretse would terminate in March 1955. The extension of the exile until a new Chief was established, proclaimed by the Conservative Government, had never been accepted by the Labour Party. They, therefore, set out to study the situation afresh and to formulate their policy on it. During the course of this study every conceivable consideration was taken into account. Not only was the attitude of the South African Government explored but also the possible effect of the return of Seretse on South African reactions towards all three High Commission territories. The fear had been expressed that if Seretse and his wife were to be returned, South Africans might take the opportunity to walk into Basutoland, and possibly interfere with the other two protectorates also. The reactions of European and Non-European opinion in South Africa and in the three protectorates were carefully tested. Discussions were held with all the Government officials concerned. Seretse himself was consulted, and it was learnt that not only was he prepared to renounce the Chieftainship on behalf of himself and his heirs if this would heal the breach, but that he had made this specific offer to the Government and that it had been rejected. The only condition on which he naturally insisted was that such a renunciation should be made in direct consultation with his own people. Discussions were held with anthropologists who had knowledge of Bechuanaland. Eventually an inquiry was conducted on the spot, with all the leading personalities amongst the Bamangwato and with chiefs of neighbouring tribes.

As a result of this exhaustive study, the Labour Party Executive came to the conclusion that, although the tribe was still divided on the issue of the correct status of Seretse's wife and children, there was a universal desire for his return. The Executive suggested that the best method of arranging for his return with the maximum support from the tribe and with the greatest chance of bringing the factions together in unity, would be for the principal leaders of the tribe to discuss the situation with Seretse and arrive at an agreed compromise. It had been discovered during the inquiry that the three main men concerned, Seretse, his uncle Tshekedi, and the Native Authority, Rasebolai, were all agreeable to this proposition. The fact was that although Tshekedi and his followers had been opposed to Seretse's wife becoming Queen or the children of a mixed marriage becoming heirs to the Chieftainship, they had discovered by experience that the tribe was not prepared to appoint anyone else to take Seretse's place as Chief. They had, in fact, been operating a colour bar against Seretse's family, and there is no doubt that the idea of a half-caste Chief came as something of a shock to many of the tribe. It had become apparent, however, over the period of five years' exile, that the bulk of the tribe were profoundly loyal to Seretse himself, and had overcome their first alarm about his family. The result was that everyone was forced to recognize that no significant progress could be made amongst the Bamangwato in Seretse's absence. The original effort made by Tshekedi and his supporters to prevent the marriage had failed; the attempt to mobilize tribal opinion against Seretse and his family was equally unsuccessful; the policy of administering the tribe in Seretse's absence was now also seen to be a failure; if any progress was to be made in this important area Seretse would have to return.

Such progress had become especially important by 1955, for not only was social and political development held up, but it was now becoming apparent that considerable mineral wealth was to be found in Bechuanaland, much of it in the tribal land of the Bamangwato. Pressure was already being exerted by important mining companies, led by the Oppenheimer Group, to secure rights over these minerals. The tribe stubbornly refused to take any decision on this matter in the absence of their Chief.

The Labour Party not only published this statement of policy, but immediately pressed it upon the Government. A conference was held between representatives of Labour's Executive and the Secretary of State for Commonwealth Relations, together with his advisers. Still the Government remained adamant and refused to consider Seretse's return until a new Chief had been appointed and was fully established.

The National Conference of the Labour Party then heard a report on the whole situation and unanimously approved the action of the National Executive. A promise was made that Parliamentary action would follow.

It was not until the first day of August 1956 that time could be found for a Parliamentary debate. In this debate both Mr James Griffiths and Mr Patrick Gordon Walker, from the Opposition front bench, pressed upon the Government the policy which had been adopted by the National Executive. It was particularly important for Mr Gordon Walker to endorse this policy, for it had been he who, in 1950 as Secretary of State for Commonwealth Relations, had had to take the responsibility for Seretse's original exile. The Government still refused to change its mind, and Commander Noble, the Under-Secretary, reiterated the Government's defence for continuing the exile.

It was made clear in the debate that as soon as another Labour Government was elected, Seretse would be allowed to return home. This fact had been clarified by the Labour Party spokesmen, and it inevitably followed that the policy of excluding Seretse could only last until the Conservatives had been defeated. Their policy was thus rendered sterile. In the knowledge that Seretse would some time return to them, the Bamangwato would certainly not agree to the appointment of an alternative Chief.

It so happened that Tshekedi was in London at the time of the debate. He recognized the new situation as quickly as anyone. He now knew that Seretse would some time return. The consequence was that his position amongst the Bamangwato was now dependent upon the attitude which his nephew took towards him.

Immediately after the House of Commons debate Seretse and Tshekedi began discussions. Nothing new emerged from their talks except that they both agreed to make a joint approach to the British Government. Tshekedi reaffirmed the renunciation of all claim to the Chieftainship for himself and his children which he had previously made. Seretse once more offered his own renunciation. On this basis both men urged the Government to allow Seretse and his family to return home. Negotiations continued for some weeks. The Government pressed both Tshekedi and Seretse to support Rasebolai as the new Chief. Both refused to do so, knowing that the tribe had rejected him as Chief and that, in any case, his position would be impossible if he tried to maintain the Chieftainship with Seretse back in the country. Eventually the Government gave in. Realizing that the whole of its policy had now been undermined and that its objectives were out of reach, it gracefully gave way and reversed its previous attitude. Seretse and his family were to be allowed to return unconditionally to their home as private citizens, but free to take a full part in the political future of their people. The restrictions on Tshekedi's activities were at the same time removed. The Chieftainship was not to be resurrected after its seven years of disuse; instead it was to be replaced by the development of a conciliar system which would gradually introduce democratic practices into the tribal government.

On 9 October Seretse left London, and the following day arrived back in Bechuanaland for the first time for over six years. He was greeted with delirious enthusiasm. Three weeks later his wife, whose dignity throughout this distressing episode had been universally admired, and her two children, Ian Seretse and Jacqueline, also left Britain. They landed in Serowe on 1 November. The tragic episode was ended—a new chapter in the history of the Bamangwato tribe, the Bechuanaland Protectorate, and British colonial relations was opened.

This incident illustrates many of the problems of British administration in Africa, but amongst them is most clearly seen the inadequacy of indirect rule in modern circumstances. If British policy is to leave decisions on tribal matters to the tribe itself, it is obviously disastrous to interfere once that decision has been taken. On the other hand, if tribal custom is to be ignored and decisions taken by the Imperial power, it is inevitably inviting trouble to allow the local people themselves to believe that they have the right to take their own decisions. In this event the worst of both worlds results, with a breakdown in tribal administration and hostility provoked towards the British authorities.

In the important developments likely to take place in Bechuanaland during the next few years this lesson must never be forgotten.

The Bamangwato area may well become a great new industrial centre in southern Africa. It will take time to bring the members of the tribe into democratic participation in economic and political life. A great responsibility now rests on Seretse to use his influence wisely and to avoid the dangers to be seen in the Copper Belt and the Witwatersrand. And in this development, the position of the British administrators must move from rulers to advisers—who are prepared for their advice sometimes to be rejected.

The first essential is to create some form of Legislative Council. It is highly significant that both Africans and Europeans, meeting in their Advisory Councils, have agreed that a legislature is now necessary. It would, of course, have to evolve its powers gradually, but it may be dangerous to delay the creation of such a body much longer. When the rest of the African colonies are advancing at such a rapid pace, to leave the vast country of Bechuanaland as a political backwoods is inviting trouble. Its people have already begun to ask whether the protectorate which Britain established over them is to be controlled by the racialist ideas of South Africa or on the principles applied elsewhere in British Africa. This is a test which will continue to be made on all aspects of British policy in Bechuanaland.

Swaziland

Swaziland is the smallest of the three High Commission territories, both in area and population. Its people number some 200,000, of whom between 3,000 and 4,000 are Europeans. The country is almost completely surrounded by South African territory, but in the east it has a short frontier with Portuguese East Africa. The land slopes from the highlands of the west to the eastern low veld, where it approaches the Mozambique coastal region. As Swaziland possesses asbestos and gold, which are already worked, and is known to have coal and iron ore, it is possible already to develop a mixed economy. Cotton is grown, there is some cattle ranching and mixed farming, two large forest station schemes, one organized by the Colonial Development Corporation, are now firmly established, whilst the introduction of vegetable and fruit-growing has begun.

It is clear from this brief summary that Swaziland has more hopeful economic prospects than the other two territories and this may in part explain the happier atmosphere in race relations. Certainly considerable confidence has been established between the administration and the leaders of Swazi opinion. It is not uncommon in this little country for mixed social gatherings to be held and, although these may also be seen on occasion in the other two territories, they are probably more numerous, more natural, and less self-conscious in Swaziland than anywhere else in southern Africa.

The one big cloud over the Swazi future is the fear of Afrikaner penetration. More than half the European population was born in the Union, three out of every four Europeans speak Afrikaans, and one in five Afrikaans only. In the southern part of the territory Nationalist Afrikaner financial backing has developed strongly amongst the farming community and there are fears that it will spread to the north.

The South African interest in Swaziland is not new. The Swazis probably moved into their present country about the middle of the eighteenth century and they also suffered from the Zulu domination at the beginning of the nineteenth century. They appealed to the British in Natal for protection and received some help, though of an unofficial nature. The Boers also were interested in Swaziland after the establishment of the Transvaal Republic, and seemed to have hoped at one time to secure the means of access to the sea through the country. In 1881 and 1884 the Transvaal and Britain agreed to recognize the independence of Swaziland, but by this time Swazi chiefs were giving such prodigal concessions to Europeans that the idea of independence seemed somewhat ironic. Inevitably, in these circumstances, corruption and bribery were very widespread, and the European advisers of the Paramount Chief were by no means always disinterested parties. In 1889 a provisional government committee was set up to deal with European interests. In a convention made between Britain and the Transvaal in the following year, it is interesting to note that any reduction in the independence of the Swazis was forbidden, even if the Swazi government consented to it, without the approval of the two signatories to the convention. Transvaal pressure increased, and in 1893 a Swazi deputation came to England to ask the British Government to take Swaziland under its protection. Britain, however, was unwilling and, in fact, in the following year, allowed the Transvaal to take over control of the administration, against the will of the Swazis.

The incorporation of Swaziland by the Transvaal was probably only prevented by the Boer War. After the defeat of the Boer Republics and the annexation of the Transvaal by Britain, a Swaziland Order-in-Council was issued in 1903. This placed the country under the protection of Britain, which took over legislative and administrative authority, but subject to respect for native law and custom. When the Transvaal received self-government in 1906 these powers were transferred to the High Commissioner for South Africa.

Since the British assumed control action has been taken towards the multiplicity of concessions which the Swazis had granted. In 1907 a third of the land under concession was restored to the Swazi people without compensation, though this still left a large part of the country in European hands. Since this time, although there has been constant discontent about the land division, more land has been restored to the Swazi people, partly as a result of their own action in collecting money in order to purchase it from the Europeans.

In 1950 the land situation was as follows:

1. Land held by the Swazi Nation, including the area of 141,380 acres purchased by the Swazi for national purposes—1,799,380 acres.

2. Land owned by individual Africans—13,548 acres.

3. Area of African Land Settlement Scheme—346,078 acres.

4. Crown land—40,000 acres.

5. Land held by the Colonial Development Corporation—218,523 acres.

6. European owned or leased land—1,881,471 acres.

The administration of Swaziland is based upon 'dual' rule, which was formally established in the Native Administration

Proclamation of 1950. The High Commissioner for the three protectorates possesses the legislative authority, and, under him, the Resident Commissioner in Swaziland supervises the administration in that country. On European affairs he is advised by an elected European council. The Swazi people, however, maintain their own traditional authorities. They have a Paramount Chief and two councils, whilst, since 1950, they have maintained their own national treasury. The Queen Mother also has a special position within the ruling system. The first council, known as the Liqoqo, has developed really from a family advisory body and has remained largely aristocratic. The second, called the Libandhla, is more popularly based, many of its numbers being members of the only serious political body, the Swazi Progressive Association.

Much of the comparative happiness of race relations in Swaziland is due to the attitude of an excellent team of administrators and to the personality of the present Paramount Chief, Subusa II. The administrative team has managed to gain the confidence of Swazi leaders and, at the same time, to develop an attitude of mind amongst some of the European residents which is best expressed in the phrase, 'We are all Swazis here'. Subusa has not only a most regal presence, with his heavy, black beard, upright figure, and royal robes, but also possesses a most shrewd and discerning mind. He boasts the title of the 'Methodist with a hundred wives', combining the advantages of both European religion and tribal tradition. He is on terms of easy friendship with many members of the administration and has recognized that the progress of the Swazi nation and its protection from South African designs depend essentially upon good relations with it.

There are many problems for the Swazi people to solve. Education is still weak, with only about 25 per cent of the children in school and again much larger numbers of girls than boys. The Swazi interest in education is much less than that of the Basutos, for example, with the exception of their three national schools, in which they have a personal interest. Economically, of course, the country is still very backward, in spite of the projects which have been started. Nevertheless, Swaziland has, in its happy race relations, one of the essential prerequisites of progress. Provided this is maintained there is reason for confidence in the steady, if slow, development of this pleasant little country.

*   *   *   *   *

Basutoland

The little mountain fastness of Basutoland is often known as the African Switzerland. It is a country of peculiarly shaped hills, dominated by a central high plateau over 9,000 ft above sea level. Its hardy people protect themselves from the cold mountainous air by wrapping themselves up in multi-coloured blankets as they ride their sturdy ponies about the rocky, stony countryside. It has a population of over half a million, only 1,700 of whom are Europeans. The country is an island completely surrounded by South African territory, and many of its able-bodied men are constantly away in the Union, working in the mines of the Rand or on the Free State farms.

The Basuto nation owes much of its cohesion and survival to the leadership of their great chief, Moshesh, during most of the nineteenth century. It was he who organized the resistance to the constant attacks of the Orange Free State after the Republic had been established on the Basutoland borders following the Great Trek. Raiding and counter-raiding for cattle and land continued throughout the middle of the century, and the Free State Government made a number of attempts to subdue the Basutos and bring them under Boer control. Moshesh realized that the survival of his nation required outside protection, which he sought from the Governor of the Cape Colony. The Imperial Government in London was reluctant to add to its financial responsibilities, but eventually, in 1868, agreed that the Basutos should be recognized as British subjects and placed under British protection. Three years later Basutoland was annexed to the Cape Colony, which found it both a financial and administrative burden. In 1884 the British Government reluctantly took over the administration from the Cape Colony and placed it under the rule of the Queen, acting through the High Commissioner for South Africa. Properly speaking, therefore, Basutoland is a Crown Colony and not a Protectorate.

Partly through the lack of administrative experience and resources of the High Commissioner, and partly because of the
independent character of the Basutos, British rule in this territory
has been somewhat looser than usual. It is usually described as
'dual' rule, dividing functions between the British administration
and the Basuto authorities. Of the latter the figure of the Paramount Chief stands at the head of a pyramid of Chiefs, sub-Chiefs
and Headmen extending throughout the country. Amongst them
the organization known as 'Sons of Moshesh', consisting of
descendants of the famous Chief, has had a particular influence.
In 1903 the Basutoland Council met for the first time, being fully
constituted seven years later. The Council, which performs an
advisory function, sits under the presidency of the Resident Commissioner, and consists of thirty-six members elected by the
district councils, fifty-two nominated by the Paramount Chief,
five by the Government, and six representing various special
bodies. It is the Council also which chooses a panel of eighteen
people from whom the Paramount Chief selects his three permanent advisers.

In 1954 a constitutional commission, known as the Moore
Commission, made a number of proposals for constitutional reform which caused considerable political ferment in the country.
The Basuto politicians had fixed their eyes on the creation of a
Legislative Council, but this was not considered by the Commission. Amidst considerable confusion the main facts to emerge
seem to have been the Basuto fear of an increase in the powers of
government at the expense of their own authority, and a desire that
their National Council should gain increased strength and become
a Legislative Council. The whole political situation is continually
confused by the fears of the Chiefs of a loss of influence, relationships between the Paramount Chiefs and the subordinate Chiefs,
and the pressure of new politicians. The oldest political body is
known as the Progressive Association and was founded in 1907. It
represents a gradualist point of view and is anxious to see a steady
development towards greater African responsibility. More recently
the Basutoland African Congress has been formed, with a wider
membership and more direct political aims. It has been the

foremost opponent of the Moore Report and has produced a scheme for an entirely new constitution, centring around the establishment of a Legislative Council.

The chiefs have obviously been considerably confused by recent political developments. Conflicts over the succession to the Paramount Chieftaincy have also divided and weakened them. At present the young Paramount Chief-designate is being educated in Britain, whilst his Aunt, Mantsebo Seeiso, acts as Regent.

In 1958 a new effort for constitutional reform was made. Professor D. V. Cowen drew up a report on Constitutional Reform and Chieftainship Affairs, and the British Government invited a delegation from the Basutoland National Council to London to discuss it. Professor Cowen accompanied them as their adviser. It had now become quite clear that the Basutos expect the normal development of a Legislative Council and governmental powers in an Executive Council to be granted to them on the same model as in other parts of British Africa. At the end of the conference in London a statement was published which declared that a Legislative Council was to be introduced with elections on a single roll. The Executive Council was also to include unofficial members. This was an historic decision, for it openly defied the *apartheid* practices of the Union just across the border. Moreover it ensured that any future decision on the incorporation of Basutoland in South Africa would be subject to the declared wishes of the Basutos through their elected representatives. 'Consultation' was thus transformed into 'consent'. The first of the three territories had been brought into the broad stream of African constitutional evolution.

A single glance at the map is sufficient to show the extreme vulnerability of Basutoland should the Union at any time decide to take more positive action in order to secure its incorporation. Its geographic weakness is aggravated by its economic dependence upon this powerful neighbour. South Africa is the chief market for its exports and the main provider of its imports. It is true that over a period the Basutos have exported more foodstuffs than they have imported, but, whilst they export crops like wheat and peas, their own diet is based almost entirely upon maize, for much of which they depend upon the Union. No doubt their agriculture can be improved by better methods and organization. Yet the fact that so many of their able-bodied males are continually absent and that soil erosion has eaten so deeply into the natural fertility of their country, constantly restricts the pace of their agricultural development. In any case, it is very doubtful whether this mountainous country can ever support its present population on anything approaching a decent standard of life.

On the other hand, it should not be assumed that the South Africans would only have to lift their little finger for Basutoland to fall to them. Basutos are not only a proud and hardy people, but have also a sound educational foundation. The percentage of their children at school is probably higher than in any other part of southern Africa, reaching a figure of over 90 per cent. Many of them only spend a short time at school, and it is significant that two-thirds of the school population are girls. Yet this educational awareness provides the basis of a social and political consciousness which is important in view of their situation. The educational work of the country is largely under the control of missions, amongst which the Paris Evangelical Church and the Roman Catholics have a particularly long history. The Catholics, indeed, have founded their own University College at Roma. This long history of missionary education has undoubtedly provided the Basuto nation with a national cohesion which would certainly unite it against any attempt by the South Africans to take over control.

What is more, if any such attempt were made, the South Africans would quickly find that they had more to lose than to gain. The strong Nationalist supporters in the Orange Free State would be deeply concerned to lose their Basuto labour, as would the Rand mines, whilst the traders in the towns surrounding Basutoland could not live without Basuto custom. The Basutos have strong weapons—if adequately backed by Britain.

The one primary danger in this situation is an internal weakness caused by the confusion of political conflict. Two weak spots are to be seen here. First, if any serious misunderstanding develops between the British administration and the Basuto leaders, resistance will be seriously weakened. Second, if the political reactions which have already begun within the Basuto nation were to take a violent form, it would provide the perfect excuse for South African intervention.

In this latter connexion a word must be said about the medicine murders which from time to time have provided morbid news for the outside world. The Basutos have a traditional faith in the protective value of supernatural potions made from human flesh. The series of medicine murders which have been discovered in Basutoland during the last thirty years or so have been frequently attributed to the influence of political changes and the desire of those in authority, particularly the chiefs, to retain their traditional powers. This cause cannot be entirely disregarded. At the same time it should be recognized that similar phenomena have occurred in other parts of the world. It might, indeed, be more useful to compare this side of Basuto life with the same impulses which produced the Mau Mau movement amongst the Kikuyu. In both cases the people concerned had attempted to adopt European religion and culture, only to find themselves constantly rejected and frustrated. Like many others outside Africa, they turned back to their traditional superstitions to seek for the strength and security which they had failed to find in the teachings of Europeans.

Once again we are brought to the conclusion that only social and economic progress, united with new political opportunities and responsibility, can develop that national strength which Basutoland, above all other nations in southern Africa, so profoundly needs. Such an understanding and progressive administration, creating hope and security, is clearly the only remedy for the superstitions which produce brutality.

*   *   *   *   *

Britain and the Three Territories

The three protectorates present Britain with one of the most direct challenges in Africa. In each case the people themselves asked for British protection and are unanimously anxious to retain it. There is not the slightest desire amongst the African peoples of any of these three territories to be transferred to the rule of the South Africans. We have, therefore, undertaken a clear responsibility, and if we were ever to give it up against the wishes of these peoples it would be a direct abdication of trust.

At the same time, the position of the three territories raises problems peculiar and difficult. Their economy is largely hinged on that of South Africa; much of their revenue comes from the collection of customs dues on their behalf by the Union; the currency, railway and postal services are operated by the South Africans; their people have been treated as South Africans in education and employment, though certain restrictions have now begun to appear; in times of maize shortage the South Africans gave them preferential rates in supplying their deficiency.

The influence of South Africa upon British policy in the protectorates was, therefore, bound to be one important factor; whether it need have been so strong a factor is open to doubt. The fact that all three territories come under the administration of the High Commissioner to South Africa, operating outside all three territories in Pretoria, is bound to confuse diplomacy with colonial administration. The High Commissioner's first task is to maintain friendly relations with the South African Government. This hardly squares with his responsibility for developing the three protectorates in the interest of their African peoples. Similarly, the Commonwealth Relations Office in London, which supervises their administration, is not fitted for colonial administration, and is frequently less concerned to see the development of the Africans than to preserve friendly relations with the South African Government. The responsibility for policy in these three territories would be much better controlled by the Colonial Office.

It is fantastic, too, that the capital of Bechuanaland should actually be outside that country, again in the Union, at Mafeking. This results in all the heads of departments and their staffs being located outside the territory which they administer, a position disliked by Africans and British administrators alike. Only fear of offending the South Africans prevents removal of the administrative capital to within Bechuanaland itself.

In administrative policy also, the influence of South Africa is constantly felt. It is obvious that South African reaction formed one of the important considerations in the British Government's decision over the issue of Seretse Khama, but it spreads much wider than in single incidents. Strong and virile development, such as has been attempted in other colonies since the war, is also inhibited in the protectorates by the fear that increased economic and political power for the Africans of these territories will upset South African susceptibilities. It is true that in certain areas, as for example in southern Bechuanaland, the action of individual administrators has succeeded in destroying certain forms of segregation introduced on the South African pattern. It is also true that in each of the three territories social activities of an inter-racial nature take place which would be impossible in the Union. In all three territories there are some devoted administrators doing everything they can to develop their areas and to assist the people within them, at the same time deliberately destroying as many South African influences as possible. Unfortunately, they are constantly hindered by the over-all direction of policy, which is continually inhibited by South African prejudices, and by scarcity of resources.

It is more than time that Britain recognized that these territories are British, that their peoples look to Britain for protection, guidance, and assistance, and that we administrate them through a policy laid down in London, uninhibited by South African racialism. The difficulties of such a principled policy should not be minimized. South Africa can make the administration of these countries very difficult. At the same time we should recognize that the South Africans only respect firm policies, having much more to lose than to gain in creating difficulties within the protectorates. The South Africans are also continually fearful of losing the friendship of Britain, their last friend in the world, leaving themselves entirely isolated.

This policy, however, in itself creates an ultimate problem. British colonial policy as a whole is designed to produce independent, self-governing states, with all external control removed. Such an achievement is hardly possible in the case of the three protectorates. None of them is capable in the foreseeable future of becoming an independent state, though each of them can un-doubtedly become more self-sufficient economically and develop political institutions giving much more responsibility to their own people. Even if they become fully self-governing internally, however, unless a revolution occurs in South Africa, they will presumably desire to retain British protection. Such a constitu-tional relationship would certainly create problems. Is a per-manent protectorate possible or desirable? In the meantime though, whilst thinking out this knotty problem, there are wide-spread opportunities for social, economic, and political develop-ment, which present a constant challenge to British justice and firmness of principle.

VI: SOUTH AFRICA

THE main interest and significance of South Africa, creating all its major problems, is the multi-racial character of its inhabitants. Broadly, the South African population is made up of Africans, Europeans, Cape Coloureds and Asians, but each of these communities can be further subdivided. Certainly one has to note the differences between the various African tribes, and also between those Africans who remain in the semi-tribal life of the reserves, those who are living on farms, and those who work in industry, living in towns. It is equally important to recognize the difference in outlook and character between the Afrikaners and the British amongst the European community. Then, even the physical features of the Cape Coloureds vary from the almost Negro to the practically white. It is also a common fallacy to believe that the Asians of Natal, and particularly from Durban, are all wealthy merchants living in fine houses and running huge cars. A few of them are, but the vast majority live in filthy slums along with their African fellow-workers.

This multi-racial South African picture has taken 300 years to paint, and its present character is the product of the thousand and one ideas, attitudes and emotions of the period during which these various people have come together and forged a South African society within one country. It represents the longest history of continual inter-racial contact within the continent of Africa and, as such, projects a more profound and direct influence upon race relations in Africa and, indeed, upon other inter-racial continents, than any other single society. Every attitude, every incident, and every law that is passed or administrative action taken in the Union of South Africa is jealously and expectantly watched wherever white and non-white people are in contact with each other. It is, in fact, little exaggeration to suggest that to the coloured peoples of the world South Africa presents the test case of the sincerity of white people.

The history of South Africa is essentially a story of race contact and attitudes. When van Riebeeck and his followers landed in the Cape in 1652, the territory which forms the present Union of South Africa was almost unpopulated. The Dutch encountered a few Hottentots and Bushmen in the Cape. Many of the former joined the settlement; the latter quickly retired to the north. But it was only at about this time that the African tribes began to move south-west into what is now the Transvaal and the Orange Free State. It was not until the eighteenth century that any significant contact was made between the Dutch settlers, now spread outwards to the north and east of Cape Town, and tribal Africans, who had moved south-west and westwards from Central Africa. For a hundred years an uneasy contact was maintained across the frontier marked by the Great Fish River until, in the 1830s, numbers of Afrikaners left the Cape and eventually established the two republics of the Orange Free State and the Transvaal in the heart of African tribalism. Meanwhile, at the end of the Napoleonic Wars, British administration and British settlers had come to the Cape and had also taken part in the establishment of Natal. Before the first half of the nineteenth century was completed, therefore, Europeans, mainly Dutch and British, had some control over the whole of the country, and race contact between white and black had become widespread and normal.

From 1860 onwards Indians were introduced into the country, first on the sugar plantations of Natal, adding a new element to the racial pattern. Moreover, throughout this 300 years' history of South Africa, miscegenation or inter-racial sexual union, with or without marriage, has taken place between European and Non-European. This has led to the creation of the fourth racial community, the Cape Coloureds, or people of mixed racial ancestry.

The main ideas on which South African society is now based are fundamentally derived from the Afrikaner people. The Afrikaners are mostly descended from the early Dutch settlers, with some mixture from French Huguenots and a few Germans who also went to settle in the Cape. All these settlers came from the Protestant communities of seventeenth-century Europe. Their social, political and religious ideas were the product, not so much of the Reformation, as of the resistance to the Catholic counter-Reformation. The result was that their outlook was based upon the strict puritanical ideas of Lutheranism and Calvinism born in the bitter struggles to preserve the Protestant faith against the powerful attacks of the resurgent Catholic Church. Their religious conceptions, which entirely coloured their social outlook, were based much more upon the Old than upon the New Testament stories.

Fundamentally, most of the Afrikaner peoples of present-day South Africa have not changed their seventeenth-century outlook. They are self-consciously and fanatically convinced that they are a chosen people, charged with a definite mission to preserve and, if possible, extend this fundamentalist conception of life. Yet, paradoxically, their experiences during the past 300 years have strongly influenced the character of their absolutist ideals. Though the original Dutch settlers were strongly imbued with a puritan religious outlook, colour prejudice had not yet entered European consciousness. The early Settlement saw nothing wrong in sexual association between Europeans and Hottentots or Negro slave women. Sometimes marriage took place, particularly when female slaves were released after conversion to Christianity. The test of social acceptance at this stage was not the colour of one's skin, but membership of the Christian Church. It was held to be morally right to enslave or to kill a pagan or a member of another faith, but baptism changed the whole relationship.

It is not, therefore, the original religious convictions of the Afrikaners which have given them their strongly rooted and quite unshakable colour prejudice. Rather is it their historical experiences in conflict with and in constant fear of tribal Africa. Yet the absolutism of their religious outlook has certainly engendered the fanatical character of this prejudice.

Four main influences during this 300 years' history can be seen as the chief causes of the colour prejudice which forms the main characteristic of the Afrikaner people. First, there was the effect of a slave society. From its beginning the Settlement at the Cape was based upon slave labour. Slaves were brought from East

Africa and from the Dutch East Indies. They performed all the hard manual labour and domestic service for the settlers. Inevitably, therefore, the Settlement took on the character of an aristocratic society in which the owning and ruling aristocracy was generally marked by its white skin. A slave society anywhere has always left a profound social influence upon the character of its members and the relations between them. It inevitably creates the growth of an arrogant assumption of superiority amongst its aristocracy.

The second influence was that of the Church. Gradually the division of humanity into Christian and pagan became modified as Christianity came to be identified with the white skin and paganism with the coloured. Social and economic pressures even brought to an end the practice of freeing slaves on baptism, whilst the Church community became much more closely identified with aristocratic white society. In the racial wars which resulted from expeditions of Afrikaners against African tribes, the Church gave to the white community a crusading zeal by supplying the excuse that they were an instrument of God for the destruction of the African Philistines. It was not a long step from this position to the acceptance by the Church that genuine Christianity was really the white man's religion, and that therefore the coloured peoples were a lower type of humanity.

Thirdly, there was the influence of frontier society. Once again we remember similar experiences elsewhere. Wherever a frontier exists between hostile forces, insecurity and fear become dominant. An attitude of racial fear became ingrained in the long period during which white settlers were established to the west of the Great Fish River and African tribes on the east. Constant cattle raids, incendiarism, skirmishes, and brutalities greatly influenced the way in which the white pioneers regarded the African. As they were a small minority faced by many thousands of tribal Africans, their fears, their insecurity and consequently their arrogance were greatly aggravated. This has continued down to the present, even though the Great Fish River lost its significance 150 years ago. The Afrikaners still feel themselves to be a small camp surrounded by the 200 million Africans of the continent.

Finally comes the reaction of the Afrikaner minds and emotions to the influence of Britain and British liberalism. The arrival of the British at the beginning of the nineteenth century, bringing with them their broad conception of equality before law and of a Christianity embracing all races, produced a violent revulsion in the majority of the Afrikaner people. It was abhorrent to them to conceive that a white man might be actually tried, convicted, and hung for the murder of a Non-European. They equally hated the experience of a strong and orderly government taxing them, abolishing slavery, and attempting to force them to accept responsibility for all members of the community whatever their race. Accordingly, many of them left the areas where the British Government established itself and formed their own states according to their own way of life in the Orange Free State and the Transvaal. The constitutions of these two republics clearly stated the first principle of this outlook in the words 'there shall be no equality in Church or State'.

Yet the Afrikaners found that the establishment of their own states did not free them from some contact with the British administration. There were frequent conflicts, constantly preserving and aggravating the initial bitterness, and eventually culminating in the Boer War. After this war, and the restoration of self-government to the Transvaal and the Orange River Colony, and surviving even the union of the four provinces in 1909 and the establishment of a single self-governing state, memories of anti-British hostility were kept alive. They became channelled into a determination to eradicate completely and absolutely every trace of British influence. The Afrikaner nation, based upon Afrikaner ideals and the Afrikaans language, had been born out of these struggles. Afrikaner nationalism could only survive on the basis of the twin emotions of anti-British prejudice and a fanatical belief in white supremacy. The Afrikaner nation was in fact created out of the attitude of mind, if not from the exact conceptions, of the mid-seventeenth century, and completely by-passed the growth of tolerance, liberalism and human understanding which had developed in western Europe during the intervening 300 years.

*   *   *   *   *

The present inhabitants of South Africa may be divided in several ways. The simplest and most significant division is that between the Whites, or Europeans, as they are called in South Africa, on the one hand, and the Non-Whites or Non-Europeans on the other. Out of a population of roughly $14\frac{1}{2}$ million people, 3 million are classed as Europeans and $11\frac{1}{2}$ million as Non-Europeans.

The European community itself is divided as we have seen, and consists of Afrikaners and British in the rough proportions of three to two. The Afrikaners are descended from the early settlers, most of whom were Dutch, with a sprinkling of French, German, and people from other European countries. Britain only took over the Cape Colony during the Napoleonic Wars; British settlers emigrating to South Africa from 1820 onwards.

We have seen something of the historical antagonism between the Afrikaner and British inhabitants of South Africa. In general, the Afrikaner is essentially a South African, having his roots in the traditions and prejudices of the country. He is largely isolated, partly by geography and partly by deliberation, from European social influences of the past 200 years.

The British emigrant, on the other hand, has usually gone to South Africa primarily in order to make a better living. Some British South African families have lived there for several generations; others are recent immigrants. Most of them, however, no matter how long they may live in the country, still retain some roots in Britain, and feel a loyalty towards the United Kingdom.

This is perhaps the main difference between the two sections of the white population. The Afrikaner is completely South African, and frequently accuses the Britisher of owing two loyalties, often placing that to Britain before his devotion to South Africa. The Afrikaner considers that the basic elements of his nation's characteristics are rooted in the society of the two Boer republics, the Transvaal and the Orange Free State.

Above all is this so in racial conviction and policy. Once having convinced themselves that on no account and in no avenue of life must they admit equality between white and non-white, the Afrikaner people have never been able to turn back. Every action taken to maintain their supremacy has inevitably increased the gulf between Boer and African, so that for many years now the Afrikaners have realized that if they once relaxed their domination over the African population they could expect short-shrift from them. They have in many ways taken on the role of slave-masters, unable, even if they wished, to allow any development within the slave population which might threaten their master status. Any relaxation, they realized, might jeopardize the whole of their stake in the country, and, as they have no other land to turn to, they would become political refugees. This fear has constantly haunted them, continually driving them on to further measures to entrench their domination.

The British, on the other hand, have always been much more concerned with business than with politics. Almost all of them accept the general colour prejudice and discriminatory attitude of the Afrikaners, and only rarely show even the friendliness possible in a master-servant relationship which is still to be seen on some Afrikaner farms. Most of them, too, are concerned to live a more comfortable life than would be possible for them in Britain and to make sufficient money either to return home to retire or, at any rate, to guarantee their future financial position and that of their families. They have usually left politics to the Afrikaners, and have taken little interest in the affairs or the destiny of their adopted nation.

Some modification of this division within the white community has become increasingly apparent over the past thirty years, during which some inter-marriage has taken place between Afrikaner and British families. This has inevitably tended to blur some of the sharper divisions between the two communities. It is also worthy of note that more Afrikaners have begun to enter the business world, and this may become increasingly important to the political scene. If the Nationalists really pursue their policy of apartheid to the point at which African labour is excluded to any extent from industrial life, there may be resistance from increasing numbers of Afrikaners as well as from the British business section. It should also be noted that there are exceptional Afrikaners as well as Britishers who pursue a liberal policy in race relations. In spite of these reservations, at present the two communities are still separate entities.

In 1910 the establishment of the Union of South Africa, as an amalgamation of the two former Boer republics and the two British colonies of the Cape and Natal, presented an opportunity for a modification of the differences between these two communities. It was hoped in Britain, and by liberals in the Cape, that the effect would be to restrain the extreme racialism of the Boers and to spread the liberalism of the Cape to the north. In the event, the reverse has taken place. Steadily the attitude and psychology of the north, based still upon that first principle of no equality in Church or State, has spread southwards. It reached its first objective in the Nationalist victory of 1924 and the Premiership of General Hertzog. Even when Hertzog and Smuts joined forces in 1933 in face of national economic crisis, the northern view had so strongly influenced its political opponents that in 1936 the first foundation stone of Cape liberalism was removed. In that year, through the joint efforts of Hertzog and Smuts, Africans, who had had the vote in the Cape on a common roll with Coloureds and Europeans since 1853, were removed from that roll and given segregated representation.

The second stage in the victory march of northern ideas came in 1948 with the election success of Dr Malan and his National Party. This firmly established the racial separation beliefs of the Afrikaners as a national policy. In the following six years, Dr Malan's government steadily imposed racial separation in every detail of national life.

The third milestone was reached at the end of 1954 when, on Dr Malan's retirement, he was succeeded by Mr J. G. Strijdom as Prime Minister. In spite of Dr Malan's rigid apartheid, he himself was a Cape man. Mr Strijdom, on the other hand, was essentially a northerner, and derived both his philosophy and his support from the Transvaal. He now had the opportunity to complete finally the penetration of the ideas of the Boer republics throughout the rest of South Africa. This may well mark the final defeat of the hopes which were entertained when Union was brought about in 1910.

Mr Strijdom led the Nationalists to their third and greatest victory in 1958. The Nationalists gained an overwhelming majority in both houses and the United Party was reduced to an almost completely ineffective opposition. Shortly afterwards Mr Strijdom died and was replaced by Dr Verwoerd, another northerner and an even greater fanatic than his predecessor. Dr Verwoerd had already shown his intransigent attitude towards the Non-Europeans when he held the post of Minister of Native Affairs. His victory over his rivals in the Cabinet, which incidentally was split over his election, was another victory for the Transvaal over the Cape and for uncompromising separation of everything European from Non-European. He soon let it be known that he intended to abolish all African representation in both houses, thus removing the handful of Native representatives who, though compulsorily all White, had been able to express some of the views of Africans in the legislature.

Dr Verwoerd is also an ardent republican, and seems likely to fulfil the oft threatened ambition of his predecessors to establish a republican South Africa. As he showed during his republican utterances during the war, his republican state would certainly be far removed from any conception of western democracy and based on the authoritarian ideas of the old Boer Republics. Under his leadership the momentum of South African nationalism is likely to increase still further and the policy of *baaskap* become the sole principle of government.

The Non-European population of about $11\frac{1}{2}$ million is also subdivided. It consists of over $9\frac{1}{2}$ million Africans, 1,200,000 Cape Coloureds and 450,000 Indians. South African inhabitants are thus divided into five separate communities: Afrikaner, British, African, Coloured, and Indian. The essential feature of these communities is that, however much we, or they, may deplore the fact, each of them feels and acts separately and differently from the others, and usually in contrary directions.

To use the term 'African' may lead to some misunderstanding. In South African terminology the usual words used are 'Native', 'Bantu' or, as a term of abuse, 'Kaffir'. The Africans dislike all these terms because of their emotional connexions and prefer the word 'African'. Nevertheless, it should not be thought that there is any greater similarity between the black people of the African continent than there is between the Europeans of the European continent. They have different shades of skin colour, they speak many different languages, they come from different tribes, which have a variety of customs, religions, observances and traditions, and they think and act in different ways.

Moreover, one should note that, in South Africa particularly, other differences have developed as a consequence of their contact with European society. Some Africans in the Union still live in primitive tribal society. Others are university professors, capable of holding their own in the international academic world. Between these extremes every different gradation of development is to be found.

For the past hundred years a deliberate attempt has been made by South African white society to induce Africans to leave their tribal life to perform the labouring tasks for the white community. The development of industry has led to a demand for labour which could only be satisfied from the ranks of the African inhabitants. Taxes were therefore imposed upon Africans to induce them to go to work in the towns so as to earn the money necessary for tax payments. The Europeans also demanded servants to do their housework, and again looked to Africans to fill this need. Increasingly, therefore, Africans have been leaving their tribal reserves, sometimes for short contractual periods, sometimes permanently, to work in the towns. It has long been the practice also for Africans to live and work on European farmsteads.

From this development, as in other countries, there gradually arose a necessity to provide at least the elements of an educational system for the newly urbanized people. It was essential to teach workers to read and write, to add and subtract, if they were to become at all efficient in urban society. Consequently, educational opportunities for Africans are greater in South Africa than in any other part of the continent south of the Sahara, with the possible exception of the West Coast. This has led, in its turn, to the creation of a small professional class of Africans, most of whom are teachers or clerks, but with a few doctors and college lecturers.

This same industrial development is the major basic cause of the increasing racial tension within the South African nation during the twentieth century. Before this century began the race relations of South Africa, though never very happy, were comparatively static. The master-servant relationship was generally accepted after military defeat, it was quite obvious to the Africans that the European master had skills, techniques, and knowledge such as had never been known in African society. The comparative calm of this racial basis was possible in a largely rural society where mass contact between the different races never occurred. Those serious conflicts which did break out occasionally were almost always on land issues, where the Africans feared that the white man was trying to take his land from him.

The real change dates from the discovery of diamonds in Kimberley in 1866 and of gold on the Witwatersrand in 1886. These discoveries changed the whole economic and social pattern of the country. They first attracted crowds of seekers after quick wealth and led to the establishment of the rough and ready, lawless mining camps, which have always developed wherever precious metals have been discovered. In these camps the African was welcomed as a labourer, but never as a prospector. Not only did he lack the skill and equipment for mining operations, but he also had little conception of the significance of this new metal. In any case, it was not difficult for the white prospectors to keep the African out and thus avoid his competition.

The industrial basis of South African race relations was thus laid from the very beginning of mining. The African was accepted as a labourer, but prevented from becoming either an owner or a skilled worker. There was another side to the early racial picture in industry which has continued down to today. The African might not be allowed into the skilled and more lucrative sides of industrial life, but he nevertheless discovered that the wages which he was paid, even as an unskilled labourer, brought him a much higher standard of life than that which he could find in his tribal reserves or whilst working for the white farmer. He was therefore soon attracted to the life of the mining camps and has continued to be attracted to urban society ever since.

This is the heart of the present racial problem of the Union.

During the twentieth century, not only mining, but secondary industries, have led to a continual growth in the numbers and size of South African towns. But town life requires a great deal of labour, in industry, in the public services, and in domestic service —for in South Africa most European families employ African domestic servants. Now the only ready supply of labour available in South Africa is that of the African. Consequently, and inevitably, the expansion of town life in the Union has necessitated a continual increase in the number of Africans leaving their own areas and going to work in the towns. Many of them, particularly in the mines, are only temporary inhabitants of the towns, brought from the reserves, and indeed, from all over southern Africa for contractual periods to work in the mines. After some months they return to their homes. This is, of course, a wasteful way of using labour, for it means that the worker is trained for his work, but only performs it for a limited period. It also has a profoundly bad effect upon the African reserves, where it is estimated that at any one time about 75 per cent of the able-bodied men are absent in the towns. Inevitably, therefore, land and agriculture in the reserves have steadily deteriorated.

At the same time, however, an increasing proportion of the Africans decide to stay in the towns and have brought their wives and families to set up homes. This inevitably leads to much greater contact between the races than ever before, and exacerbates that colour prejudice which is felt by almost all white South Africans.

This increasing urbanization of the African population has led to many evils. In brief, a large number of Africans have been cut off from the security, discipline, and inhibitions of their tribal society, and find themselves in a vacuum in the new town life, with nothing to take the place of their tribal standards and values. White society has recognized its need for African labour and has continually set out to attract it. Yet, at the same time, it has resisted any acceptance of the Africans' right to be considered a part of urban society. Too often Africans have been attracted to employment in the towns without any social provision being made for their life there. Most South African municipal governments, supported by the central Government, have built African housing estates, provided medical facilities, and laid on some elementary public services. Most of the education has been left to the religious bodies. Yet in no town in South Africa has the provision of social amenities ever kept pace with the number of Africans entering. The inevitable consequence has been that vast, appalling slums have grown up, the only shelters being rudimentary shanties made of flattened paraffin tins, sacking, bits of iron and wood, knocked up by the inhabitant himself. Sanitation and hygiene have frequently been almost non-existent, drainage and pure water very rare. The result is that disease has become rampant, and in these surroundings criminality spreads widely.

All governments since the time of Union have attempted to deal with this problem according to their racial prejudices, rather than from the standpoint of the needs of these new communities. They have based their approach upon the almost universal desire of the South African white community to avoid recognition of Non-European existence in town life. They have, therefore, attempted to adopt policies of segregation to make entry into the towns more difficult for Non-Europeans, to expel those whom they can, and to refuse the rights of citizenship to Non-European urban dwellers.

This policy has, of course, been diametrically opposed to the needs of industrial development on which the prosperity of the nation, and particularly of its white section, largely depends. It might be possible for a time to maintain the industrial colour bar by which Non-Europeans are prevented from entering the semi-skilled and skilled ranks of industry in any numbers. What has proved to be impossible is to increase the standard of life of the South African people and, at the same time, prevent Non-Europeans from entering and living in the towns. This became clearly apparent during the years of the Second World War, when industrial expansion was accelerated, though the provision of social amenities was drastically restricted. Even before the end of the war General Smuts had to admit publicly that the policy of segregation had utterly failed. During the thirty years between 1921 and 1951, the number of Africans living in South African towns increased from 587,000 to 2,325,388, and at the end of the latter year it was estimated that 165,000 houses were required to accommodate the homeless Africans already in these towns.

This is some measure of the central South African problem. The Africans are needed, indeed, demanded, to perform the labouring tasks of the townships; yet the urban areas neither provide the necessary social facilities, nor accept them as members of the urban community.

It was these conditions which the Nationalists inherited when they came to power in 1948 under Dr Malan. Their policy was described by the word 'apartheid'. It was a new word, not even appearing in the Afrikaans dictionary, and was given many different interpretations. Briefly, it may be seen to embrace three separate interpretations. The first, which is supported by a small group of academics, by the leaders of the Dutch Reformed Church, and by those who speak for South Africa overseas, envisages the separation of the South African nation ultimately into completely self-governing states based upon race. There would be separate states for Europeans, Africans and Coloureds, at least. The second interpretation is that of the Government, which publicly denied in 1950 that it envisaged this total apartheid as its practical policy. Its intention is to separate the races wherever possible in every detail of national, local and personal life, to insist on the use of separate amenities in post offices, public transport, entertainment, education, and hosts of other aspects of life, and, so far as possible, to restrict African urbanization, concentrating as many Africans as possible in the reserves. The third view of apartheid, which is held by the die-hard Afrikaner supporters of the Government, mainly in the rural areas and usually expressed at election time, is simply that it is another word for traditional South African *baaskap*. This simply implies the maintenance of white domination at all points and at all costs throughout the nation.

It is the Government's interpretation, often in conjunction with *baaskap*, which has, of course, the most practical effect. It has been put into operation since 1948 in such measures as the Mixed Marriages and Immorality Acts, which prohibit marriage or any form of sexual intercourse between European and Non-European; in the Population Registration Act, which classifies all inhabitants according to racial origin; in the Separate Amenities Act, which makes it legal to provide inferior facilities for Non-Europeans; and, above all, in the Group Areas Act, which gives the Government power to institute racial zones within which only persons of a particular race may live, own property, or carry on business. Measures have also been taken to strengthen the tribal authorities in the reserves, to control all African education through Government direction, and to begin to remove Africans from certain urban areas in proximity to Europeans, resettling them at a greater distance from the town centres. One or two experiments have also been made, as in the Sasol Scheme at Coalbrook, to establish new patterns of industrial life, with separate townships for Africans and Europeans at a considerable distance apart. Emphasis is also being placed upon the encouragement of industrial development in those towns which are close to the African reserves, like East London, at the expense of others which draw their labour from a distance, as in Port Elizabeth. Finally the government has taken powers to prohibit any forms of private or public mixing of European and Non-European.

Meanwhile, the Government has taken tremendous powers in order to suppress any opposition to its policy by the removal of its leading opponents, particularly Non-European, from positions of leadership, and by taking power to impose very heavy penalties upon opposition movements and individuals.

To understand the background of South African nationalism, one has always to remember that the Afrikaner leaders and many of their supporters have always felt they were fighting a continual battle for the establishment of an Afrikaner nation against the control or interference of the British Empire. This was a struggle which began in the days of the Great Trek in the 1830s, in the establishment of the separate Boer Republics in the Transvaal and Orange Free State, which reached a climax in the Boer War, but which still continues today. The Afrikaners were defeated in the Boer War by military means, but they have always been determined to avenge that defeat in the political field. Even though South Africa has been an independent state since 1931, many Afrikaners still feel that it is subject in some way to British influence. They determined, for instance, to remove the Cape Coloured voters from the common electoral roll, not only because of racial policy, but because the South Africa Act, which protects the Cape Coloured voters, was passed by the British Parliament. In the same way, they are determined to establish their state as a republic, which alone, they feel, will give them complete independence. Their leadership of the country is thus fundamentally influenced by the two basic principles of independent Afrikaner nationhood and permanent white domination.

In pursuing these objects the Nationalists are greatly assisted by the weak, divided, and vacillating opposition of the United Party, which represents a conglomeration of views and interests, but basically accepts the same racial principles as the Nationalists.

The United Party was originally the product of the fusion in 1933 between Hertzog and Smuts in the face of the economic crisis. Most of the Nationalist followers of Hertzog and most of the South African Party followers of Smuts joined their leaders in this new party. The party split on the war issue in 1939, when Hertzog returned to the Nationalist fold. After the war its continued existence depended almost entirely on the magic of General Smuts, but it very rapidly deteriorated into a collection of individuals with very different ideas linked together only in the hope of regaining office under the mantle of Smuts. When the General died in 1950 the Party deteriorated still further, unable to find any sharp policy to offer as an alternative to that of the Nationalists. It is generally supported by the British community who fear Afrikaner control and the destruction of all British institutions, including the English language. It is also supported by some Afrikaners who are revolted by the narrow outlook of the Nationalists. On every major issue of principle, however, the United Party has collapsed as a political force under the conflicting internal pressures within it. It does not speak with the blunt voice of the Nationalists and opposes the policy of apartheid and *baaskap* with its alternative of 'white leadership'. It is very difficult to find any genuine difference between the two conceptions. On the other hand, the United Party is always more sympathetic to the industrial future of the country and continually points out to the Nationalists the need for Non-European labour in industry. This is not surprising, as most of the industrialists who are interested in politics are members of the United Party, though over the last few years many of them have come to recognize its political futility.

There are also three other political parties in opposition to the Nationalists—the Labour Party, the Liberal Party, and the Federal Party. Until after the war the Labour Party had been a firm supporter of racial separation on the grounds that only by this policy could the interests of both white and black workers be safeguarded. It was usually more concerned with the interests of the former than the latter. More recently, however, there has been a revolution within the Labour Party, which is now moving clearly towards a recognition of the need to represent white and black alike, and to oppose at every point the racialism of the Nationalists. The handful of Labour Party members in Parliament owed their election to the electoral agreement of their Party with the United Party at the last elections. At the 1958 election, in the absence of such an agreement, they lost their seats. Nevertheless, they are coming to recognize that only by fighting alone can they retain any political significance in South Africa today. They are making strenuous efforts to associate closely with Non-European organizations and form a common anti-racialist front. In this effort they are, unfortunately, constantly hampered by the divisions in the trade union movement, which is split between those supporting apartheid, on the grounds that the trade union function is to protect the white worker; those who consider that white and non-white unions should exist side by side; and those who are trying to maintain mixed unions.

The Liberal Party was formed after the 1953 General Election and is supported by the handful of individuals who have always opposed the racialism of the majority of the white community by a liberal racial outlook. Non-Europeans are free to join this party and a few have done so. The Federal Party is almost entirely confined to Natal and was formed really in order to protect the British outlook of Natal from the encircling forces of the Afrikaners.

The Nationalist strength is also a reflection of the weakness of the opposition of the Non-Europeans. So far, in spite of their greatly superior numbers, the Africans, deprived of almost all opportunities for significant development, and constantly under the shadow of the powerful white man's law, have been unable to devise either a strong organization or powerful tactics to oppose the domination of the white man. Their only real friends amongst the white population consist of a handful of Socialists, Liberals, ex-Communists, and people of independent thought from various walks of life, who, though an important expression of common-sense South African views, nevertheless are almost entirely unimportant in the white political arena.

The Non-Europeans are continually weakened politically by their own divisions. They have never found it possible to form a common political front, although the Nationalists are rapidly forcing them to recognize its necessity. The Africans and the Indians generally work closely together in politics through their two Congress movements. The Cape Coloureds are always hopelessly divided between various political movements, none of which makes much impact. This division within the Non-European ranks has probably been aggravated by social and political factors. As a community the Cape Coloureds have always considered themselves to be on a higher social level than the Africans, whilst there has been some similar tendency amongst the Indians. Politically, too, the Africans were separated from the Cape Coloureds when they were removed from the common electoral roll in 1936 and given the separate representation of three white members of the House of Assembly. Now, however, the Cape Coloureds have suffered the same fate. After many attempts from 1951 onwards to remove the Cape Coloureds from the Cape roll, each attempt being frustrated by the courts, the Nationalists succeeded in their objective in 1956. The previous year they laid the foundations for their success by first packing the Appeal Court, and then packing the Senate with their own supporters. This enabled them to pass with the requisite two-thirds majority an Act removing the Cape Coloureds from the electoral roll and giving them separate representation.

The greatest success in organization achieved by Non-Europeans in modern times was the passive resistance campaign of 1952 organized by the African and the Indian Congresses. In this campaign Non-Europeans were urged to break discriminatory laws deliberately, offer no resistance to arrest, and thus obstruct the administration of the country and pack the gaols. It is remarkable that in the second half of 1952, 8,000 Non-Europeans voluntarily went to gaol in this object. The movement was killed, however, at the beginning of 1953, by a characteristic tactic of the Nationalist Government. They passed two new Acts giving themselves much greater powers of arrest and of imposing emergency regulations, whilst savagely increasing the penalties of flogging, fining, and imprisoning anyone who opposed their laws. The threat was sufficient to kill the passive resistance campaign, incidentally casting doubts on the willingness of some of its leaders to accept martyrdom.

It seems certain that the organization of Non-Europeans, together with those Europeans who are courageous enough to associate themselves, will be long, slow, and painful. In the conditions of South Africa it seems inevitable that nothing short of martyrdom can succeed. The leaders themselves will have to show an example if they are to gain the support demanded. With the drastic and all-embracing powers now in the hands of the white Government, and with the opportunities for increasing their powers at will, only a revolutionary movement led by such idealism is capable of challenging white dictatorship. The arrest of 156 opponents of the Government at the end of 1956 on charges of treason still further emphasized this fact. The Nationalists are clearly determined to strike fear into the heart of anyone bold enough to oppose South African racialism. How this challenge is met will determine South Africa's future.

The Treason Trial went through many vicissitudes during its first two years. Charges were dropped against some of the defendants. Then the indictment was withdrawn and a further one introduced first against thirty of the ninety-one remaining. It was indicated at the same time that the rest would also be charged again. This is only one method by which the Nationalists are showing their determination to cow all genuine opposition raised to them. It typifies the character of Nationalist administration. They are determined to subject every element which can in the slightest degree undermine their conception of a racialist state, and yet they are not efficient enough to be able to carry through such measures with either the speed or thoroughness witnessed in fascist or communist régimes.

This South African problem directly affects Britain and the British people. It was we who were originally responsible in 1909 for passing over political power to the white minority of the Union and entrusting them with the responsibility of the future of the vast Non-European majority. We took that action on the basis of the liberal principle of self-determination. Today we have no further power to interfere, for South Africa is now a sovereign independent state. Nevertheless, the lesson of our mistake in 1909 should not be lost on our policy towards other similiar situations.

We also still have the responsibility for the administration of the three High Commission territories, commonly known as the Protectorates. The three countries of Bechuanaland, Basutoland and Swaziland were given the protection of the British Crown largely because their people did not wish to be placed under South African rule. The opening was left for them to be transferred to the Union at some future date, for economically and geographically they are obviously a part of South Africa. Basutoland, indeed, is a little mountainous country completely surrounded by the Union. Many efforts have been made by South African governments to effect this transfer. If this were ever done whilst the South African white community maintains its present attitude towards Africans it would be a complete betrayal of African trust. When Seretse Khama was exiled from Bechuanaland after his marriage to a white girl there is no doubt that the South African prejudice was an important factor.

Meanwhile, we are responsible for the well-being of the inhabitants of these territories, many of whom at present depend for their livelihood upon work in the Union. One of the few influences which the British people can have upon the South African racial situation is to see that these people are given much greater opportunities to build a decent standard of life in their own countries and are treated entirely differently from their brothers in the Union.

The situation in South Africa is profoundly significant for the rest of the African continent, in the Commonwealth, and throughout the whole international world. The white community of South Africa has laid down its basis of relations with the Non-Europeans in the form of complete social segregation, almost entire denial of political rights, and as much segregation in the economic field as can be reconciled with white comfort. This pattern of race relations has been observed and, in one degree or another, adopted by every other white community settled in the African continent. They have been persuaded and impelled in this direction partly by the presence amongst them of a considerable number of South Africans themselves, and partly by the impact of the South African attitude which is felt wherever white and non-white are in contact throughout the continent.

During the last few years, since the Nationalists gained power in the Union, a yet stronger racial influence has spread from the south. Every country south of the Sahara, with the exception of West Africa, is facing some form of troubled racial problem. A variety of solutions have been proposed and attempted, none of them with much confidence. The Nationalist slogan of apartheid is now the strongest, most dynamic, and clearest ideology offered to white settlers in Africa. It is a policy which the Afrikaner Nationalists believe offers the sole hope of maintaining white settlement in any part of the continent. They believe and they preach that this policy provides a solution, not only for their own problems, but for those of white communities throughout Africa.

Whilst no other white settler community has openly accepted this ideology, and many of them even fear that its acceptance will lead to equal racial tensions to those which now trouble the Union, this breeze from the south has ruffled the brows of Africans in every part of the continent. They regard it as a sign of militant white nationalism. They fear that it is strengthening the determination of their own white masters to maintain permanent dominance over their African majorities. South African influence is, therefore, agitating the nerves of race relations all over the continent.

Since 1947 the Commonwealth has ceased to be merely an extension of Europe overseas and has become a vast multi-racial organism. Today, with the inclusion of Pakistan, India, Ceylon, and Ghana, there are far more Non-Europeans than Europeans within the Commonwealth. South Africa, in spite of her racial policy, is still a member of this organization, which is based essentially upon multi-racial equality. South African Prime Ministers have to sit next to the Non-European Prime Ministers at Commonwealth conferences. Although there is no rule of unanimity, or even of agreement on policy, the presence within this new Commonwealth of a state whose whole foundations are based upon white domination inevitably raises many vexed problems.

Some people argue that South Africa should be expelled from the Commonwealth. This would be a policy of complete despair. It would presuppose that the Commonwealth can never exercise any influence on the South African racial position. It would abandon any protection for the Non-European victims of the white *herrenvolk*. It would expose the Protectorates to attack and drive the whites to further excesses. It is not a policy which finds support amongst Non-Europeans or liberals in the Union.

Finally, the South African stage is seen throughout the world to be the focal point of White-Coloured relations. Two-thirds of the world's population is Non-European. In every part of this section of the world's people heated emotions are aroused by the attitude adopted towards Non-Europeans by the white people of the Union. This is taken to be the supreme test of the white man's genuine willingness to allow the coloured person, so long his slave or servant, to attain a position of full human equality.

Consequently, at international gatherings such as the United Nations, the South African situation is frequently a matter of emotional debate. On the issue of the mandated territory of South-West Africa,* which the Union refuses to place under the Trustee-

*See Appendix 2. South-West Africa is a country of nearly half a million people. It was mandated under the League of Nations to be administered by the South African Government, having previously been a German colony. Since the war there has been a continual dispute between the Union and the United Nations as to whether it should become a Trust Territory. All South African governments have refused to sign a Trust Agreement.

ship Council of the United Nations; the regular Indian complaint about the treatment of Indians in South Africa; and in debates on South African racial policy, not only is the Union Government on trial, but the attitude towards Union policy of every other member state is closely observed. Those states which do not actively condemn Union policy are held to be approving it. Inevitably the whole of this issue heats the fires of racial tensions throughout the world. As these tensions divide the one-third white from the two-thirds non-white, it is obvious that the South African situation ultimately endangers the peaceful relations of the entire world.

VII: AFRICAN MISCELLANY

St Helena, Ascension and Tristan da Cunha Islands

In the southern Atlantic there are two islands, St Helena and Ascension, which, together with the Tristan da Cunha group, can be considered part of British Africa. St Helena is well known for the fact that Napoleon was exiled there from 1815 until his death six years later; Tristan da Cunha is known as one of the loneliest places left in the modern world.

St Helena is a mountainous island which was originally discovered at the beginning of the sixteenth century by the Portuguese. It has since passed through the hands of the Dutch and English East India companies. Its roughly 5,000 inhabitants are of a distinct racial type, the descendants of racial mixture between Europeans, Africans and Asians. In 1922 Ascension was made a dependency of St Helena, and in 1938 a similar decision was made about Tristan da Cunha.

The constitution of St Helena is headed by a Governor who, since 1939, has had the aid of Executive and Advisory councils. The former consists of two ex-officio members, a number of nominated officials, and three unofficial members. The Advisory Council is made up of thirteen members, ten of them being unofficials, two nominated by the friendly societies, and one by the important hemp industry; but it is the Governor alone who makes all ordinances.

Ascension was discovered on Ascension Day 1501 by the same Portuguese expedition which later found St Helena. It has only been inhabited since 1815, and even today has a population of merely 196 people, of whom forty-six are Europeans. The island is really run by Cable & Wireless, Ltd., who use it as a relay station for transatlantic telecommunications.

Tristan da Cunha was discovered in another Portuguese expedition in 1506. It is situated about halfway between South Africa and

South America, and, like the other two islands, is of volcanic origin. The island is largely made up of a great volcanic cone which rises to 6,760 ft at its summit and is covered with thick vegetation up to 5,000 ft. It has been inhabited since 1810, but suffered from the appearance of steamships and the opening of the Suez Canal, and has now only 292 people living on it. During the Second World War a meteorological and wireless station was built by the South Africans and has been operated ever since. Since 1950 the Colonial Development Corporation has stimulated the fishing industry, many of the fish now being canned and exported. In 1952 an elected Island Council was set up, consisting of ten men and five women, together with a headman, a headwoman, a chaplain, two company representatives and an administrator. Ships call here on an average of about once every six weeks.

Mauritius

The second group of African islands is that of Mauritius and its dependencies. Mauritius has had a very chequered history. It may have been known to the Arabs and possibly to Malayasians in medieval times. It certainly became a Dutch port-of-call on the route to the East Indies from the end of the sixteenth century. It was settled by the Dutch in 1638 and four years later it was from Mauritius that Tasman set out to discover Australasia. Early in the eighteenth century, however, the Dutch abandoned the settlement which was soon taken over by the French, who governed it through the French East India Company. Settlement was made by French planters who imported African slaves. The island was then captured by the British during the Napoleonic wars and was ceded to them in the peace settlement. With the abolition of slavery in 1833 Mauritian slaves were released and Indian labour imported to work on the sugar cane plantations. As early as 1886 a Legislative Council, including elected members, was established.

The population of Mauritius reflects its varied history. Of the total population of over half a million, 362,000 are Asians, or Indo-Mauritians, as they are sometimes called. Europeans, Africans and people of mixed descent account for 158,000, and there are 19,000 Chinese immigrants or Sino-Mauritians.

Mauritius has a special significance in colonial constitutional-ism. In 1948 a new constitution was introduced consisting of the Governor with an Executive Council and a Legislative Council. Under the presidency of the Governor, the Legislative Council consisted of nineteen directly elected members, together with twelve nominated and three ex-officio members. The Executive Council was made up of the three officials and four members elected by the Legislative Council. From 1951 two new members were added to the Executive, nominated by the Governor from the elected and nominated members of the Legislative Council. After 1951 also, the Governor chose four of the unofficial members of the Executive to act as 'liaison officers'. These members kept in touch with government departments and took some share in forming policy as a step towards a ministerial system.

In 1956, after considerable discussion with the Colonial Office, new constitutional proposals were published. The force of these would have been to restrict the nominated members in the Legis-lative Council to a maximum of twelve, to increase elected members to twenty-five, and to appoint a Speaker. The Executive Council would have had seven in place of four unofficial members, would have exercised collective responsibility with all these seven unofficial members taking the title of Minister, six of them being entrusted with portfolios.

The main argument was centred upon the new franchise pro-posals for this new constitution. The 1948 constitution allowed qualified adult franchise with simple majority election in multi-member constituencies. It was now proposed to introduce universal adult suffrage but to use the single transferable vote instead of a simple majority. This was bitterly opposed by the Mauritius Labour Party. Although most of its members are Asians it has made strenuous efforts to develop as an inter-racial party. It has been opposed by a conservative group, largely backed by planters of French origin. The single transferable vote was expressly de-signed to prevent any party from gaining an over-all majority in the fear that this would lead to Asians ruling the country. At the 1953 elections the Labour Party secured thirteen of the nineteen elected seats. It has consistently maintained, however, that it is not a single racial party and that this method of election would prevent the development of genuine party government. At the same time it feared that racialism would be stimulated in politics by the encouragement given to an electoral appeal for the support of candidates on racial grounds. This might well have led to racial group politics, but without any party majority able to form a government. It would certainly have encouraged electors to vote for racial rather than party candidates.

The constitutional argument is important because of its significance for all those colonies with a mixed racial population. It could have led to a constitutional crisis in Mauritius, for the Labour Party believed that it was not only fighting on constitutional principles, but against the threatened economic stranglehold of the French planters. Such an outcome would have inhibited social development in the island, for sugar dominates the economy and only strong government can produce the social progress essential if a healthy community is to be developed.

In 1957 the alternatives of single or multi-member constituencies were referred to a commission and the Labour Party agreed to operate a ministerial system within the Executive Council. The Council was enlarged to include nine unofficial members along with three officials, six of the nine holding portfolios, and the other three becoming Ministers without Portfolio. Early in 1958 the commission reported in favour of single member constituencies. The island has therefore been divided into forty constituencies, which will be contested by party candidates. The commission also suggested that twelve extra members of the Legislative Council be appointed by the Governor to ensure that representation is broadly in proportion to the communities composing the electorate. The Labour Party thus won its important fight on the principle of establishing modern party government and it can be expected that party systems will develop in the island along similar lines to those followed in Britain.

Seychelles

The colony of the Seychelles used to be a dependency of Mauritius. These granite and coral islands in the Indian Ocean were also taken by Britain during the Napoleonic Wars. Until 1903 they were attached to Mauritius, but since that year they have been a Crown Colony with a Governor, Executive and Legislative councils. The population of just over 37,000 people consists of the descendants of eighteenth-century French settlers and African slaves, Creoles of mixed racial origin, Indians, Chinese, and a number of other Europeans.

The Executive Council has the Governor as its president, three officials and some other members—one of the latter must be an unofficial member of the Legislature; in 1956 there were three unofficial members, two of whom were members of the Legislative Council.

The Legislative Council consists of thirteen members. The Governor is president; there are six official and six unofficial members, four of the latter being elected and the other two nominated by the Governor.

Most of the people of the islands work in agriculture. A variety of tropical products are grown for local consumption and the main export industry is the production of copra, the price of which has enormously increased since the Second World War.

In 1956–7 widespread scandals were revealed within the administration and the House of Commons heard scathing attacks on conditions in the Seychelles.

Zanzibar

Zanzibar is one of the most colourful and romantic islands in the world. It probably has the longest history of any part of Africa, other than Egypt. It is believed that the Egyptians, Phoenicians, and Sumerians all traded down this coast. Certainly the Arabs and Persians came here to settle as early as the seventh century A.D., and the Mohammedan religion spread from the beginning of the tenth century.

When the Portuguese began to explore the southern African coast on their way to the Indian Ocean they quickly took control of Zanzibar and Pemba islands. The Portuguese retained their control until the end of the seventeenth century when they were replaced by the Arabs. In the early eighteenth century Ahmed bin

Said founded the Al-Busaid dynasty from which the present Sultan of Zanzibar is descended. In 1741 Ahmed became Imam of Muscat. In 1832 the Imam's capital was transferred to Zanzibar and the modern Zanzibar town was founded. It was from this date that the famous clove industry was first established. At this time, too, Zanzibar became probably the most important slave market in the world. In 1873, however, the Sultan made a treaty with Britain agreeing to prohibit the export of slaves and closing all his public slave markets. Thirteen years later Britain and Germany, both of them interested imperially in East Africa, recognized the sovereignty of the Sultan over Zanzibar and Pemba and a ten-mile wide strip on the East African coast. In 1890 the Sultan asked for and obtained British protection over the two islands.

The present Sultan Seyyid Sir Khalifa Bin Harub, one of the most remarkable rulers of the British Empire, has been on the throne since 1911. He is assisted by a British Resident, who is directly responsible to the Colonial Office. Since 1926 Executive and Legislative Councils have also existed. The Sultan has been president of the Executive Council, the Resident being vice-president. The latter is also president of the Legislative Council. Under a new constitution adopted in 1956, however, the Sultan and his heir have withdrawn from the Executive Council, and to advise the Sultan a Privy Council has been established consisting of the Resident, the Chief Secretary, the Attorney General, and three nominated members. The new Executive Council now consists of the Resident, seven officials, and three unofficials drawn from the Legislative Council. The latter are to concern themselves with particular departments as a step towards the introduction of a ministerial system. The new Legislative Council, with the Resident presiding, has twelve officials and twelve unofficial members.

The election of these unofficials is of some constitutional importance to multi-racial Africa. The plan for these elections was made by Mr W. F. Coutts, the same man who made the proposals for African elections in Kenya. He suggested that six of the twelve seats in Zanzibar should be filled by members elected on a common roll. Franchise has been restricted to males, with certain educational and economic qualifications. The other six seats are to be filled from representatives put forward by the different racial communities, and appointed by the Sultan on the advice of the British Resident. To the surprise of the Arabs, the first elections in 1957 resulted in members of the Afro-Sharazi Party, an African party, winning all six seats.

Zanzibar has a population of about 150,000 and Pemba Island about 115,000. The racial composition of the inhabitants reflect their varied history. Three-quarters of them are Africans, and of the remainder some two-thirds are Arabs, nearly one-third Indians, and a few Europeans and various other nationalities. In general, relations between the different races are extremely happy, although the Arabs, perhaps the most politically conscious, were strongly critical of the constitution until recently and boycotted it from 1954 till 1956. The narrow streets, picturesque arches, the large brass studs on the great oak doors, the mingling of the colourful, cosmopolitan peoples, and the all-pervading scent of cloves, together with the seasonal appearance of the ancient dhow fleet in the harbour, preserve the romantic association of Asia and Africa, of ancient and modern, in a delightfully exotic setting.

Somaliland Protectorate

On the horn of Africa lives a community of about 640,000 nomadic Somalis whose chief occupation is tending their herds of camels, their flocks of sheep and goats. These people came under the protection of Britain in 1887 following the conclusion of a number of treaties between their tribes and the British Government. The history of this area is largely shrouded in mystery, and is still mainly speculation, but it certainly goes back to the most ancient of human times. Britain's connexion with the Somali people dates from the period in which the British and French were competing for spheres of influence in the strategic areas of the African continent. Later negotiations were conducted concerning the boundaries of the Protectorate with Italy, in 1884, and Ethiopia, in 1897.

The administration of the Protectorate is comparatively primitive, executive and legislative power are vested in the Governor, who is advised by a council consisting of government officials.

There has also recently developed a Protectorate Advisory Council, with representatives of the different sections of the community purely in an advisory capacity.

Some interest has been centred on the Somaliland Protectorate recently because of the dispute over the Haud area. This area is used by Somali tribes as grazing lands, but, according to the Abyssinian treaty of 1897, it actually belongs to Ethiopia. It was occupied during the Second World War by Britain, but handed back to Ethiopia in 1955. This brought considerable protest from the Somalis, who feared that the Ethiopians would interfere with their grazing rights. The Somalis seem to have had some considerable reason for such fears, for there are signs that the Ethiopians, in spite of their pledges, are trying to bring the nomadic Somalis who use this area under their jurisdiction. The question has also been raised as to whether Britain has any right under international law to transfer the land of a protected people to another state. In view of the fact that Somaliland as a whole is scheduled to become an independent state in 1960, the whole situation is considerably complicated and might well lead to this becoming a tragically discontented area. Somalia was transferred by the U.K. to Italy in 1930 and will become a sovereign state at the end of 1960. What is then to happen to the British Protectorate?

One problem is raised by all the small territories, with the exception of Somaliland, which will presumably join a new Somaliland state.* There may be no more than 192 people living on Ascension. Yet they are 192 human beings. They have the same human rights as any member of a great state. These include the right to a share in the governance of all their affairs. But how can such a right be put into practice?

No one can imagine Ascension, or St Helena, or Mauritius as independent nation states. They are clearly non-viable economically and politically. Yet no one has the right to presume that they will always remain as dependent territories, ruled by alien states.

---

*In February 1959 it was announced that constitutional progress in British Somaliland was to be accelerated and the possibility held out of it joining the new Somali state after 1960.

For this would permanently deny their inhabitants their basic rights.

There is no easy solution for this problem. Yet it is one which must be faced frankly and demands both thought and imagination. There have already been suggestions from Mauritius that the Maltese policy would be appropriate, with these small communities sending members of parliament to Westminster to share in the policy-making which inevitably affects these colonial peoples. It may be that internal self-government can be achieved, with special relations agreed with Britain for defence and external affairs. Whatever the solution may be—and it may differ in different circumstances—the challenge still faces British colonial thinkers.

VIII: THE OTHER EUROPEANS IN AFRICA

THE people of the African continent are divided nationally according to European rather than African influences. The frontiers of almost every African state were drawn up by the various European governments who coveted the resources, markets and strategic values to be found in nineteenth-century Africa. These frontiers were fixed according to the balance of power which obtained between the different European states at various periods. All those states in Europe urgently concerned with the problems arising from their industrial revolutions sought to use control of African territory as one solution. Thus, all the main European industrial countries of the nineteenth and early twentieth centuries have been concerned in African colonization.

Germany and Italy were eliminated from the colonial world as a result of their defeats in the First and Second World Wars. In the twentieth century it has come to be accepted that one price of military defeat is to lose colonies. The effect of this loss, particularly on Germany, has perhaps been rather to damage national prestige than to suffer any severe economic disability.

The general practice has been to place the colonies of a defeated state under some form of international control. After the First World War the League of Nations established a Mandates Commission which supervised the administration of Germany's former African colonies, although the administration itself was handed over to one of the victorious allies. Later, after the collapse of the League of Nations, the United Nations set up a Trusteeship Council to take over this work. Thus what used to be the German colonies of the Cameroons, Ruanda-Urundi, South-West Africa and German East Africa, and the Italian colony of Somalia have come under this system, although there has been a continuing dispute about the status of South-West Africa. Eritrea, Ethiopia and Libya, previously Italian colonies, have become independent states.

In addition to the British, with which this book is mainly concerned, there thus remain in Africa French, Belgian, Portuguese and Spanish colonizers. Their principles of colonial policy and their practice of administration show important differences. In particular, whilst British colonial policy is broadly based on the intention, however long delayed, to train the peoples of her dependencies for self-government and ultimately to establish their countries as independent states, this objective is by no means completely accepted by the other European imperialists. We should, therefore, look at the peoples and territories which they govern and examine the objectives and the policies they pursue to achieve them. The broad outline of non-British colonial policy in Africa will be described, but deliberately not in such detail as has been used in British Africa.

French Policy in Africa

French colonial policy in the African continent should be divided into two sections, very roughly corresponding to the division between British West Africa and her East and Central African territories. The French rule a number of territories inhabited solely by Africans—Equatorial and West Africa, the Cameroons, Togoland and Madagascar; but they had also several 'plural societies' or countries in which white settlers as well as black Africans lived. These are the North African Mediterranean territories.

The French territories where the racial problem is particularly prominent because of white settlement consist of Algeria, Morocco and Tunisia. Algeria has a population of over $9\frac{1}{2}$ million, of whom about 1,100,000 are European residents, the remaining 8,400,000 being Moslems. Algeria is not constitutionally a French dependency, but actually forms a part of France itself, in spite of the fact that it is about four times the size of France. In Morocco over ten million people live, including 350,000 of French or European origin. Morocco had the status of a French protectorate until the

Franco-Moroccan Agreement was signed in March 1956, when it became an independent state. A few weeks later Tunisia followed suit, ending its former protectorate status. It has a population of 3,800,000, of whom 180,000 are European settlers.

Algeria

The Algerian problem has become particularly notorious since the revolt broke out in 1954 and rose to a climax of world interest as being the focus of the revolutionary French crisis in May 1958. It has become an issue in international politics, a matter of debate at the United Nations, to the open disgust of the French, and now plays an increasingly vital part in the internal political life of France. The French indeed were shocked and chagrined when the rebellion broke out. They already had trouble in Morocco and Tunisia and had assumed somewhat complacently that Algeria was safe and secure. In this they somewhat resembled the British attitude towards Kenya before 1952. Bands of well organized nationalists began to murder Frenchmen and attack French garrisons. The French thereupon followed the familiar pattern, banning the most militant political organization—the Movement for the Triumph of Democratic Liberties—interning its leader, Messali Hadj, in France and sending large numbers of troops to Algeria. Terrorism and reprisals have continued ever since, with successive French governments completely failing to deal with the root causes of the problem.

The Algerian problem is somewhat different from those of Morocco and Tunisia, although its main causes may be very similar. Algeria has been under French rule since 1830. One in every eight of its inhabitants is European. Above all, Algeria is constitutionally a part of France.

Like all plural societies the relation between France and Algeria has been full of prejudices. Only within the last few years has any French government contributed to the education of the Arab population and even now only one in six of the Arab children are at school (the schools, however, show a sharp contrast to the practice in the British African territories in that there is no segregation, Arab and French children being taught side by side).

According to the latest figures there are double the number of Moslem children compared with European pupils in the primary schools, but this still leaves Moslem education proportionately far behind that of European, a constant source of racial grievance.

French policy in Algeria has been similar to that of Britain in another direction. The reaction of the French government to the revolt, like that of the British Kenya government, was to combine military measures with some social and economic reform. Sub-division of the administrative departments has for the first time taken government service out of the urban areas into the rural districts. Free medical services, social assistance, and housing allocations have thus been brought to wide areas for the first time. New communes or district councils have been set up, together with their offices and schools, whilst agricultural settlements are improving the land.

On the other hand, of course, as usual, it is the French settlers who occupy the most fertile coastal land, whilst the oil, gas, iron and other minerals now being widely developed in the Sahara provide a deeply-rooted foundation for French desires to retain the territory. As in other parts of multi-racial Africa, the settlers and metropolitan power have a deep economic interest in preserving control whilst the indigenous inhabitants, though still needing European wealth and technical skill for their development, have begun to realize that ultimately their country could provide the basis of modern life and are consequently determined to rule it for themselves.

As the Moslem birth-rate is three times as high as that of the Europeans, the proportions of the population are rapidly altering in favour of Moslems. As elsewhere, this high birth-rate, which is increasing the population by something like one million every four years, has been produced partly by the improvement in medicine and hygiene brought by European skill. It produces the same problem as in other parts of the continent, with the number of mouths increasing faster than the production of food to feed them, thus making any rise in the standard of living extremely difficult to achieve. So far this has only served to increase European fears, but not in any way to diminish their determination to retain their power and the French connexion. In this respect the situation approximates more to that of South Africa than to any other part of the continent.

The French, following their policy of assimilation, claim that Algeria is fully a part of metropolitian France and that Algerians are Frenchmen. Thus thirty of the 626 members of the French Assembly were elected in Algeria and half of these were Algerian Arabs. Yet the hypocrisy of claiming that assimilation was based on equal French citizenship is exposed in the fact that, if the Algerian representation had been proportionate to its population, it would have had 125 deputies instead of thirty in the Assembly. In practice the Algerian members had little effect on French policy towards their country for they were divided amongst the French political parties and did not unite to bring co-ordinated pressure on the government.

This attitude of assimilating Algerians into the French nation exists side by side with a moderate degree of local autonomy. There is an *Assemblée Algérienne* which exercises authority over local finance and some other domestic issues. It is divided into two houses, one consisting of Arabs and the other mixed between the Arabs and French settlers. It is very largely controlled by the French administration and partly exists as a sop to the desire of the settlers to control local affairs on the spot.

There is no official racial discrimination in Algeria such as is experienced in other parts of multi-racial Africa. Social integration, however, hardly exists except that the French settlers are more subtle than their British counterparts in patronizing the handful of educated Arabs. The settlers themselves regard Algeria as a valuable economic prize; they own two-thirds of its arable land and almost entirely control the wealth of the country. They regard the Arabs as a legitimate supply of cheap labour which is the explanation for the contrast. between the development of the health services whilst education has been neglected.

The Algerian Nationalist Movement has been active in one way or another since the 1920s. It has been supported by Algerians both in Algeria and amongst those living in France. Vacillation, weakness and complete neglect have marked the policies of successive French governments, building up the spirit of revolt which eventually erupted in 1954. A series of reforms was proposed in 1936, but then pigeon-holed, whilst in 1947 a new progressive statute which might have had constructive results was never put into the form of operation originally intended.

The nationalist movement, however, although confined as usual to a group of politically conscious people, had widespread simmering discontent on which to play. The movement itself had been dispersed among a number of organizations, including an insignificant Communist Party. The *Union Démocratique du Manifeste Algérien*, known as the U.D.M.A., was founded soon after the Second World War by Ferhat Abbas, appealing mainly to the intelligentsia and with a parliamentary reformist programme; the M.L.T.D., or *Mouvement pour le Triomphe des Libertés Démocratiques*, was the mass organization led by Messali Hadj, the Algerian nationalist hero who has been either detained or exiled for most of his life; and there was a group of liberals organized under the name of Ulema, mainly concerned with spreading Arabic culture particularly through the foundation of independent schools. In 1954 the M.L.T.D. was split on the issue of tactics and another organization known as the *Comité Révolutionnaire pour l'Unité et l'Action*, or C.R.U.A., demanded unity within the nationalist forces and armed rebellion. Out of this organization the National Liberation Front, usually known as the F.L.N., and its military wing, the Army of Liberation, were born. They quickly took charge of the political and military direction of the revolution.

These two organizations represent a philosophy which approaches the anarchist in its fundamental individual democracy. They are essentially egalitarian, disregarding religion, races, nationality or colour in their claim for equal rights. They demand that the large estates, mainly European, should be broken up into small-holdings. They are constantly suspicious of individual leadership or personality cults. Their discipline is the discipline of democratic collective responsibility. In many ways they represent the essential radicalism of French tradition or even the Levellers of early Cromwellism.

The nationalist movement recognizes that it is extremely unlikely ever to be able to match French military might. Nevertheless, it maintains that time is on its side, that it can always replace its losses in manpower from the sympathetic population, and that ultimately it will force France to recognize her inability to continue the war. Its demands are simply for the recognition of Algerian nationality, after which a provisional Algerian Government will be set up to negotiate a peace settlement and organize elections. It is willing to protect French culture and those settlers who decide to stay either as Algerian nationals or as protected foreigners, though there has been no clear picture given of the structure which such an Algerian state should take. In the meantime, the increasing intransigence of the French settlers or *colons*, together with the Army officers, not only prevented any settlement being discussed but precipitated a revolutionary situation in metropolitan France itself. The F.L.N. at the same time has consistently rejected French offers of a cease-fire and elections, unwilling at present to attempt the effort of overthrowing French rule from inside by constitutional means. Consequently, the bitterness has steadily increased; tortures, massacres, and atrocities have continued on both sides; and the situation has reached that impasse of tragedy where victory for either is impossible, but an end to its pursuit would be considered by both as disastrous defeat.

After his assumption of authority it seemed for some time that General de Gaulle thought he could come to terms with the Algerian Nationalists and make his peace with the Arab world. He soon changed his mind, however, and in his constitution allowed clauses to be introduced which firmly barred the door to any deal with the Nationalists. Article 89, for instance, specifically vetoed any interference with the 'Frenchness' of territories which at that moment formed an integral part of the Republic. It seemed that he hoped to isolate the rebels and persuade the majority of Algerians to accept his constitutional proposals under the promise of improved economic and social opportunities and a greater degree of local self-government.

At the end of September 1958 Algeria took part in the French referendum on the new constitution. The administration used all its efforts to obtain as large a vote as possible, whilst the F.L.N. was campaigning against voting.

On 19 September a 'Provisional Government of the Algerian Republic' was proclaimed at the Headquarters of the F.L.N. in Cairo. Ferhat Abbas was designated Prime Minister, together with a Government which included four members who were in the hands of the French and three engaged in military operations in Algeria. The provisional Government was immediately recognized by Iraq, the United Arab Republic and Libya, followed by other governments supporting the rebels.

In the event Algerians voted in favour of the new constitution by 3,356,169 to 118,615. Abstentions varied generally from 10 to 20 per cent, though in certain areas it was more than 40 per cent. The figures were immediately claimed by the extreme right wing, who had originally been responsible for the uprising in May, as a victory for their claim that Algeria must remain French, though it seems more reasonable to suggest that it proved the efficacy of the Army's psychological campaign in organizing the vote and persuading the people that this was their only hope of economic progress.

General de Gaulle refused to commit himself to any clear future policy on Algeria. He rejected the demand of the Algerian Europeans to destroy the unity of the country, ignored the creation of the government in exile, but left the way open to future negotiations with the rebels. He stressed the importance of economic and social progress, but left the political future in a vacuum. Shortly afterwards General de Gaulle offered cease-fire talks, which were quickly rejected by the rebels, who declared that the fight would be carried on until independence was won. The ultimate future of Algeria will depend partly on French policy and practice under the new constitution, and partly on developments in the rest of North Africa, the Arab world, and in other French African colonies. It is as obscure as that of South Africa at the opposite end of the continent.

Morocco

Most of Morocco—there was also a Spanish and International zone—became French as a result of early twentieth century

European bargains over colonial possessions. In 1902 Franco-British agreement gave France a free hand in the country in exchange for leaving Egypt to the British. During the following ten years the Germans made strenuous efforts to interfere in Morocco and gain a share in its spoils. The French eventually bought them off, partly by allowing German firms to associate with French in Moroccan exploitation, and partly by allowing them to expand their energies south of the Sahara. In 1912, therefore, the French were free to establish a protectorate over Morocco with the acquiescence of the Sultan and without international interference.

Morocco has an Atlantic and a Mediterranean coastline, and standing at the entrance to the Mediterranean, has an obvious strategic value. It has been isolated from the rest of the African continent by the Atlas Mountains, and, unlike the rest of North Africa, never came under Turkish rule. For these historic and geographic reasons Moroccans have, therefore, been more isolated than many other North African peoples. Much of the country still remains very backward and dominated by the older forms of the Moslem religion. On the other hand, the strongest European cultural influence in the country is Spanish rather than French and, although it is nearly 500 years since they left, it should not be forgotten that the Moors occupied Spain from the eighth to the fifteenth century.

The economic value of Morocco is largely derived from minerals, including zinc, lead, manganese, phosphate, cobalt and antimony. The Americans are particularly interested in this mining activity which involves the production of strategic materials. It may be that this mineral wealth will become even more important in the future when the massive hydro-electric schemes come to fruition.

As in all other African countries colonized by the European powers, a profound dichotomy has developed in their relations. Morocco is still a very backward country socially and economically. It was much more backward when the French established their protectorate less than fifty years ago. Roads, railways, harbours, airfields have been built; industries have been developed, health services provided and irrigation produced to assist agriculture.

This has cost France large sums and Morocco is still dependent on French capital for development.

On the other side of the balance sheet, Morocco has been extremely lucrative to French industry, valuable in building up French national morale and important strategically both for its own situation and for its provision of troops to the French army.

Again, Morocco has provided an outlet for over 300,000 Frenchmen to settle abroad and find a life of economic and social privilege. They have taken land and almost all of the skilled jobs during the development of the country; the civil service was exclusively their possession.

Of course, the French politicians used the age-old apologia of imperialists in arguing that the Moroccans were incapable of self-government, that they had no trained technicians or administrators, that the nationalist demands expressed the wishes of only a small minority concerned with personal power, and that the achievement of the French in transforming Morocco from barbarism to stable government would have been destroyed if the French were to have left.

Moroccan nationalist opinion was mainly led by the organization known as Istiqlal. This organization was banned after the riots in Casablanca in 1952, but it continued to exercise a considerable influence from behind the scenes. One of its leaders, Allal el Fassi, sought refuge in Cairo and another, Hadj Ahmed Balafrej, in New York.

The Moroccan nationalists had no constitutional outlet for their ideas. This, of course, is always the most combustible of situations. There were no elections and no representative assembly, nor were Moroccans in the same position as their neighbours in Algeria, for being protected persons they were not allowed to elect members to Paris. The French, therefore, created the worst of two worlds; they did not promise eventual self-government, as the British had done in their African territories, yet neither did they apply the policy of assimilation which they usually claim as their specific alternative to British policy.

Nor could Moroccans claim the rights of French citizenship; freedom of movement, of press, of speech, of assembly did not exist. Thousands of Moroccans were detained without trial and there was no appeal against arbitrary arrest.

Again we find the emphasis placed by Moroccan nationalists on education starvation, for only one child in ten of school age was at school in 1956. Again the complaint was made that of the money spent by the French in the protectorate a grossly disproportionate amount went directly or indirectly to the European settlers.

In the trade union field a curious situation arose; the French apparently preferred Moroccans to come under the influence of Communists than to face the risks involved in establishing their own trade unions. Moroccan trade unions were prohibited, but Moroccan workers allowed to join French unions. As most of the unions in Morocco were affiliated to the Communist *Confédération Générale du Travail* this prohibition, in fact, brought the Moroccan workers under direct Communist influence. The depth of French fear for any kind of Moroccan organization could not be more clearly exposed. It also, of course, gave the French the opportunity of labelling the nationalists 'Communist'.

Once again, it was evident that French colonial policy in North Africa was directly undermining the interests of the French people themselves. No doubt Morocco was still a very backward country and although urban life was increasingly characterized by European forms, the mass of the people in the rural areas still lived under Moslem feudalism. Old-fashioned Moslem traditionalism was dominant and women were normally treated as slaves and chattels. This is a problem of the whole Moselm world and one which is particularly important in the midst of nationalist revolutions. The nationalists inevitably weaken their cause by denying the rights they claim for themselves to their womenfolk.

This was the background to Franco-Moroccan relations before the independence settlement of March 1956. By this agreement Morocco became an independent state, although at first the French preferred to talk about interdependence. However, the central feature of the agreement was that, although French troops remained in Morocco, its own Government became responsible for its destiny internally and externally.

It will take the Moroccans some considerable time to establish

anything approaching a modern state. The central figure in the
country's life since independence has been the Sultan, who has
taken the title of King Mohammed V. He has been a unifying and
stabilizing influence both in the internal situation and in the
periods of friction which have arisen between Morocco and Spain
and through the continuing suspicions of France. The King himself has appeared wise and enlightened, even though surrounded
by a court still largely feudal and mainly incompetent. He has
declared that he wishes to become a constitutional monarch with
an assembly elected by universal suffrage, and preparations have
been made to hold elections. The party system, however, is still
very rudimentary and continues to be dominated by the Istiqlal.
This party, which took the leading role in the nationalist movement and the achievement of independence, has provided almost
all the ministers in successive governments. For a time it accepted
M. Bekkai as Premier, though he was an independent, but after a
government crisis in April 1958, when all the Istiqlal ministers
resigned, the King called on M. Ahmed Balafrej, Secretary-
General of the Istiqlal party, to form a new government. M.
Balafrej had previously been Foreign Minister and retained this
post as well as that of Prime Minister in his new Government.

Istiqlal, like Nehru's Congress in India, is a national movement
rather than a unified political party. Stresses within it began to
appear before it had been in office many months. The left-wing, in
particular, led by Mehdi ben Barka, a leading trade unionist,
criticized the Government for not taking more positive socialist
measures, for its subservience to the Americans over the bases,
for leaving control of the police and army to the crown, and for
postponing elections to the National Assembly.

Meanwhile there had been a small-scale revolt led by ben
Miloudi in the countryside. The fact is that Istiqlal is largely an
urban movement, led by the small French-educated class of in-
tellectuals, and somewhat remote from the rural areas. It is
natural too that criticism should have developed in the Spanish
zone, where transference to the franc economy has led to steeply
increased prices, whilst there is also still much antagonism amongst
the Berbers towards any kind of central government.

The Balafrej Government fell towards the end of 1958 and the King was left to deal with the political crisis.*

Morocco is thus feeling its way towards the establishment of a stable state. It has a tremendous task in raising the economic level of the masses, destroying their illiteracy and introducing them to democratic practice. It still largely depends on French capital and loans if its economic plans are to have any immediate hope of success. Although the Moroccans are anxious to retain their French settlers they are still nervous about the presence of French troops and continually worried about the effect of the Algerian revolution. They are in the delicate position of sympathizing with the Algerians whilst fearing to offend the French, on whom they still depend. In spite of differences in constitutional status and relations with France, Moroccans, like Tunisians, increasingly recognize that nothing short of a general agreement on North Africa can provide them with the security in which to build their new life.

Tunisia

The basic problems of Tunisia are much the same as those of Morocco, but there are a number of important differences between the two territories. Whilst the Tunisian nationalists had the same grievances, complaining about discrimination in favour of settlers, lack of social provision, in particular the slow pace of education for responsibility and the absence of civil liberties involving the arbitrary detention of 6,000 political prisoners, the character of the nationalist movement took a somewhat different form. In the first place, Tunisians are much more sophisticated than the Moroccans, their feudalism has had a much lighter hand and even many of their women have begun to emerge into a less restricted sphere. The nationalist leaders are, moreover, more experienced in the outside world and particularly of France. Whilst they continually criticized the French policy for not doing enough for their country, they always recognized their need for French assistance, provided that it was devoted to giving Tunisians greater opportunities to learn techniques for themselves.

*At the end of 1958 the King called on Abdullah Ibrahim, leader of the left-wing of Istiqlal and prominent in the trade union movement, to form a new Government.

Perhaps because of the greater self-confidence and higher standards of Tunisian nationalists, some of the French settlers there took a more reactionary attitude than those of other parts of French North Africa. The organization known as the Red Hand had a strongly Fascist character, attacking not only nationalism, but the Americans, because of their support for nationalist leaders, and every French government which was considered sympathetic towards any aspect of the nationalist cause.

The dominant Tunisian nationalist movement both before and since independence has been the *Néo-Destour*. The word *destour* is the Arabic equivalent of constitution, and the *Destour* party was founded shortly after the First World War. Its name represents its policy, which concentrated on the demand for responsible parliamentary government in line with the world political mood of the time. From time to time this organization has been banned by the French government and was only legalized for the first time since the Second World War by Mendès-France in 1954. Most of its leaders have been educated in France and have close connexions with the French. The party divided in 1934, *Néo-Destour* representing the more modernist, radical approach, in keeping with French traditions, whilst the other section, calling itself *Vieux Destour*, was conservative and traditionalist. *Néo-Destour* in fact reflected the new intellectual and political trends of the middle-class and the masses.

It has been this party which has taken control of the direction of nationalist politics over the last twenty-five years. The party is highly organized right down to its local branches, and significantly includes women in the same branches as men, a clear break with Moslem tradition. Its organization is democratic and is governed by a central bureau of fifteen members, elected every two years at a national congress representing all branches. The party has linked to it a wide variety of organizations representing different sections and groups of the community, and since independence was attained has taken an increasing role in social reforms through such interests. The success of the party is due not only to its strong organization, but also to the popular appeal of Habib Bourguiba, now Party leader, Prime Minister and President of the Republic.

Bourguiba is a colourful, flamboyant figure, who has spent much of his life in exile and has drawn deeply on French as well as Arab influence. He is an appealing demagogue, evokes enthusiastic responses in town and country audiences, and at times can also deploy his less conventional talent as a satiric mimic and comedian.

In 1952, when Bourguiba was most recently exiled, the trade unionist Farhat Hached took up the leadership until he was murdered in December of that year. It is widely believed that the Red Hand was responsible for his murder which immediately stimulated riots in Morocco and bitter resentment throughout Tunisia. The prominence of Hached was a reflection of the trade unions' strength in Tunisia, where independent unions were allowed, in contrast to the situation in Morocco. Hached was the leader of the *Union Générale des Travailleurs Tunisiens*, which was affiliated to the International Confederation of Free Trade Unions and was opposed by the Communists. The trade union movement inevitably became the centre of nationalist organization.

In 1954 the new French Prime Minister Mendès-France flew to Tunis to try to prevent the imminent civil war and promised home rule for the Tunisians. A government composed of Tunisians was formed with the moderate Tahar ben Aner as Prime Minister and members of *Néo-Destour* in the cabinet. Although there was a cabinet form of government in Tunisia there were no elected representatives and the French still maintained control through a director. The French also continued their struggle to maintain control by constant pressure on the Bey, for whose support they had to contend with the nationalists. Although the palace had less authority than that of the Sultan in Morocco, it thus provided the stage for political intrigue and contention between the French administration and the nationalist forces.

In spite of the fact that terrorism, particularly that of the Fellagha, kept the Tunisian countryside in an acute state of tension, with Tunisians and Frenchmen killing each other every day, there was more hope for a settlement here than in the rest of French North Africa. The Moslem world brought strong public pressure to bear on the French over their policy in Tunisia. Local elections were held with 60 per cent vote in the rural areas and

Mendès-France went so far as to pledge ultimate autonomy for the country.

The Tunisian nationalist movement gained its objective in March 1956, when, less than three weeks after the Franco-Moroccan declaration, independence was recognized by the French. Once again France talked about interdependence, but in fact, as Tunisia was to have her own army and to control her own foreign affairs, security and defence, her independence was real. Some French troops remained in the country, causing suspicions and fears, particularly during the crisis of May 1958, whilst on the other hand the French have been continually annoyed about Tunisian support for the Algerian rebels. Nevertheless, the type of society developed by independent Tunisia has continued to be influenced by its French connexions and, under the leadership of Bourguiba, has remained strongly attached to the Western European cause.

As an independent state, Tunisia has had to face the problems which we have seen elsewhere. About 100,000 of its French residents left the country following independence, whilst the French army was drastically reduced. This may have led to an easing of tension, although Tunisians still welcome the presence of Frenchmen, but it certainly increased economic difficulties. Unemployment is high, as is the birth rate, and the development plans which alone can ease this situation depend heavily on French capital. This is not always forthcoming, partly no doubt due to recurrent tension between the two states, seriously aggravated by such disastrous incidents as the bombing of the village of Sakiet.

In spite of this grave problem of the poverty of most of the people, after independence the Tunisian Government put a number of radical reforms into practice. It has removed religion from the political field, emphasizing the secular nature of education and youth training, and has revolutionized the status of women: polygamy has been forbidden, one-sided divorce by husbands made illegal, and adult women given the right to make their own marriage contracts. The trade union movement, the U.G.T.T., has continued to flourish with a membership of about 120,000 Abroad Tunisia has now been firmly established in internationa

councils, and President Bourguiba has become the leading expo-
nent of the doctrine of North African unity. For a time the
Algerian nationalist F.L.N. maintained its offices in Tunis, and its
removal to Cairo was something of a blow to Bourguiba's leadership. He showed his independence of Cairo by breaking off diplomatic relations with the United Arab Republic in October 1958,
partly at least through his fear of the danger of communism in-
filtrating through Egypt.

As in the case of Morocco, so in Tunisia we come back to the
Algerian headache. Tunisians fear that a victory for the French
over the Algerian rebels might be followed by French reconquest
of Tunisia. On the other hand, if the intransigent Algerian
nationalists succeed, Tunisian links with Western Europe might be
loosened and the Pan-Arabism, which lost face with the elimina-
tion of Salah Iben Yusuf, former Secretary-General of *Néo-Destour*,
could again become dominant. Certainly everything which exacerbates Tunisian national pride and weakens the leadership of Bourguiba will tend to drive French North Africa towards Cairo and
Moscow and away from its traditional links with the west.

French Black Africa

It is significant that there is no word in the French vocabulary
equivalent to 'self-government'. The central aim of French colonial
policy is to train the colonial subjects not for self-government but
to be Frenchmen. Thus in French Black Africa—i.e. French
Equatorial Africa, French West Africa, French Cameroons,
French Togoland and Madagascar, which are distinctly African as
opposed to Mediterranean—political representation is in Paris
rather than in the territory itself. The French no longer term these
countries colonies, but 'overseas territories'. Each of them elects
members to the National Assembly and Senate and to the Assembly of the French Union. Most of these representatives are black
Africans. It is significant, and indeed to British eyes remarkable,
that one of the men selected by de Gaulle as Minister of State
during the crisis of May 1958 was M. Félix Houphouët-Boigny, a
Negro from the Ivory Coast.

The roots of this system can be traced back to the decree of 1792 abolishing slavery and declaring that 'All men, without distinction of colour, domiciled in French colonies, are French citizens, and enjoy all the rights assured by the constitution'. This principle of equality has never been put into full practice and with the extension of French colonialism over wide areas of western and equatorial Africa in the late nineteenth century was largely supplanted by authoritarianism. The new colonial Africans became subjects instead of citizens. Only recently and particularly since the Second World War has practice significantly begun to approach principle. In January of 1944 a conference was held at Brazzaville in French Equatorial Africa where General de Gaulle and his supporters radically altered French colonial policy in black Africa and laid the foundations for subsequent reforms. It is interesting to note that the host of this conference was the distinguished Negro Félix Eboué who served in the French colonial service as Acting-Governor of French Sudan, Governor of Guadaloupe and Governor of Chad. It was Eboué who had declared for General de Gaulle and Free France in 1940 and thus led French Equatorial Africa, in contrast to the other French territories, against Hitler and Pétain.

In 1946 the French colonials were declared equal citizens with French nationals. They thus came under French law and were entitled to enjoy freedom of speech and assembly. They were also now entitled to representation in the legislative institutions of the French Republic and in the local government councils now known as *Assemblées Territoriales*. As French West Africa and French Equatorial Africa were both federations a *grand conseil* was established in each, but without control of economic affairs of the territory. Meanwhile, in order that French Africans should be gradually brought up to the standard of life of French nationals, an organization similar to the British Colonial Development and Welfare Fund, known as the Investment Fund for Economic and Social Development, was established to promote large-scale capital investment. Another inevitable result of this new attitude was the abolition of forced labour.

In 1950 a further law pursuing the same principle gave equal salaries and conditions to African civil servants at the end of 1952;

labour legislation was brought closer into line with that of France. In June 1956 Guy Mollet's Republican Front Government introduced the law which has come to be known as the *loi-cadre*. The young French Socialist, Gaston Defferre, who had become prominent in the non-communist resistance movement in Marseilles against the Nazis, was mainly responsible for the introduction of this legislation. It may have marked a turning point in French colonial policy, for its central object was to bring the colonial peoples into much closer association with the government of their own areas. It gave the French Government powers to initiate by decree reforms in colonial policy. Whilst continuing their representation in the French Parliament, the inhabitants of French overseas territories, excepting Algeria and the West Indies, were to be granted direct universal suffrage and a single electoral college for the elections to both their local assemblies and to Paris. The powers of the local assemblies were to be extended and executive councils responsible for government set up. In addition, the Overseas Civil Service was to be reformed by the introduction of increasing numbers of Africans.

Practice naturally varies over these huge areas. French West Africa, for instance, is eight times the size of France itself and covers a sixth of the area of the whole African continent. Political activity is probably at its highest point in Senegal which has a longer experience of representation than the other areas. The French Cameroons have perhaps the highest degree of trade union organization and labour legislation. So far the French have never faced up to the logic of their own policy. If representation were genuinely equal as between the French colonies and metropolitan France, the colonial members would control the French government. They have been prevented from doing so by various thinly veiled stratagems designed to keep them under-represented. The extremes to which the French have been driven in their illogicality may be judged from the fact that before adult suffrage was granted the qualification for the African woman's vote was to have two or more children. So far the colonial members in the French Assembly have divided according to the French party system and have not formed a single bloc. It may be that reaction to French policy will eventually be to force African representatives into a single group. Certainly there is a sharp contrast between this method which permits Africans to sit with full rights in the French parliament and the British parliamentary susceptibilities. It took several years' pressure and political diplomacy for the British parliament to accept the idea of admitting three members for Malta.

Yet even if the French are successful thus far they have still to meet the real logic of their own policy. How can they continue to insist on political representation from their colonies being concentrated in Paris once political consciousness has risen to the point of demanding equal representation ? It seems inevitable that a contrary strain will develop in the French colonies similar to that of other parts of Africa. Already some Africans denounce the French attempt to channel all their political activity to Paris. They believe that this is an attempt to weaken the national ambitions of their people. The link with France may well be maintained provided that French policy does not discourage the political, social and economic progress which the Africans will demand. But it would have to be through some form of federal structure with autonomy at home. It has been suggested that a type of commonwealth might develop within the French Union on the same lines as the British model. The clear distinction, however, is that the British Commonwealth has developed on the essential principle of a right of secession largely contrary to French colonial thought.

In spite of the advantages of the French system which are seen particularly in the comparative absence of colour prejudice and colour bars, the Africans in the French territories have inevitably begun to follow the same processes as those in other parts of Africa. They have also been provided by the French with excellent terms of reference, for they can constantly contrast the principle of equality with the practice of lower living standards, meagre education and lesser political rights. In their efforts to reach genuine equality it seems probable that nationalist movements will develop despite the French assimilation context. Such movements are unlikely to be any more satisfied with under-representation in Paris than are other Africans with under-representation in their local legislative councils. The momentum of agitation is bound to create new political movements which will ultimately face the French with the logic of their own policy.

The publication of the new de Gaulle constitution in 1958 marked a step nearer to a clear definition of the relationship between French Africa and Paris. It certainly offered a more definite relationship than that under the 1957 outline law, with its limited home rule in the twelve French African territories. Under the de Gaulle constitution these territories were offered a choice of accepting or rejecting the new constitution, rejection to be followed by independence within a 'system of free peoples', a kind of Commonwealth. General de Gaulle, however, made it plain that those who chose independence would be deprived of all further French administrative and technical assistance. Those who accepted the constitution would become members of 'the Community', a form of federation, but would retain the right to leave the Community and become independent in the future. Internal autonomy was guaranteed to members of the Community, together with representation in its institutions. Overseas territories would also be entitled to group themselves in federations.

The African leaders were divided on their attitude towards the new constitution. At a conference in 1957, held at Bamako, French Sudan, most of the leaders of the African Peoples Rally, the R.D.A., and largest inter-territorial party, agreed that there should be central federal governments for French West Africa and French Equatorial Africa and that these should have a federal relationship with the Republic. This view was not held by M. Houphouët-Boigny, who became one of de Gaulle's Ministers, but was very strongly held by Léopold Senghor from Senegal. Early in 1958 at Cotonou in Dahomey the latter formed a new party, the Regroupment of African People or P.R.A. The primary aim of this new organization was independence. Senegal, with a strong left-wing socialist trend, led the opposition to General de Gaulle, together with smaller elements in Niger and Dahomey. Independence, however, was to be followed by association with metropolitan France. Nevertheless, there were strong suspicions of African central government in many states, and both parties were split on their attitude towards the new constitution.

In the referendum, the constitution was approved by a very large majority in all the overseas territories except French Guinea. The latter was immediately taken to have seceded from France and to have become independent, and all French aid was immediately stopped, whilst the French Government stated that French officials would be withdrawn within two months. Houphouët-Boigny, President of the R.D.A., was naturally very pleased with the result, whilst Senghor immediately said that P.R.A. support for the constitution was in reality support for African unity, and that membership of the French community would only be a passing phase used to prepare for independence. Shortly afterwards M. Sékou Touré, Prime Minister of French Guinea, announced in a joint statement with Dr Nkrumah that a union was to be formed between Ghana and French Guinea, though it is doubtful whether initially this union will be more than some form of treaty of alliance. It has helped Guinea to overcome her immediate financial difficulties with a loan of £10 million from Ghana. It has also stimulated ideas of a West African Federation.

It was now left to the territorial assemblies to decide what their new relationship with France was to be. They could become French departments, preserve their existing semi-autonomous relationship in the Loi-cadre, or become members of a federal Community. All chose the latter alternative. Under the constitution such a Community has a president, executive council, senate, and court of appeal. The president is elected by an electoral college including overseas members, though only as a small minority. The Prime Ministers of overseas member states are members of the Executive Council. The Senate is chosen by parliaments of the member states in proportion to population and 'responsibility'. Foreign policy, defence, currency, over-all economic policy, strategic materials and, possibly, justice, higher education and communications are all controlled by the Community government. Otherwise the member states have full autonomy.

Probably the central factor on which the African leaders are relying is their right to leave the Community and become independent. This, they believe, can be used as a bargaining counter with the French in order to avert the danger of domination by the metropolitan country. If this proves the case, some genuine Afro-French community may be developed and could influence the development of relations between other imperial powers and Africa. It would have a much stronger central direction than the British form of Commonwealth. Its length of life, however, depends almost entirely on the extent to which each member feels that they have a genuine share in its direction. Its members will, of course, also have available to them the economic and technical aid which the French can supply. On the other hand, if this sense of genuine collective partnership and responsibility is not created, and particularly if it is seen that France dominates the Community, M. Senghor's prediction will surely be proved and the member states will simply use the time of their membership in order to prepare for independence together with further efforts to create federations among themselves.*

Belgian Colonialism

The Belgians have one African colony, the Congo, and administer Ruanda-Urundi as a United Nations Trust Territory. The Belgian Congo is one of the largest countries in the world, almost as big as India, but with a population of only 12 million. It became notorious for misgovernment and atrocities when it was the personal possession of King Leopold II. Eventually in 1908 Leopold was forced to hand over the administration to the Belgian government, which has retained it ever since.

Belgian colonial policy is based upon state-directed paternalism. The Belgians believe themselves to be realists and consider both the French and British to be romantic in the idea that Africans are yet ready to run their own states or to elect representatives to the metropolitan parliament. They consider political responsibility can only be exercised by experienced, well-educated and prosperous persons. They do not doubt Africans can attain these qualifications, but regard it their responsibility to train them gradually towards this attainment, starting with the economic foundations.

*This trend was borne out in January 1959 when four of the seven French West African states, Senegal, Sudan, Dahomey and Upper Volta, formed the 'Federation of Mali' and representatives of four Equatorial African states, Gabon, Congo, Chad and Ubangi-Shari formed a customs union.

Thus, Africans in the Congo have probably better economic opportunities than anywhere else in colonial Africa. Education is largely directed towards vocational training and a wide variety of careers is open to them. There is a very sharp contrast between the economic opportunities of the African in the Congo and his neighbour in the Rhodesias. As both the Congo and Northern Rhodesia are mining centres it is seen particularly here where the strong colour bar in the Northern Rhodesian Copper Belt is strikingly absent on the other side of the frontier. It is also very apparent on the railways which, in fact, cross the frontier. As far as the Congo boundary Africans are allowed to drive the locomotive. Once the frontier is reached white crews have to take over from them.

The Belgians, of course, have considerable advantages in pursuing this policy, for the Congo is a very rich territory. Its uranium, copper, diamonds and palm oil supply Belgium with a strikingly favourable balance of payments. Most of this wealth is controlled by five gigantic trusts in which the Belgian Government holds a very strong interest. The Government is thus able to pursue through big business its paternal policy of economic progress and social welfare. It does so, however, in a consistently autocratic manner and does not allow the Africans to develop their own trade union movements.

The second autocratic welfare influence is the Roman Catholic Church which has a privileged position only slightly modified since the Second World War. The Church controls almost all the schools and is heavily subsidized by the state for running them. By comparison with other territories, school provision is very good, but its whole direction is to condition pupils to their place in the hierarchical structure accepted by both Church and State.

Politically, the Congo is controlled directly and completely from Brussels. There is no local parliament although a modified electoral system has been started for a mild form of local government. The governor-general has political and administrative power responsible to the Minister of the Colonies and through him to the Belgian parliament. The Minister is advised by a colonial council composed of elder statesmen drawn entirely from Belgium. In the Congo itself, although there is a government council and provincial councils, they are purely advisory and do little more than provide shadowy outlets for the expression of opinion.

It is significant that in recent Congo local elections *Abako*, mainly a Bakongo tribal organization, won two-thirds of the seats in Leopoldville, its leaders demanding immediate independence. Their opposition, the *Conscience Africaine*, however, only asked for independence at the end of thirty years. The President of *Abako*, M. Kasavuvu, was arrested in January 1959 during the riots which revealed a new political awakening in the Congo. The Belgians immediately announced new reforms leading 'without ill-considered haste' to eventual independence.

The Belgians argue that eventually the Africans in the Congo will be trained to take over responsibility for their own country, but this training must be slow and based upon economic security. They therefore deliberately discouraged their Africans from visiting Europe where they might be influenced by forces of discontent. They also sharply divide the *evolué*, or educated minority, from the backward masses. There is no formal colour bar, yet no one would suggest that the Africans have equality. The cities are divided into black and white communities and a variety of limitations are placed upon the liberty of the majority of Africans. Even in employment there are some vocations closed to the Congo African.

This is all justified by Belgium on the grounds of cultural differences which they claim are slowly being ironed out. Nevertheless, it is the type of differentiation which is increasingly being seized upon as political awareness develops. Nor can the Belgians much longer maintain their attempt to isolate the Congo from developments in other parts of the continent. The Congo is after all a cross-roads of African communications. Whilst many Congo Africans still see the economic and social advantages which they enjoy compared with their Rhodesian neighbours, increasing numbers of them have begun to realize that even Africans in Rhodesia have political rights denied to them. Nor are they unaware that farther north in Uganda and Nigeria, not to speak of Ghana, Africans have begun to rule their own countries. Political fever is highly infectious and in spite of the deliberate isolation of the Congo the germ is already across the frontiers.

Portuguese Africa

The Portuguese have been in Africa longer than any of the other present European colonizers. They were the pioneers of exploration in the fifteenth century which eventually brought Europe to the continent. They have been in Angola since 1482 and in Mozambique since 1505. These now remain their two African colonies apart from one or two small enclaves hardly worth mentioning.

Both territories are very large, but like most of the continent sparsely populated. Mozambique has a population of about 5,700,000 and Angola about 4 million. Nearly 50,000 Europeans live in the former territory with about as many Asians and half-castes. In the latter there are nearly 90,000 Europeans.

Portugal is a dictatorship under the control of Dr Salazar. Its African colonies are now no longer colonies, but a part of Portugal. This was made plain when the Portuguese refused to report on them to the United Nations. They are thus also ruled by the dictator. This change took place in 1951 and now both territories are considered an integral part of metropolitan Portugal. A façade of representative institutions exists in Mozambique, but it has no more effect than similar institutions in Portugal itself. The same press censorship applies; there is a similar system of secret police and political parties are unknown. The Salazar régime considers that Mozambique and Angola are now permanently a part of Portugal.

It is significant that under this authoritarian régime the colour bar as such is practically non-existent in the Portuguese territories. Black and white mix together indiscriminately in public and mixed unions with or without marriage are common. Segregation is virtually unknown except in social circles where a culture rather than colour bar applies. The fact that, in contrast to so many other territories, distinction between culture and colour is genuine is shown by the fact that Africans can qualify for full civilized rights by passing certain simple tests. They then become known as *assimilados*. Of these there are 30,000 in Angola and over 4,000 in Mozambique.

On the other hand both territories are amongst the most backward in the continent. Very little effort is made to provide any reasonable kind of education and this, of course, reduces the opportunities for Africans to qualify as *assimilados*. The Catholic Church is very strong in its influence and virtually controls education. Forced labour is openly admitted and is organized on a percentage basis by recruiting agents. The Government itself employs a forced labour system for work on the roads in addition to the use made of it by the planters.

The Portuguese policy is a reflection of the system in Portugal itself strengthened to deal with a more backward people. It is essentially hierarchical in which the good of the mass of the people is determined and enforced from the top. Civil liberties and rights are non-existent and political ideas suppressed amongst the masses and seduced amongst the intelligentsia. If such a system were enforced on the basis of a complete colour bar one would forecast an eventual revolutionary explosion. The lack of colour bar provides a moderating influence and opens a safety valve. It also emphasizes once again the fundamental place which colour consciousness has throughout the continent. It may be that eventually ideas of political rights will spread from outside, but at present this possibility seems remote and unreal.

Spanish Africa

The Spaniards still hold a number of small colonial enclaves in the African continent. The only important one was Spanish Morocco, with a million people, which sometimes enabled General Franco to pursue his policy of embarrassing the French. Morocco was mainly used by Spain for military purposes and it was, in fact, the Moorish troops who won the civil war for Franco. The Spaniards and Moors get on well together and there was virtually no colour bar.

In 1956 the Protectorate was ended when French Morocco was granted independence. Since then there have been a number of minor tensions over the presence of Spanish troops and the definition of boundaries. For a short time in 1958 conflict between Morocco and Spain flared up over the tiny territory of Ifni, but, in general, Spanish colonial policy no longer has any important influence in Africa.

The Influence of the Independent States

This book is primarily concerned with colonial Africa and as we have seen the major influences on African development up to the present have been European. This situation, however, is changing and one of the major forces of the change is the growing influence of the independent states in the continent. We have already seen the newly independent state of Ghana juxtaposed against the hated influence of South Africa, but there are other independent states in the continent with a very wide variety of impacts. It is significant that these independent African states met together for the first time at a conference held in Accra in April 1958.

Ethiopia has the longest history of genuine independent status in the African continent; but it is bound up in its mountainous fastnesses occupied in overcoming immense problems to establish itself as a nation in the modern world. It has had comparatively little influence outside its own frontiers until recently. However, it has the prestige of seniority amongst independent African states, who decided to hold their second conference at Addis Ababa in 1960. As this Ethiopian capital has also been chosen as the head-quarters for the United Nations Economic Commission for Africa, approved by the General Assembly in March 1958, it may be that Ethiopia will now have greater contact with the outside world and a more direct influence on other African peoples.

Libya is the child of the United Nations and its million nomadic bedouins have a long way to go before they emerge into the modern world, still less have any influence on other parts of the continent.

Libya had never been a national entity until created by United Nations' decision on Christmas Eve 1951. The Italians began the conquest of the region in 1911 and completed their operations after savage wars against Sanusi in 1932. The British invasion of 1942 removed Italian rule, leaving Britain and France to occupy the territory with a United Nations Commissioner until it was created an independent state. It has a two-chamber parliament representing the three provinces of Tripolitania, Cyrenaica, and Fezzan, with a lower house of elected members and a senate divided equally between the King's appointees and members elected from the provincial councils.

The main problem for Libya is whether it can bring together its diverse elements into a single national consciousness. The King, Idriss I, symbolizes national unity. Education is developing amongst both boys and girls; the British trained Civil Service and the police force have a national outlook. For the time being, however, the foundations of the state depend very largely on the British annual subsidy and military base together with the American air base and its gradually increasing economic and technical aid. Whether the three provinces with little common history or interest can hold together is still to be seen.

Liberia is constantly held up by white racialists as an example of what happens when an African state is given over to the control of African rulers. It has become notorious for corruption and inefficiency. It would be more relevant to suggest that Liberia shows the inevitable results of dumping detribalized and denationalized slaves in a barren land and then allowing the state to be run by an American rubber company.

The Sudan has begun an exciting experiment in combining the southern primitive pagans with the northern Moslems who have been strongly influenced by Egypt. Lack of imagination in British policy thrust them out of the Commonwealth community.

The problem of trying to sustain the heritage of a British democratic system whilst still building a sense of nationality became too much for the Sudanese by November 1958. Parliamentary government was breaking down because the three main groups, none of which had an absolute majority, refused to cooperate with each other. In the north the two large religious sects whose co-operation was vital to the survival of the Government split over the issues of co-operation with Egypt and the future constitution. The Negroes of the south never co-operated with the other groups, aiming only at independence from the north.

When General Abboud took over from the politicians, therefore, his main object was to preserve the integrity of the Sudanese state. The fifty-seven-year-old General is conservative and religious, but above all a Sudanese nationalist. Desert nomads still dominate the Sudanese scene and, together with the discontented southerners, can only be welded into a national state by unified central government. It is far too early to say whether the democratic experiment in the Sudan has come to a final end. Certainly the somewhat unrealistic hopes that were entertained for the democratic régime have been too optimistic. The lack of a well established political party system or, indeed, of a strong centralized nationalist movement with the prestige of having gained independence, left a vacuum as the foundation of the democratic system. It may be that after a period in which national unity is strengthened, attention will be fixed on the tremendous economic and social problems facing the people and a democratic structure emerge from their consideration. This, however, is guessing at the future.

Egypt has perhaps the most dynamic influence on Africans after that of Ghana. The Egyptians also have colossal internal problems to solve, particularly that of developing the foundations of a national economy together with the system of wealth distribution and organization which will raise the mass of their people from the depths of poverty. Yet because Egypt has been faced by the military might of France and Britain she has taken the guise of a hero to many Africans in spite of Nasser's dictatorship. The present régime in Egypt believes it to be in her interest to take an active part in fermenting nationalist movements in the French and British colonies and the radio in Cairo is especially used for this purpose. Africans also remember that it was the refusal of Britain and America to finance the Aswam Dam which really began the quarrel with Egypt. They attribute this to meanness and imperialist motives on the part of the westerners. They regard it as further proof that Africans and Asians can never expect the help of a reliable western hand in pulling themselves out of the mire of poverty. Many of them are now watching to see whether the Volta River scheme in Ghana will be treated in the same way as the Egyptian dam.

It is impossible, therefore, to generalize as to the impact of the independent African states on the development of the continent as a whole. Most of the independent states will be very largely devoting their energies to their own problems for many years to come. They are likely to condition their external influence according to a domestic need as do all other states. They will certainly be expected by colonial Africans to represent the demands of their brothers at international assemblies such as the United Nations. They will equally be expected to disprove by example the contention that Africans are not capable of ruling themselves through good government. It may be that as an increasing number of African states become independent the same kind of suspicions, jealousies and conflicts will develop between them as have been seen between national states in Europe and elsewhere. On the other hand, they may learn from the lessons of other continents. Certainly at present there is some sense of fellow feeling amongst them drawn from the fact that they all feel themselves to be a part of an exploited and oppressed continent. If they can turn that defensive sentiment into a constructive understanding and fellowship they may well teach other continents a lesson of value in international living.

The first conference of these states in Accra in the spring of 1958 marked a mood rather than showing a policy. It revealed the desire of these states to develop an African attitude to international affairs. Ghana as the host country and initiator of the conference took the immediate leading role and clearly intends to impress on other African states their common continental responsibility. At the same time inevitably, although the conference itself by its very existence showed that Arabs and Negroes have begun to think of themselves as belonging to one community, the interests of the two groups were still seen to have marked differences. The Arab states were principally concerned about the situation in Algeria and gave considerable moral uplift to the Algerian rebels by recognizing them as the true representatives of their country. The Negro states counter-balanced this North African emphasis by introducing the problems of Togoland and the Cameroons. There was clearly ignorance as well as considerable lack of concern for those Africans still living under colonial régimes and the conference as a whole was more significant as a pointer to future activities than for what it achieved itself.

IX: THE AFRICAN CONTINENT

THE unwritten and often unspoken thought which arises in most white people's minds when they begin to become conscious of black people is, 'Are these people the same as us ?' An already large and constantly growing set of influences frequently lead the ordinary person to feel confused over the answer. Most of us who were at school before the war received our first impressions of coloured people in the form of the mission boxes we used to collect for the 'poor little black boys and girls in Africa'. We were taught at school by good-willed but ignorant teachers of the black cannibals and savages encountered by explorers. We learnt of the bravery of Kitchener and Gordon and similar generals who withstood the primitive brutality of coloured hordes in defence of the Queen, Flag and Empire of the white man. We read and heard stories of 'Little Black Sambo', 'Man Friday' and other semi-amusing, semi-pathetic coloured inferiors. Perhaps such teaching still continues, though it must have been considerably modified by the increased knowledge of and contact with coloured peoples of the colonies during and since the war.

There was nothing vicious in the ministers, teachers, and parents who imparted such early knowledge. Yet ignorance can often have more profound and tragic results than sheer viciousness. Generations of white people have received their earliest impressions of the peoples whose skins are coloured in this manner. Condescension, patronage, paternalism, exoticism, and fear have been amongst the first emotions provoked. They have been accompanied by the belief that all coloured people are primitive, ferocious, ignorant, dirty and savage. Many of us, therefore, have been led from infancy to believe that they are essentially different from us.

During the last thirty years a war on minds has been declared on this issue. Racialists, based mainly on Nazi Germany, Fascist Italy, the southern states of America, and southern Africa, have deliberately taught that the differences between white and coloured people are inherent, arising from definite physical, mental, psychological, and spiritual characteristics. They have, of course, added the corollary that people with white skins are inherently superior.

It is always more difficult to prove a positive than a negative, but it must be admitted that there has never been the same determined, cohesive effort to prove the unity of the human race as there has been to establish the permanence of its divisions. Many have opposed the racialists, but frequently their opposition has been based on different grounds, and most of them have avoided the ultimate issues.

How often, for instance, have we heard it said that, 'Of course white people are not superior to black. But the races are different and no good can come from mixing them.' Those who genuinely and fully believe in racial equality will accept mixed marriages as natural. That there may be social difficulties in such unions is undeniable, but similar difficulties exist in marriages between people of different nations or different classes. The essential point is that if one really believes in racial equality consciousness of race and colour disappears, and people are seen as individuals, not as members of separate groups. The answer to that hoary question 'Would you like your daughter to marry a Negro?' is not 'Yes' or 'No', but 'It depends what kind of a man he is, no matter whether he be white, brown, black or yellow'.

The half-formed fears of many people have been aggravated by other influences besides those of the racialists. The difference of skin colour is the most obvious of physical differences. Consequently, when an influx of coloured people suddenly settles in a district which previously has known very few of them, all the prejudices and fears which were similarly aroused by Poles, Americans, and Italians as foreigners, are considerably aggravated. It is also true that a much larger proportion of coloured than white people in the world are poor and ignorant of modern conditions. This is, of course, due to the fact that most of the coloured people live in under-developed territories and have never had anything approaching the same opportunities as have most of the people descended from the European nations. The consequence is that the habits of some of them are different from what is now conventional in European countries.

Such factors tend to lend weight to the arguments of the racialists. In such arguments, as in all dangerous propaganda, there is a tithe of truth, constantly distorted and twisted, but many people tend to recognize the small element of truth and ignore the distortions. Thus it is perfectly true that most of the whites of the world are superior to the coloureds in techniques, skills, the control of natural forces, education, health, and the general organization of society. What is untrue is that this factor rises from the inherent characteristics of people of different skin colours or that the white man is superior to the coloured when equal opportunities are available. In short, nations and groups have reached varying stages of development for a variety of historical reasons. But each human being within them is a separate entity to be judged not as a colour or race, but as an individual.

Fortunately, more determined and better organized effort has been made in recent years to study scientifically the basis of racial and colour difference and to establish an authoritative explanation for it, as an alternative to the emotional mumbo-jumbo used by the racialists. The most serious effort in this respect has been the work sponsored by the United Nations Educational, Scientific and Cultural Organization, which has set up a number of committees, composed of some of the leading scientists in the world, to study all the issues involved. It is worth quoting their findings fully as the clearest and most authoritative analysis of this whole vital racial issue yet produced.

1. Scientists are generally agreed that all men living today belong to a single species, *Homo sapiens*, and are derived from a common stock, even though there is some dispute as to when and how different human groups diverged from this common stock.

The concept of race is unanimously regarded by anthropologists as a classificatory device providing a zoological frame within which the various groups of mankind may be arranged and by means of which studies of evolutionary processes can be facilitated. In its anthropological sense, the word 'race' should be reserved for groups of mankind possessing well-developed and primarily heritable physical differences from other groups. Many populations can be so classified but, because of the complexity of human history, there are also many populations which cannot easily be fitted into a racial classification.

2. Some of the physical differences between human groups are due to differences in hereditary constitution and some to differences in the environments in which they have been brought up. In most cases, both influences have been at work. The science of genetics suggests that the hereditary differences among populations of a single species are the results of the action of two sets of processes. On the one hand, the genetic composition of isolated populations is constantly but gradually being altered by natural selection and by occasional changes (mutations) in the material particles (genes) which control heredity. Populations are also affected by fortuitious changes in gene frequency and by marriage customs. On the other hand, crossing is constantly breaking down the differentiations so set up. The new mixed populations, in so far as they in turn become isolated, are subject to the same processes, and these may lead to further changes. Existing races are merely the result, considered at a particular moment in time, of the total effect of such processes on the human species. The hereditary characters to be used in the classification of human groups, the limits of their variation within these groups, and thus the extent of the classificatory subdivisions adopted may legitimately differ according to the scientific purpose in view.

3. National, religious, geographical, linguistic and cultural groups do not necessarily coincide with racial groups; and the cultural traits of such groups have no demonstrated connexion with racial traits. Americans are not a race, nor are Frenchmen, nor Germans; nor *ipso facto* is any other national group. Moslems and Jews are no more races than are Roman Catholics and Protestants; nor are people who live in Iceland or Britain or India, or who speak English or any other language, or who

are culturally Turkish or Chinese, and the like, thereby describable as races. The use of the term 'race' in speaking of such groups may be a serious error, but it is one which is habitually committed.

4. Human races can be, and have been classified in different ways by different anthropologists. Most of them agree in classifying the greater part of existing mankind into at least three large units, which may be called major groups (in French *grandes races*; in German *Hauptrassen*). Such a classification does not depend on any single physical character, nor does, for example, skin colour by itself necessarily distinguish one major group from another. Furthermore, so far as it has been possible to analyse them, the differences in physical structure which distinguish one major group from another give no support to popular notions of any general 'superiority' or 'inferiority' which are sometimes implied in referring to these groups.

Broadly speaking, individuals belonging to different major groups of mankind are distinguishable by virtue of their physical characters, but individual members, or small groups, belonging to different races within the same major group are usually not so distinguishable. Even the major groups grade into each other, and the physical traits by which they and the races within them are characterized overlap considerably. With respect to most, if not all, measurable characters, the differences among individuals belonging to the same race are greater than the differences that occur between the observed averages for two or more races within the same major group.

5. Most anthropologists do not include mental characteristics in their classification of human races. Studies within a single race have shown that both innate capacity and environmental opportunity determine the results of tests of intelligence and temperament, though their relative importance is disputed.

When intelligence tests, even non-verbal, are made on a group of non-literate people, their scores are usually lower than those of more civilized people. It has been recorded that different groups of the same race occupying similarly high levels of civilization may yield considerable differences in intelligence tests. When, however, the two groups have been brought up from childhood in similar environments, the differences are usually very slight. Moreover, there is good evidence that, given similar opportunities, the average performance (that is to say, the performance of the individual who is representative because he is surpassed by as many as he surpasses), and the variation round it, do not differ appreciably from one race to another.

Even those psychologists who claim to have found the greatest differences in intelligence between groups of different racial origin, and have contended that they are hereditary, always report that some members of the group of inferior performance surpass not merely the lowest ranking member of the superior group, but also the average of its members. In any case, it has never been possible to separate members of two groups on the basis of mental capacity, as they can often be separated on a basis of religion, skin colour, hair form or language. It is possible, though not proved, that some types of innate capacity for intellectual and emotional responses are commoner in one human group than in another, but it is certain that, within a single group, innate capacities vary as much as, if not more than, they do between different groups.

The study of the heredity of psychological characteristics is beset with difficulties. We know that certain mental diseases and defects are transmitted from one generation to the next, but we are less familiar with the part played by heredity in the mental life of normal individuals. The normal individual, irrespective of race, is essentially educable. It follows that his intellectual and moral life is largely conditioned by his training and by his physical and social environment.

It often happens that a national group may appear to be characterized by particular psychological attributes. The superficial view would be that this is due to race. Scientifically, however, we realize that any common psychological attribute is more likely to be due to a common historical and social background, and that such attributes may obscure the fact that, within different populations consisting of many human types, one will find approximately the same range of temperament and intelligence.

6. The scientific material available to us at present does not justify the conclusion that inherited genetic differences are a major factor in producing the differences between the cultures and cultural achievements of different peoples or groups. It does indicate, on the contrary, that a major factor in explaining such differences is the cultural experience which each group has undergone.

7. There is no evidence for the existence of so-called 'pure' races. Skeletal remains provide the basis of our limited knowledge about earlier races. In regard to race mixture, the evidence points to the fact that human hybridization has been going on for an indefinite but considerable time. Indeed, one of the processes of race formation and race extinction or absorption is by means of hybridization, between races. As there is no reliable evidence that disadvantageous effects are produced thereby, no biological justification exists for prohibiting inter-marriage between persons of different races.

8. We now have to consider the bearing of these statements on the problem of human equality. We wish to emphasize that equality of opportunity and equality in law in no way depend, as ethical principles, upon the assertion that human beings are in fact equal in endowment.

9. We have thought it worth while to set out in a formal manner what is at present scientifically established concerning individual and group differences.

(a) In matters of race, the only characteristics which anthropologists have so far been able to use effectively as a basis for classification are physical (anatomical and physiological).

(b) Available scientific knowledge provides no basis for believing that the groups of mankind differ in their innate capacity for intellectual and emotional development.

(c) Some biological differences between human beings within a single race may be as great as or greater than the same biological differences between races.

(d) Vast social changes have occurred that have not been connected in any way with changes in racial type. Historical and sociological studies thus support the view that genetic differences are of little significance in determining the social and cultural differences between different groups of men.

(e) There is no evidence that race mixture produces disadvantageous results from a biological point of view. The social results of race mixture, whether for good or ill, can generally be traced to social factors.

(Text drafted, at Unesco House, Paris, on 8 June 1951, by: Professor R. A. M. Bergman, Royal Tropical Institute, Netherlands Anthropological Society, Amsterdam; Professor Gunnar Dahlberg, Director, State Institute for Human Genetics and Race Biology, University of Uppsala; Professor L. C. Dunn, Department of Zoology, Columbia University, New York; Professor J. B. S. Haldane, Head, Department of Biometry, University College, London; Professor M. F. Ashley Montagu, Chairman, Department of Anthropology, Rutgers University, New Brunswick, N.J.; Dr A. E. Mourant, Director, Blood Group Reference Laboratory, Lister Institute, London; Professor Hans Nachsheim, Director, *Institut für Genetik, Freie Universität*, Berlin; Dr Eugène Schreider, *directeur adjoint du laboratoire d'anthropologie physique de l'École des hautes études*, Paris; Professor Harry L. Shapiro, Chairman, Department of Anthropology, American Museum of Natural History, New York; Dr J. C. Trevor, Faculty of Archaeology and Anthropology, University of Cambridge; Dr Henri V. Vallois, *professeur au Muséum d'histoire naturelle, directeur du Musée de l'Homme*, Paris; Professor S. Zuckerman, Head, Department of Anatomy, Medical School, University of Birmingham; Professor Th. Dobshansky, Department of Zoology, Columbia University, New York; and Dr Julian Huxley contributed to the final wording.)

The short answer to our question is, therefore, that Africans and other coloured people have the same human qualities as white-skinned people. They may be poor; for generations they have been riddled by tropical diseases; they have been cut off from contact with developments in other parts of the world and most of them are, therefore, ignorant. Although many of their religions, cultures, traditions, and social organizations bear little resemblance to those of the European world, yet each of them is individual, subject to the same emotions, capable of the same form of development, and included in the same range of human characteristics as the European.

Many will feel that much of this need not have been said. Unhappily in the present tempest of racial propaganda and argument the facts cannot be too often repeated.

Having established the common basis of Africans with non-Africans, we can now proceed to consider the major problems of the continent on exactly the same grounds as we would approach similar problems in any other part of the world.

Africans are human beings in exactly the same way as are Europeans, but much of their continent corresponds more closely to the early Middle Ages in Europe, or even to more ancient periods, than it does to modern European life. Although it is in Africa that have been found nearly all the diamonds in the world, more than a half of the gold and a fifth of the copper, together with many other minerals, and although the continent is an important producer of cocoa and palm oil, a vast majority of its 200 million people are desperately poor. Less than a tenth of its land area can be cultivated; the mineral wealth which it has produced has been developed from the outside by immigrants and foreign companies, and only a tiny proportion finds its way to the service of the Africans themselves.

In many parts of the continent there are simply no roads at all and where they do exist they are usually rough tracks cut in the bare earth, deeply rutted in the dry season, and impassable quagmires in the wet. The few railways are largely single-track lines, capable of sustaining only very low speeds with their severe gradients and curves.

Soil erosion is in parts of Africa worse than anywhere in the world, and the vast deserts which already exist are rapidly spreading. Water supplies are very scarce in many areas where, paradoxically, the tropical rains regularly denude the hillsides of their fertility and wash thousands of tons of top soil into the rivers.

The African people themselves are divided into hundreds of tribes, speaking a multitude of different languages, and owing allegiance to a wide variety of religions. It has often been said that the most dynamic influence in Africa is that of Nationalism. Yet genuine Nationalism hardly exists in any part of the continent; the very national frontiers which appear on the maps have all been drawn by Europeans, without reference to any African reality. They are the result of the European balance of power and were drawn according to European considerations. They cut across tribal areas, they divide up natural economic units, they pay no attention to geography. Little basis is therefore left for the growth of any form of national loyalty.

The five European imperial powers in the continent administer their colonial territories in vastly different ways. The French try to make their African subjects into Frenchmen and persuade them to take part in French political life by sending members to the National Assembly in Paris. The Belgians, Portuguese and, to some extent, the Spaniards, believe in ruling directly from their metropolitan capitals. They allow neither white nor black in their territories to have individual political rights. The British base their rule on the general principle of developing self-governing institutions, although where there are considerable enclaves of white immigrants it is they who, in the first place at least, gain the major political influence.

Then there are the ten independent states, Morocco, Tunisia, Egypt, Ethiopia, Ghana, Guinea, Liberia, Libya, the Sudan, and South Africa, nine of them governed by Africans, the tenth by a European minority. All of them have tended to be the playthings of European influences. One should perhaps also note that the United Nations has a stake in Africa through the administration of its trust territories, Tanganyika, Togoland, the Cameroons and Ruanda-Urundi, though in each case the administration is undertaken by a European power on behalf of the United Nations itself.

To this political division of control should also be added the growing economic and financial influence of overseas capital, particularly from the United States. Many of the companies engaged in various forms of economic development are based in overseas countries. Their influence on African development is inevitably large, but their decisions may well be taken on considerations which bear no relation to African situations. It is frequently the economic needs of an overseas people rather than the needs of Africans themselves which determine the form and purpose of development.

Africa has largely, therefore, taken on the aspect of a passive continent played upon by the European and American world. Its people have never been much more than pawns moved according to the strategic, political, and economic aims of external powers. Slowly the leaders of world events are beginning to realize the dangers which this situation presents. It is becoming almost an acknowledged *cliché* to say that Africa is a vacuum which will inevitably be filled by one of a number of forces. Western Europe and America, African racialism, Communism, Arab nationalism, all contend to influence the pattern of thought and habit of this, the last continent of the world to join international civilization.

It is generally, though not universally, agreed that a determined effort must be made to lift the mass of Africans from their existing deep-rooted poverty. There are still some Africans who so fear the influence of the external world that they would prefer poverty to the impact of external influences. There are still some Europeans who consider that the 'noble savage' is a happier and better being than a tribesman suffering from the pangs of transition to modern society. There are many other Europeans who still keep their eyes fixed within their own countries, paying scant heed to what is happening to the millions of people dependent upon them who have contributed in their suffering to the comfort of European life. Yet generally there is a gradual awakening to the fact that on grounds of expediency alone the world can no longer afford an Africa characterized by endemic poverty, dispossession, discrimination, widespread disease, and illiteracy. It is from such conditions that the fabric of civilization has so often been shaken in the past, and it is to such a vacuum that contending national blocs so often turn their eyes as a new field of conflict.

The general acceptance of the necessity for African development poses many questions. Much of the economic aid to initiate development projects can only come from outside the continent. In an era when the peoples of Europe in particular are desperately competing with each other to maintain and, if possible, to raise their own standards of living, who will be prepared to devote a proportion of their production to the far greater, but more remote, needs of the peoples of Africa? When tractors are needed to improve the production of European agriculture, increase European food supplies and decrease European dependence on imports, will European peoples be prepared to send tractors to Africa? So long as there is full employment and democratic institutions are maintained in the metropolitan countries, it is difficult to visualize the self-denying effort being made to provide the considerable help which is urgently required. Full employment implies the existence of a market for all goods that are produced. To provide such goods as a gift or loan to the under-developed peoples of Africa must inevitably, in the short term, restrict consumption in the metropolitan country. And so long as politicians have to sell their policies competitively in democratic elections it needs foresight, wisdom, and statesmanship for a party to be courageous enough to tell the electorate that it proposes to follow such a policy.

Nevertheless, it should be recognized that some slight move towards this attitude has been made since the end of the war. As a matter of fact, in the middle of the Dunkirk crisis of 1940, the British Parliament still found sufficient time and interest in its colonial responsibilities to pass the first Colonial Development and Welfare Act. This established the principle that the British Treasury—which in fact means the British taxpayer—should contribute to both the social and the economic development of colonial peoples. The Act has been renewed several times, on each occasion with additional grants. All the colonies are now assisted by it and can plan their development programmes in the knowledge that these funds are available to them.

Although the Colonial Development and Welfare Acts are a step in the right direction, this effort has always been weakened by lack of sufficient funds. The development programmes of the colonies are drawn up, but their expenditure is always scaled down. It is certainly right that the resources should be used to their best advantage, but there are many cases in which this scaling down has retarded the progress in development demanded and which could have been achieved. It is true that there are often difficulties in the application of this money, particularly in securing the services of the trained technicians essential to its constructive employment. It is equally true that much more money is required if the desperate poverty existing today in these colonies is to be effectively attacked. There is also a strong case for associating the Colonial Development Corporation with the C.D. and W. in this work. The C.D.C. is often regarded as a purely financial organization. It should not be so; it should be enabled to invest in schemes which do not bring profit, but do supplement the work of the C.D. and W. in raising the standard of living of the colonial peoples.

Whilst this is certainly a step in the right direction, there is no cause for the British people to feel complacent. It is not generally recognized that Britain still gets more material benefit from her colonies than she returns to them. Apart from the invaluable sources of raw materials and food which the colonies supply cheaply to the British people, it should be remembered that without the sale of cocoa from Ghana and rubber from Malaya to the Americans, the dollar gap would have been unbridgeable. Then again, Britain, whilst loaning long-term capital to the colonies has at the same time been borrowing heavily from them at short-term rates. Between the end of 1949 and the end of 1955 the sterling balances in this country rose by about £1,700 million, whereas the total grants and loans and our contribution to the United Nations' special agencies have never been above about £25 million a year. What is more the lack of saving within the United Kingdom, the consequent shortage of capital, and the economic policy of this country which led to the raising of the bank rate, all directly affect the colonies. Remember that they also have to pay these increased interest rates on the essential investments which they need for capital developments.

It is also an important fact that much of the investment in Africa is concentrated on the most developed, and therefore the least needy, territories. Just as in the Commonwealth as a whole investment has been attracted to the well-developed areas like Australia and Canada where profits are highest, rather than to the Asian countries, whose need for capital is so much more urgent, so in the African continent it has been comparatively wealthy South Africa, the Congo and the Rhodesias which have mainly attracted private investment. These three territories, whose total population amounts only to about 33 million, have in fact secured half the total capital invested in the whole continent, whose population numbers about 200 million. To a certain extent it can be asserted that the earnings and savings of poorer colonies have been used to finance the development of the better developed areas. This surely points directly to the need for increased public investment channelled where the need is greatest, where there may be smaller profits and longer to wait for them. It equally points to the necessity for some control of the direction of private investment if such capital is to have its most constructive effect.

It should also be clearly noted that many of the African territories, like other under-developed countries of the world, still rely very heavily on single-factor economies. Many of these factors are in the range of primary products, whose prices fluctuate enormously according to world conditions over which they have no control. Thus the fall in the price of commodities like cocoa in Ghana or copper in Northern Rhodesia, prices determined according to international circumstances, have drastically cut the standard of living of their people, suddenly increased unemployment, and more than wiped out all the benefits of external aid. Without some means of regulating commodity prices and ensuring that such countries can rely on reasonably steady returns for their goods over a period of years, any other planning is impossible and their people will remain at the mercy of international whims.

Moreover the Treasury showed the utmost meanness when it discouraged some colonies from increasing industrial taxation. It feared that extra taxes on British companies in the colonies would mean less tax revenue here. Considering that considerable wealth is still taken out of the colonies by companies operating overseas, whilst colonial needs are so much greater than those in this country, this represents a most unjust attitude on the part of the British Government. Even on grounds of expediency, it should be recognized in Britain that by curtailing a rise in the standard of living in the colonies we are denying ourselves potential markets. If the living standards of every colonial person were raised by only £5 per year it would create well over £400 million of extra spending capacity.

Whilst Britain has slowly begun to recognize her responsibility as a colonial power and to make free gifts through these channels, the United States of America has also been contributing to the same field. There has always been a tremendous fund of warm-hearted generosity amongst the people of the United States for peoples in need, but the major motive of the administration in providing aid to the under-developed areas has undoubtedly been their fear of Communism. There are occasions on which this object can sour and distort the effort. Whatever the motive, however, the funds made available have been invaluable.

The United Nations too, through their various agencies have provided funds for development in Africa. The main difficulty of their provision has perhaps been the high cost of administration which has absorbed far too large a proportion of the funds allocated. Yet both Britain and the United States have been niggardly in the extreme in their approach to the imaginative scheme of the Special United Nations Fund for Economic Development. Only £90 millions is required from thirty countries to begin this international scheme to help the underdeveloped peoples. As yet Britain and America have refused to contribute a penny.

In spite of all these doubts and drawbacks and the inadequacy of the funds available, it is still important to recognize that Africa, unlike previous continents in history, is being consciously and deliberately assisted to develop by the outside world. Of course it is true that much African wealth has been and is still being removed from that continent, but it is nevertheless an important new principle in modern international affairs to provide voluntary aid to other peoples.

Arising out of this important feature of African life comes quite another consideration. Capital is entering the continent from a number of sources. The question now arises as to who should control it and on what conditions. Many Africans themselves are beginning to ask this pertinent question. There is a natural fear of creating conditions such as have developed in the Union of South Africa, where the white men control all the capital and coloured workers, particularly in the mines, are regimented in conditions of semi-slavery. Even if such extremes are not repeated, there can be no doubt that the establishment and expansion of industry and urban life inevitably undermine the traditional African social system of tribalism. If such a breakdown is induced too suddenly and without thought and preparation, psychological distortions similar to that of the Mau Mau movement become inevitable as all foundations of African security are suddenly removed.

Africans also fear a repetition of the experiences of the Northern Rhodesian Copper Belt. They are frightened that the white man will monopolize skilled work, keeping them permanently as unskilled labourers and removing vast quantities of wealth from their land.

There is a parallel to such fear in the agricultural world, where not only is further European settlement opposed as resulting in yet more loss of land, but there is wide suspicion that if the Africans themselves apply methods of agricultural improvement their improved lands will be taken from them by the whites.

The deduction from these trends is that although African communities, with very few exceptions, today desire continued economic aid from the European states, they have begun to expect that conditions will be laid down for its operations. They expect from their respective governments the establishment of industrial charters which will ensure full opportunities of training and promotion for African workers in the new enterprises. They claim that increased proportions of the profits made shall be devoted to the development of their own territories. They demand the protection of their land rights against the claims of immigrants.

Not only do they make abstract demands for these conditions, but it naturally follows that, in order to ensure that they are carried out, the Africans themselves demand increased participation in the governments concerned. They have also begun to organize trade union movements to further their claims, often with the help of parent bodies in Europe. This raises the further social question as to whether trade unions can, in fact, be instituted and developed from the outside. Can the genuine spirit of trade unionism develop amongst trade union members unless they have gone through the trials and struggles which have produced trade union loyalty in the European nations? Or will the colonial trade union members look upon their organizations simply as a means to securing better wages and conditions for themselves and lose interest in them once these have been obtained?

The whole of this trend of thought towards outside assistance in economic development raises the immense question of the relationship between the indigenous African majorities and the immigrant minorities. No other continent has ever had to face the same complexities as are raised by this issue in Africa. In every part of the continent, with the possible exception of British West Africa, small enclaves of white immigrants from the highly developed, sophisticated, and technically advanced European states are living amongst vast majorities of Africans, most of whom live in an entirely different age, with hardly any points of contact in culture, religion, language, or tradition. Yet all over the continent, the pressure for social justice, and its necessary accompaniment of political rights, is rapidly growing. These feelings are no doubt themselves an export from European life, very largely due to British influence in the continent, bringing the conception of political representation, parliamentary institutions and eventually self-government. They are spreading to those African colonies ruled by the French, Belgians, Portuguese, Spaniards, and South Africans.

A variety of names has been used to describe different phases of the British attitude to her colonial peoples. 'Imperialism', 'paramountcy', 'trusteeship', 'partnership', 'multi-racialism' are some of them. They mark a gradual transition from the dominating to the paternalistic attitude, to the recognition that the colonial peoples are now beginning to take an active and individual part in the political life of their countries. The word that has been least heard, but is most revered by those Africans who are politically conscious, is 'democracy'. It is an inevitable consequence of teaching in the

British pattern that pupils will ultimately claim for themselves the same rights as Britons themselves have gained. Thus, where Britain still claims to be the trustee for her African wards, whether she believes that the indigenous and immigrant races must establish some form of division of responsibility on a partnership basis, or whether she should try and maintain separate racial communities each with their respective representation, the Africans have by today so seized hold of the British conception of democracy that nothing less will satisfy them. It may be that they will concede that so long as the educational, organizational, and technical gap remains wide between the different communities, these multiracial arrangements must be accepted as temporary expedients. But they all demand that they be recognized as nothing more than expedients and so always be regarded merely as steps on the path to the establishment of full democracy.

Democracy to the African politicians means a British form of democracy, based upon universal suffrage, on the principle of 'one man, one vote'. This implies that, although cultural differences may remain, in politics there can be no room for privileged minority groups. There is no real desire in any British African territory to expel the white men or the Asians. What is simply demanded is that the privileges of these communities be brought to an end and that all accept the common loyalty to a new nation, irrespective of race or colour. In short, the primary demand is the destruction of all racial and colour discrimination.

The attack upon political discrimination is only one aspect of the total effort aimed towards the establishment of social justice. It has a multitude of forms, involving not only politics, but all aspects of social and economic life. Whether in theory political equality should precede or succeed the abolition of colour prejudice has already become a purely abstract question. Africans in all parts of the continent have begun to realize in differing degrees that they are frequently the victims of a vicious circle. They are told that it would be dangerous to give them political equality before they have attained equality in education, skills, technique, experience, and economic life. Yet they believe that they will never obtain equal opportunities in any of these spheres until they have gained at least sufficient political power to ensure governmental action to guarantee equal chances. They have, therefore, fixed their eyes first upon political equality, as a prerequisite for equality in the other departments.

In their efforts to secure equality of opportunity, the Africans are already meeting many difficulties. Because of the historical backwardness of the continent, they realize that they still require the technical, educational, medical, and economic assistance of the immigrant peoples. Yet, if they force the pace of political advance too fast, they are bound to provoke fear amongst many immigrants. Not only so, but they may risk those protections which are still essential to the life of many of their own people. To destroy all discrimination in landholding in East Africa immediately would not only open the 'White Highlands' to non-European tenure, but would also destroy the application of tribal custom and the protection of tribal land.

African advance has, therefore, to be carefully planned and shrewdly directed. It will normally attack first the weakest bastions of privilege. It is a significant fact that, particularly in East Africa, dislike of the Asian immigrants has increased in places and sometimes overshadows the antagonism towards the European. There are two main reasons for this fact. The first results from what has been said above about privilege. The Asian immigrant is also disliked by the European and has established only a precarious hold in his new country. He somewhat resembles the Jew of medieval Europe in that he has turned usually from the frustration of competition with the more politically powerful European to commerce. A very large proportion of the commercial and financial life of East Africa is today in the hands of the Asian. He not only owns large hotels and stores in the towns, but takes his small shop right out into the heart of the bush. As the African advances economically, the first hurdle he encounters is competition with the small Asian businessman.

The second reason arises from the character and exclusiveness of Asian life. The African has found his progress in European guidance and has fixed his aims upon European achievement. He has already begun to accept and participate in European culture. He therefore develops an antagonism towards the oriental cultural structure which the Asian preserves. The African frequently feels that the Asian community sets itself apart from national development. It should be said that the most intelligent Asian leaders recognize this danger and are making strenuous efforts to persuade their own people to take a full share in the development of these new multi-racial nations and to participate socially in the new societies.

One further point should be mentioned in connexion with the efforts to abolish colour prejudice. There has developed amongst some groups in Britain, known selfconsciously as 'Friends of the Africans', an emotional paternalism which is really only a reverse side of colour prejudice. The general attitude is that the black man must always be right. This is, of course, naturally resented by intelligent Africans. It is another form of treating the African as a race instead of as an individual. It is often linked to fanaticism and lack of judgment which can only harm African movements and the whole cause of racial equality. If the black man is equal to a white man he is equally prone to be wrong, and has the right to expect that his genuine friends will be as willing to disagree with him and to criticize him as they would a person of any other skin colour. The gushing sentimentalists, with their pathological 'personality cults', can be a greater menace to Africans than open racialists.

On the other hand, Africans too have some readjustments to make. At present many of them are still understandably extremely sensitive to criticism and disagreement with their ideas. This is perhaps inevitable amongst a people emerging from the enforced status of inferiority, still lacking in self-confidence and having to insist aggressively on their right to equality. Nevertheless, Africans, like everyone else, must recognize that one of the first tests of equality is the readiness to accept criticism without rancour, consider it objectively, and argue rationally rather than emotionally. Anyone in Britain who fails to criticize the views of an African because he has a black skin and may be sensitive is no friend of the African people but as much a racialist as those who speak of 'kaffirs'. Every African, whether it be in his continent or abroad, who shows resentment to criticism because it comes from a white man equally subscribes to the racialist philosophy.

One aspect of African life particularly open to criticism is the status of women in African society. In every primitive society labour has to be spread much more widely through the community than is possible in the technically advanced nations. The sharp division between the 'able-bodied' and the 'weak' can only come with technical development. Thus in all primitive societies women and children are widely used for comparatively heavy labour. It is also a normal division in primitive society for women to work in the fields, whilst the men go hunting and fighting.

In tribal Africa these conditions have inevitably developed. Yet since tribal warfare was abolished and hunting died out, the necessity for this type of division has disappeared. Nevertheless, the habits have persisted. It is still quite a common sight in many parts of the African continent to see the women performing heavy labour whilst the men, released from their obligations of hunting and defending, take life easily.

Then again, most African tribes are based upon the patriarchal principle. Government and decision reside entirely in male hands, whilst the female is expected to obey.

It requires a much closer study of anthropology than is possible here to understand fully the social organization of tribalism. It is too superficial simply to assume that the practice of the 'bride price', or what is commonly known as 'buying a wife', reduces the female to the position simply of a chattel. This practice is often a form of social security from which the wife herself benefits. Nor can polygamy simply be condemned out of hand as an unmitigated evil. The fact is that the closely woven structure of the tribe usually gives a security to all members of the family, but particularly to the women and children, unknown in western life. It avoids many of the dangers of juvenile delinquency, spinsterhood, and widowhood. It provides its own deeply rooted and all-embracing social security. Within it the women have their special influence and secure position. Most of them, including many of the educated women, oppose its breakdown.

Having said this, it is nevertheless clear that without a revolutionary change in the position and status of women, African society cannot graduate into any form of modern civilization. Not only are the superstitious and prejudiced traditions of the past harmful to the individuals concerned—female circumcision and heavy labour are two obvious examples—but the whole effect militates against the emergence of a half of the African population into the sphere of social, economic, and political responsibility. It is futile for African politicians to claim modern equality for their peoples and to deny it to their own women. Unless women come to be regarded as equal and individual human beings with the men, all the claims for individual human rights made by the male politicians are fundamentally spurious.

What is more, no modern society can emerge from Africa so long as it tries to retain the superstitious prejudices of primitive tribalism. Many of the younger educated Africans are beginning to recognize this fact. They find in their own personal life that there are so few educated African women that it is often impossible for them to find a wife with the same social background as they have gained themselves.

The first attack on this problem must, of course, come from a rapid increase in the education of African girls. Some Africans have even gone so far as to say that, if necessary, the speed of educational advancement of the boys must be slowed down in order to give a first priority to girls' education which is today lagging so far behind. This is, of course, not simply an African problem; the same barriers to female education exist all over the world in some degree. It is indeed curious that one of the few exceptions is to be found in the African continent itself. In Basutoland there are far more girls than boys at school, as the Basutos need their boys as herdsmen.

It would obviously be preferable to maintain the security and common responsibility of tribal family life, whilst raising the status of the women. Whilst this problem is too deep a question to be discussed fully here, it would certainly seem that once you begin to treat all people as individuals, at the same time distinctly separating urban and rural life, the ties which bind a tribal family must be cut. Initiative and individual personality do not usually go together with traditional collective responsibility. Nevertheless, the African, in his leap from tribalism to modern life, may be able to produce some new and higher forms of social responsibility than those seen in western industrial society. It can be imagined that profound psychological issues are at stake here. At the same time, the African cannot risk leaving the female half of his population in superstition and ignorance for fear of what the revolution in social life may bring.

It is a humbling fact that for some years to come, in spite of all that may develop in the African continent, the decisive decisions, on which the whole future role of the African peoples depend, will be made not in Africa but in Europe. The British people have only just begun to realize that we have a greater responsibility for the 60 million British dependents in Africa than for the 50 million people of the British Isles themselves. Much of the comfort of our modern life, and a great deal of the economic margins on which our comparatively smooth development to democracy has been based, stem directly from the suffering of British colonial peoples. We have used them as cheap labour, as customers for our goods; we have taken the wealth out of their countries, used them for strategic bases, and called on their help in war. Now the urge towards social justice which has played such a large part in British history is called for on the international stage. We have a debt to pay to the peoples whom we have exploited in the past, and, if we have any concern for a peaceful and healthy international society, on grounds of expediency as well we shall recognize and repay this debt.

Africa today is a continent caught up in the momentum of revolution. It is in the process of transformation from primitive static tribalism to modern dynamic industrialism. The foundations of ancient tribal agriculture, with all their social implications, have already been undermined. Thousands of Africans every year now stream into the new towns, some of them having travelled thousands of miles from their villages. Many return after a period of urban life; others remain in a growing settled urban community. All have some experience of modern mass organization to contrast with the parochial tribal structure in which they have been brought up.

The effect of this new and increasing movement of the masses is to begin the process of destroying the ancient pastoral life of the continent, to introduce new methods of land tenure and husbandry, to create new urban communities, and to shatter the mirror of traditional African life. The social pattern of the tribe, with its hereditary authorities and disciplines, is cracked. New organizations, like trade unions, co-operatives, political parties, are taking its place. Sometimes there is conflict between the modern political leaders and the traditional chieftains. At others they work together for a common national purpose.

The political organizations and the other forms of association may be badly organized, may only have a transitory life, and their leaders may be brash, self-assertive and demagogic. Some may be bribed or corrupted. The same characteristics have been seen in similar circumstances in other continents. No one, however, can doubt the depth of this revolutionary upheaval, nor that it is transforming the whole character of African society. There can be no return to tribalism. A modern society, with all its pressures, its arguments and its potentialities, is in process of being created.

The Western world has a unique responsibility and a special opportunity in this continental revolution. It has so far been conducted in the languages and according to the conceptions of Western democracy. The slogans, ambitions and ideologies of nascent Africa have been taken from the Western European tradition. Yet Western Europe still slumbers beside the turmoil which it has created in this continent. Many of its reflex actions when it has been disturbed have been destructive of its own influence. When the French resist in North Africa the same demands which created French nationhood, or when the British support in East and Central Africa the claims of aristocratic caste which they had to break in their own country before a democratic society could be created, the ideals of Western tradition are undermined in African eyes. When the Western developed economy refuses to give active and substantial support to African development, the sun of Western democracy is seen to be setting. All Africa is becoming conscious of this apparent lack of Western interest. A common African front, facing the problems of the continent, is already visualized by the African intelligentsia. If they cannot fulfil their needs from the West, they will turn elsewhere. Although European nations have particular opportunities through their intimate contact with the continent, they also have the particular disadvantage of an imperialist heritage. Some Africans already look to the Soviet Union and more especially to China as having themselves solved the dramatic problems of the under-developed masses; they also observe the communist's clean sheet on colour prejudice; others look to Egypt as a dynamic nationalist force; still others regard India as the champion of the coloured peoples. There are the beginnings of an 'African Personality' cult which could easily turn away from the rest of the world into a racialist fetish.

The choice rests with the West. If it really believes in the values of its society and recognizes the profound significance of adding the African continent to the Western way of life, it will throw off its languor and participate enthusiastically in the dramatic revolution which is taking place. It will recognize Africa as an addition to the society which it has created, bringing a new dynamic contribution. To face this challenge it is essential that the paternalistic tradition be discarded. If the West makes the unimaginative assumption that Africans will blindly follow its example rather than building upon it, understanding can never be established. If the West in its complacency assumes that the new African nations will simply ally themselves to anti-communist military blocs, it will continue to live in its own little world, barred by its own arrogance from African minds. If anything, the African leaders are attracted by the concept of 'positive neutralism', for they have no quarrel with the communist world, though as yet no desire to accept its pattern. At present they wish to be on friendly terms with the West, the communists, the Arabs and Israel.

If the Western world genuinely wants to retain the African as a partner it can only be on the basis of the complete equality of friends. This demands an entirely new effort in understanding and active participation in the African revolution. Even the efforts of progressive forces in Europe have so far savoured of little more than tired liberalism. European socialists have never thought beyond the preconceptions of their liberal predecessors in their relations with Africans. Achievement has been measured solely in terms of 'independence' and 'new national states'. The lessons of balkanized Europe might never have been learned. Now that the process has gone so far it would be impossible to turn back, for the minds of Africans too are fixed on the creation of independent national states. Nevertheless, the Africans have already shown signs of recognizing the basic danger of repeating European folly. They are unlikely to remain content with state frontiers which make no sense economically, geographically or socially. New frontiers will be drawn, old ones rubbed out, and new constitutional forms projected. If this process frightens the West and, worse, if they attempt to interfere with it, it will be basic Western ideals which suffer. To understand Africa one must be prepared for adaptation, experiment, and entirely new conceptions.

There is no longer any place in Africa for the old imperialist or colonial concepts. The imperial powers have a straight choice. Either they can assist the African revolution by lending their technical skills and capital to its African protagonists in their efforts to overcome centuries of primitivism and human inequality, which still bar the continent's progress; or they can take their stand along with the White racialists of the continent in trying to stem the flood. If they accept the former choice, they may establish a new relationship based on mutual and equal respect with the new African world; if they take the latter, they will be swept away into the dustbin of history along with the other refuse of a bygone age.

In the past empires have been marked by conquest, occupation, decline. If the twentieth century European imperial powers are to escape from historical precedent, they can do so only by transforming the imperial relationship into one of human service through a partnership of equals. Yet if Europe is to face seriously the challenge of Africa today, present tentative efforts in economic assistance and political opportunity will have to be revolutionized in speed and volume.

The African peoples may take any one of three roads. They may accept the communist model of dealing with the problems of an under-developed people; they may embrace Black racialism, determined to rid themselves of all White and Brown men, so many of whom have been their oppressors; or they may accept the basic principles of the democratic life, adapting them and producing new forms to fit their particular needs. At present there is little attraction in communism for the African, for he has grown up usually within the concept of a Western democratic society, even though often he has been barred from full participation. Racialism is equally foreign to the African character, though there are signs of its beginnings which will be fostered wherever the White man attempts to maintain his caste system. To deal with the tremendous social and economic problems of the continent through the democratic medium is a terrific task, which will require all the energies of African, European and Asian combined. It is, in fact, to try and provide the material revolution accomplished in Russia and China whilst using the slower and less decisive methods of democratic representation. The reward is to combine material prosperity with individual liberty. Its success depends on the Western world even more than on the Africans. If either communism or racialism prevail, or if, as seems more dangerously possible, the racialism reaction is seized upon by the communists for their own ends, the African continent will be lost to the democratic world. The West must awaken to the fact that the character of a new continental society is at stake. What will history's verdict be on the Western impact: the plunderer of its wealth, or the creator of its soul?

In the British parts of Africa a special opportunity awaits the new African states. They can look forward on gaining independence to becoming full and equal members of the Commonwealth. The new Commonwealth which has grown up since the Second World War, which already includes the Asian states and Ghana, is the most progressive conception in British history. It holds out the opportunity at one and the same time of independent statehood and membership of a genuine international community. In so doing, it meets the several needs of the new African states. Not only can they achieve the independent existence to which they all aspire, but at the same time they can become members of a free, voluntary and equal association of states, able to lend strength, wisdom and protection during their early years.

The admission of the new African states to this community will increase its heterogeneous nature, adding to it new ideas and fresh contributions. It may well be that the Africans will decide to establish their own new constitutional structures within the African continent and erase many of the artificial lines of division previously drawn by the Europeans. This need not in any way inhibit their full membership of the Commonwealth, and indeed should enhance its strength.

It is true that in some ways the Commonwealth is still more of a concept than an actuality. Much thought and discussion is needed to project its full impact on world affairs. It is not easy to equate national sovereignty with international collectivity. Nevertheless, a start has been made and each member is fully autonomous without any inhibition of its internal or external policy, whilst at the same time gaining new strength from the free discussions it participates in with fellow members. Moreover, because membership is voluntary, secession is possible at any time.

The Commonwealth now bestrides the five continents of the world. Its potential as a mediating force for peace is limitless. Within its bounds all the most dangerous and urgent of our international problems, colour prejudice, racial discrimination, relations between developed and under-developed peoples, can be solved. They will only be solved, however, if the Commonwealth is virile enough to face them squarely. The immediate challenge of racialism in South Africa and Central Africa are focal to its whole existence as an international community. If Central Africa were to follow the example of its southern neighbour no African state would remain in the Commonwealth longer than sheer necessity demanded. Such an eventuality and its train of consequences would be sufficient to destroy the whole basis of the Commonwealth association and every shred of British influence in Africa.

Africans will only seek or retain Commonwealth membership so long as they believe that it is based on complete racial equality and dedicated to remove racial intolerance.

The Commonwealth community has grown from the experiment of democratic evolution and is founded on the principles of racial equality and free institutions. So long as these remain the positive ideals for which the community strives it will prosper through common effort towards agreed goals. Its success in establishing a genuine international community will be greatly enhanced by the inclusion of the new African states, whilst they will find security, comradeship and stimulating ideas through their membership. On this success may well depend man's chance to avoid dividing the human community into two armed camps, separated by colour, race and wealth. Africa, as the new keystone of the Commonwealth, will play a vital role in this greatest human drama.

X: FUTURE PERSPECTIVES

THE kaleidoscope of African situations is changing so rapidly that any attempt to describe them can only be ephemeral. The main purpose of this book has not been to describe current situations, but rather to provide a background from which the changes that are taking place in Africa can be understood. Nevertheless, in the short time since the preceding chapters were written, a number of events have taken place in the continent which, though foreshadowed in the earlier chapters, may be studied with advantage because of the light they shed on the problems and development of the continent as a whole.

The most important recent developments have certainly been those in Central Africa, Kenya, the Congo, and the French territories. Their importance lies not simply in the fact that they have all hit the headlines at one time or another, but that their problems lie at the roots of the African enigma, whilst the solutions to them will significantly influence the progress of the rest of the continent.

In this last chapter, therefore, we shall concentrate not so much on the details of recent events but rather on their significance to the reshaping of Africa's destiny—a process in which all parts of the continent are currently engaged.

West Africa

The most interesting trend in West Africa has been the series of tentative attempts to secure some form of closer association of the various states. Starting with the projected Ghana-Guinea union late in 1958 and continuing with the project for the Federation of Mali early in 1959, this trend reached its highest point so far with a meeting of Dr Nkrumah of Ghana, President Sékou Touré of Guinea, and President William Tubman of Liberia in July 1959.

There has been little practical outcome of the proposal of union between Ghana and Guinea, and although Mali has been established, there were early defections on the part of Dahomey and Volta. It seems likely that, from this experiment, the West African leaders are turning their minds more to the establishment of a loose federal structure which will enable other states to join as the idea of closer association takes firmer root. At their meeting in July the three leaders proposed that a special conference of African states should be held in 1960 to lay the foundations for a community of independent African states. This proposal followed the decision of Dr Nkrumah and M. Touré at a former meeting to propose a union of such states within which each would preserve its own personality and internal structure. All independent African states are to be invited to the conference, together with those which already have a fixed date for independence.

The future of any form of West African association will depend very heavily on the attitude taken by Nigeria when she becomes independent in 1960. So far, Nigerians have held largely aloof from such moves, and the Federal Government in particular has shown considerable scepticism of their value. The Nigerians are heavily preoccupied with preparations for independence. They have already negotiated a loan of £15 million with the British Government in order to complete their four-year development plan. The parties are preparing for the elections, and already the N.C.N.C. and N.E.P.U. have come to an agreement which will enable this combination to fight on a national basis in all three regions. When Nigeria, with its 32 million people, becomes an independent state it is bound to have a very important influence on the whole of West Africa, and its attitude towards an association of states will be crucial.

Sierra Leone and the Gambia have not yet shown any direct interest in associating with the other West African states. In 1960 there are to be further constitutional discussions in each country which will certainly result in more representative constitutions. They will then have the opportunity of defining more clearly their attitudes towards the other states.

In Ghana, which has so far taken the lead in this wider community, there have been certain critical rumblings regarding the interest being shown by the Government in other states. The promise of a loan to Guinea was by no means universally popular, even inside the Cabinet. More serious are the doubts which continue to be raised about the sincerity of some Ministers' and party officials' democratic pretensions. The Granville Sharp Committee, appointed to investigate the allegations of an assassination plot against two leading members of the Opposition, found that there was a conspiracy but was divided on whether there was evidence to show that it was specifically to assassinate Dr Nkrumah. The continued detentions without trial and the new state-controlled structure of the trade union movement, together with various other indications of intimidating opposition, have led some people—both inside and outside Ghana—to fear for the future of genuine democracy there. Guinea has become an openly dictatorial state, ruled by decree, and there is some fear that this may influence the development of Ghana. The main weakness continues to be the inefficiency of the Opposition, whose leader, Dr Busia, has now left the country.

The main issue determining the future of Ghana seems to be whether the current strong Government measures are to be used in order to safeguard the democratic foundations of the state or whether their use itself will lead to the habit of using power and thus to the destruction of democracy in both practice and spirit. There are in Ghana—both inside and outside the Government—those liable to take both these roads. The future of democracy in the country will depend on the outcome of the struggle between them. The environment in which the struggle will be won, and which in itself is likely to influence the outcome, will depend very heavily on the degree of success attained by the new development plan—designed to expand industry and agriculture, promote the Volta River Hydro-electric Scheme, and, if some capital still remains, expand other services. If this, together with the sound organization of the cocoa industry, provides sufficient resources for an expanding standard of life for Ghanaians, it may well be that there are sufficient powerful democratic voices in the country to preserve and develop a genuine democratic system. This is really much more important for Ghana and the whole of West Africa than the decision, which will be made in 1960, to create a republic in the country, presumably with Dr Nkrumah as President and Prime Minister, acknowledging the Queen as head of the Commonwealth but not of the Ghanaian state.

East Africa

The progress of events in the three East African territories is so different that their contrasts are much more marked than their similarities. In Uganda there is no cohesion in African political organization, and the Province of Buganda is constantly at loggerheads with the rest of the country. In Kenya the battle for power continues between African and European, with the Asian unhappily ground between the two. Yet, in Tanganyika there is a strong African political party which has secured the friendship and cooperation of both European and Asian and is well on the way to proving conclusively that three separate races can join together in the establishment of a new nation state. It is almost becoming an anachronism to talk about 'East Africa' when the problems and policies of the three different territories diverge so drastically. The fact is that the development of the three territories has been so different recently that their basic problems today are no longer identical.

Uganda

Uganda is developing steadily but slowly towards self-government. The constitutional committee is due to report shortly on the electoral system and the composition of the Legislative and Executive Councils. It is almost certain that this will lead to a widening of the franchise, a greater degree of representation in the Legislative Council, and an increase in the number of elected Ministers in the Executive.

This progress, however, is sustained almost entirely by the Provinces other than Buganda. Buganda is the richest and commercially most prosperous area of the Protectorate. It is also the most stubborn, and in some ways the most anti-democratic. The

Kabaka and his Court are still the most powerful political influences, and they—together with the Lukiko, which largely reflects their views—are stubbornly opposed to the creation of a unitary Uganda state, even though it would be self-governing. They fear that the hereditary feudal power of the Kabaka and his followers will be inevitably diminished by association with the other Provinces in a single-state structure. They therefore continue to refuse co-operation in the constitutional developments of the country and continually put forward demands to the British Government for an end to their agreement.

The most significant, and in many ways the most tragic, development of recent months has been the affair of the Uganda National Movement. This movement was initiated by Eridada Mulira, who has been one of the foremost opponents of Buganda feudalism and has suffered persecution for his opposition. In the spring of 1959 he decided that open opposition to the system was yielding no results, so he told his friends that he had decided to change his tactics and try to influence the feudal system from within. Accordingly he formed the National Movement, which was little more than a political front for Buganda national feudalism. It adopted the disastrous policy of persecuting the Asians, ostensibly in protest against the proposal to reserve special seats for the minority groups as African representation increased. Whether this policy was adopted with the object of securing popular support or was derived from the personal prejudice of some leaders of the movement towards Asians, it is impossible to say. It may be recalled that in 1955, when it was first proposed that an Asian Minister be appointed, the same kind of prejudices were displayed. The Asians are often unpopular in Uganda and in other parts of East Africa because of their wide-spread control of trade, particularly amongst small commercial enterprises selling to Africans even in the most remote parts of the country. Not only does this lead to suspicion of profiteering, but as the Africans begin to develop commercially they find the small Indian trader in the way. The social exclusiveness of the Asian community is also resented.

An appeal to anti-Asian feeling is thus apt to be popular in spite of the valuable public work known to have been done by leading

Asians like Sir Amar Maini. Whatever may be the causes of popular anti-Asian prejudice, this is a despicable political tactic, designed to hinder greatly the harmonious development of a new Uganda state. It is widely disliked by African leaders in other parts of East Africa than Buganda. It led to the imposition of a boycott on Asian shops, and this in turn led to bribery, corruption, and blackmail. Out of the tense situation which developed, violence arose, the National Movement was banned, further attempts to organize it under different names were prevented, and some of its leaders were detained.

The whole situation leaves Uganda in a dilemma. It seems unlikely that the healthy constitutional development leading directly to self-government and eventually to independence—a development supported by the rest of the country—will secure the support of Buganda in the foreseeable future. Yet, without Buganda the Protectorate is impoverished. Even if a federal system were devised, the federal government would be largely at the mercy of Buganda's wealth and influence. The responsibility now lies with the Africans, who have the opportunity—if they will take it—to create a newly independent state in their country. Some of the leading Africans from other provinces and, indeed, some of the more intelligent Baganda are so irritated by the intransigence of Buganda nationalists that they are seriously considering some form of federal system or allowing Buganda to secede. Unfortunately for healthy political development, the strongest of the national political movements, the Congress, is continually developing schisms, fragmenting itself, and thus weakening its influence. Without at least one well-organized national political party, it seems that healthy democratic development for the state as a whole is bound to be retarded. It may be that ultimately the Africans of Kenya and Tanganyika, who have already shown deep concern for the weaknesses of Uganda, will have to intervene more directly if Uganda is to be saved from the follies of its own politicians.

Kenya

The political battle which rages today in Kenya stems directly from the original decision of 1956 to allow Africans elections. Once

it was admitted that Africans could take part in democratic pro-
cedure, a political momentum was inevitably created. Even though
they were originally allowed only eight seats in the 1957 elections—
subsequently increased to fourteen the following year—and although their franchise was limited, these restrictions were insignificant compared with the political consequences which must follow
from the acceptance of the principle. It was quite obvious that as
soon as there were any number of elected Africans, pressure to
increase their numbers was bound to develop and could not be
withstood. So long as Kenya was anywhere within the orbit of the
British political system, it was unthinkable that a community of
over 5 million people should continue for long to be represented
by only as many members as the European community of 50,000.

Thus the original acceptance of the principle of African election
was bound to herald an era in which political pressure and resistance
to it would provoke a series of constitutional crises in which the
initiative would always be on the side of the Africans, with the
Europeans, fighting a defensive rearguard action to maintain white
privilege, constantly on the retreat. Whether these crises would
deteriorate into a complete breakdown depended on the extent to
which the British Colonial Office was prepared to modify its
support of European privilege, walking the delicate tightrope of
granting some measure of the Africans' demands without arousing
undue antagonism among the immigrant communities, but satisfying the Africans that genuine progress was being made.

It is in this context that the deadlock which had developed by
the end of 1958 was broken in 1959. Although the British Colonial
Secretary as late as November 1958 had refused the demands of
the Africans for a constitutional conference, by April of 1959 he
had been forced to change his mind and agree that such a conference would be held late in that year or early in 1960. He agreed,
too, that a constitutional expert should be sent to Kenya to consult
with all parties to the dispute and to advise on the next constitutional steps to be taken.

He even went so far as to declare that he saw no reason why
responsible self-government should not ultimately be granted to
Kenya, although he could not foresee a date on which any British

Government could surrender ultimate responsibility. He added that conditions necessary for self-government were a sufficient understanding of parliamentary institutions to produce responsible self-government; a sufficient measure of co-operation among the communities; a reasonable prospect that any government would be able to ensure for the people of Kenya a fair standard of living in an expanding economy; and a competent and experienced civil service.

The first reaction of the African elected members was that this statement marked a considerable advance over previous British promises. They were particularly pleased with the assurance that Kenya was to develop as a self-governing nation with parliamentary institutions, though they still demanded some indication of when the objective of self-government was to be achieved. So satisfied were they with the statement that they immediately called off their boycott of the Legislative Council.

Meanwhile Michael Blundell, the leading European politician, had announced his decision to resign as a Minister in order to lead a new organization called the New Kenya Group. The Group's principles and aims were somewhat vague, but they included recognition of the need for African advancement in the political field and some breakdown in the barriers around the White Highlands. Not only were the Group's aims vague, but the members who originally formed it—including Ministers as well as members of the Legislative Council—were immediately divided on their interpretation. The fact was that the Group represented European members and those Africans and Asians elected to the crossbench who foresaw that African pressure was becoming irresistible but hoped that they could modify the speed of its progress. The main significance of this group has been that it has broken up the solid white front and led to discussion within European circles of the various alternative methods of constitutional progress. Shortly afterwards all the more conservative Europeans came together under the leadership of Group Captain Briggs, with the firm intention of preserving white privilege to the end, proposing as a means the decentralization of political power so that the Europeans would be able to maintain their positions in their own areas. The principal feature of the methods on which this group is based approximates that of South African apartheid, with each race developing local self-government.

The African reaction to the formation of the New Kenya Group was first to establish a Constituency Elected Members Organization, which included African and Asian elected members and also one European. It was not long, however, before the non-European elected members began to divide amongst themselves. At the time of the first favourable reaction of African members to the British Government's new statement, one of the most powerful African members, Tom Mboya, was on a lecture tour in America. When he returned to Kenya he expressed much stronger doubts of the Colonial Secretary's statement than had been entertained by his colleagues. In particular he would not accept the Colonial Secretary's words as an indication that Kenya was to be allowed to develop as a genuine British-type democracy with universal adult suffrage and a Government drawn from the majority of elected members. Moreover, he and some of his colleagues were influenced by the remarkable progress of Tanganyika, and obviously feared that their neighbour was likely to achieve internal self-government and then independence before they could attain the same status themselves.

Inevitably, with the new surge of political activity amongst Africans in Kenya, personal rivalries have developed, and there is keen competition for leadership. It is therefore the case now that if one leader makes extreme demands, his competitors dare not risk appearing any less devoted to the progress of their people, for fear of being outbid in appeal to the masses. It was certain, therefore, that once Tom Mboya took this line it would be followed by other African leaders such as Oginga Odinga and Julius Kiano. What was less expected was that some of their elected colleagues would decide to go their own way. Yet, this in fact has happened. Early in August a new party named the Kenya National Party was formed by a number of African, Asian, and European elected members. This party was pledged to work for a democratic Kenya, with equal rights, a common electoral roll, multi-racial education, and a thorough examination of the land problem. The party was not

joined by the three main leaders, who issued a separate statement
a fortnight later calling for a common roll, single-member constituencies, cabinet government, a definite date for independence,
the opening up of the White Highlands, a ban on further immi-
gration of European farmers, multi-racial education, an end to the
emergency, the immediate release of Jomo Kenyatta, the re-
organization of the judiciary, an end to foreign military bases, and
either the dissolution of the Kenya Regiment or its opening to all
races.

The immediate significance of these moves is that for the first
time an open breach has occurred amongst the African elected
members. The first group, who formed the Kenya National Party,
have been impressed by the fears voiced by the Asian members
that the African leaders were becoming intransigent and demanding advance so fast that all the immigrant communities would fear
expulsion from the country. The Asians have maintained an
uneasy common front with the Africans in their major demands
over the last few years, but they now clearly believe that the leading
African personalities have become too extremist for the welfare of
the country. Nevertheless, this decisive if extreme lead given by
Odinga, Mboya, and Kiano has forced their African colleagues into
a very difficult position. If they try to sustain a more moderate
policy, they run the risk of being denounced as traitors by their
leaders, with a subsequent loss of popular support. As soon as the
leaders' statement was issued, two of the founder members of the
National Party associated themselves with it. Shortly afterwards
these three leaders and their supporters formed the Kenya Independent Movement as a competitor to the National Party.

Professor Mackenzie of Manchester University, who is mainly
responsible for the recent constitution of Tanganyika, was appointed constitutional adviser in August 1959. His task is colossal,
for it will be seen that although the position is more fluid now than
it has been for years, the racial groups are organizing themselves
increasingly for an all-out political battle. It is to be doubted
whether any Africans can secure popular support whilst maintaining a policy of moderately paced advance, designed to secure the
support of progressives within the immigrant communities. The

weakness which has previously beset European politics, the inability to withstand the popular pressure of their electorate—and which still besets them—has now extended to the Africans. It is an ironical paradox that whereas until recently the Europeans were demanding a reduction in Colonial Office control, believing they could establish independent government in Kenya on the Central African model under permanent white leadership, whilst the Africans were appealing to Britain to continue her authority until they were strong enough to take an active part in the political field—the positions are now reversed. It is the Europeans who now see British control as their protection and the Africans who are demanding its reduction in order to create an independent state ruled almost entirely by Africans. The fact is that in Kenya, as in other African countries, the existence of a trained African civil service, a large African professional class, and Africans trained in economic and commercial practice is no longer considered an essential for African independent government. Pressure for the majority community to rule the state and equally to get rid of not only European direction but British control is rapidly increasing month by month. It is irresistible, and the only practical issue that remains is how to order affairs during the brief transition period so that a state will emerge that is likely to sustain the basic principles of democratic practice and guarantee the essential liberties of every one of its inhabitants.

Tanganyika

For several years Tanganyika has been potentially the most hopeful country in multi-racial Africa. It is certainly the happiest in race relations and, apart from a few minor incidents, has avoided those tensions and explosions which have beset East and Central Africa.

The constant moderation and far-sighted tolerance of African nationalism, dominated by the remarkable personality of Julius Nyerere, have produced a climate in which the delicate manoeuvre of advancing African political rights with the co-operation of the European and Asian candidates has been possible. Since the new Governor, Sir Richard Turnbull, took office in the middle of 1958

Tanganyika has begun to realize its potential. In the elections of September 1958 and February 1959 the Tanganyika African National Union (T.A.N.U.) won all the African seats, and T.A.N.U.-supported candidates won all the European and Asian seats. This was a remarkable achievement, considering the opposition which the Government had offered to the organization of T.A.N.U. in many areas and the irritating tactics which it had too frequently employed against leading T.A.N.U. members. What was much more remarkable was the fact that after the elections all thirty elected members formed a genuine team, organized in the Elected Members Association, and co-operated in preparing for the next constitutional advance. It is an astounding commentary on race relations in Tanganyika that whereas the African elected members were anxious to ensure protection of the minorities by continuing to reserve certain seats for them under the next constitution, it was the Europeans and Asians who objected to this and expressed themselves satisfied that this was unnecessary and that politics could now be moved into a completely non-racial atmosphere.

Following the elections, a committee was set up under the chairmanship of Sir Richard Ramage to consider further constitutional changes, including an increase in the number of constituencies and an extension of the franchise, but without being allowed to consider complete adult suffrage. On July 1 five unofficial members drawn from the elected members were appointed as Ministers in the Executive Council. Three of them were Africans, one was European, and one Asian, but all considered themselves, first and foremost, members of the Elected Members Association rather than representatives of their races.

The way now seems open, therefore, for Tanganyika to prove possible what has so often been considered impossible—by creating out of a multi-racial society a new nation state in which all people will come to feel national loyalty more strongly than racial consciousness. Much still depends on maintaining the momentum already created, without any irritating hindrances which could still sour tempers. T.A.N.U. has shown itself prepared to compromise on speed and tempo, though not on principle. The Governor has won the confidence of all races in a remarkably short time and despite his Kenyan history. In particular he has established a relationship of mutual respect and regard with Julius Nyerere which is the key to harmonious progress. If he has one weakness, it is in being too sensitive to panic reports from district officers— as yet unable to appreciate the new circumstances of the country— and thus paying too much regard to 'law and order'. On the other hand, he counter-balances this failing with a recognition quite remarkable in colonial circles of the necessity for producing a colonial police force with the same friendly relations with the public as are traditionally seen in Britain.

T.A.N.U. has put forward its proposals for the next constitutional step to the Ramage Committee. They suggest that the Legislative Council should be increased to eighty-two members, of whom seventy-nine should be elected. Of these, twenty-one seats would be reserved—thirteen for Asians and Arabs, and eight for Europeans. The rest would be seats open to all races. They further propose that a majority of elected members should be appointed to the Executive Council by the end of 1959, and that after the general election for the newly constituted Legislative Council, which they hope would be held in 1960, only three ministries would be retained by officials—those for defence, external affairs, and legal affairs. The way would then be open for an early grant of internal self-government, leading soon afterwards to complete independence. T.A.N.U. draws its support from such a wide cross-section of the community, including the tribes, chiefs, and all races, that this can now be represented accurately as a national demand. Most of its features would be readily conceded by the leading administrators. There is now complete confidence in Julius Nyerere, who has shown himself always highly intelligent, tolerant, moderate, unfailingly good-humoured, prepared to discuss, negotiate, and compromise, but unshakeable on principle. He has always set his people a shining example in personal life: he has no big cars or houses to distinguish him from the masses, is scrupulously honest, mixes unself-consciously with all classes, and is essentially a servant of his people. His big lack has been high-calibre lieutenants who are capable of sharing some of his overwhelming responsibilities. He devotes himself to training and building up his colleagues instead of competing with them.

Tanganyika, therefore, has all the elements to provide a decisive answer to those who ask whether it is possible to create genuine nation states out of multi-racial societies. If it is left to develop on its own, there can be no doubt as to its success. The one dark cloud overhanging its future is the interference in its progress by influences in Central Africa and Kenya. It is significant, for example, that the Ramage Committee was not allowed to consider adult suffrage, though it is quite apparent that adult suffrage for the Africans with reserved seats could not endanger minority protection. There is a growing suspicion that in Central Africa and Kenya Europeans are frightened that the example of Tanganyika will expose the basic fallacy of their apologia for the maintenance of white privilege, and that the Colonial Office listens to their whispers when giving orders to their Tanganyikan servants. Such interference in the healthy development of this fine and successful experiment in race relations would be an unforgivable betrayal of British democratic principle and of those fine men and women of all races in Tanganyika who are setting an example of living together in unity.

Central Africa

The affairs of Central Africa have suddenly broken into the world's headlines in 1959. No one who has had any knowledge of the realities in Central Africa since 1951 is surprised. The only change in the situation is that a point was reached in the frustration of the Africans, on the one hand, and the nervous determination of European leaders, on the other, at which a resort to force was inevitable. The use of force and the consequent violent reactions provide world news. But, in fact, they illustrate nothing more than a further stage in the struggle for power. They are an integral part of the policies which have been followed for many years and, even though more spectacular, cannot be dissociated from them.

It would be a slight exaggeration to say that the history of Central Africa has followed the same pattern as that of South Africa. In the latter case, the Europeans have always been more numerous, more powerful, and more fanatically convinced of the morality of white supremacy. Nevertheless, the struggle in the two areas is based on an identical principle. It is simply that a white minority should so control the political, economic, and social affairs of the country as never to be in danger of rule by the black majority.

Ever since 1915, moves have been afoot to establish a single Rhodesian state out of Southern and Northern Rhodesia, sometimes including Nyasaland. At first the Southern Rhodesians were frightened that amalgamation with the north would bring them into dangerous contact with a society in which Africans might advance in skills and techniques. At that time they favoured much more the idea of uniting with the south. In fact, by a small majority, they decided in 1923 to set up their own state, virtually independent of Britain, leaving Northern Rhodesia and Nyasaland to follow the normal line of colonial development which would gradually bring Africans into positions of responsibility. They were soon attracted, however, by the remarkable boom in Northern Rhodesian copper mining during the twenties and thirties. The idea of Rhodesian amalgamation was revived. So strong was the pressure of Rhodesian whites that in 1927 and again ten years later the British Government had to set up Royal Commissions to study the whole question of closer association. Even at the earlier date Northern Rhodesian Europeans had begun to join their Southern Rhodesian brothers in expressing fears that Britain intended to bring Africans into the Government. Both Commissions reported against the policy of amalgamation, pointing out the differences in native policy of the three territories. This did not, however, deter the Europeans from pursuing their objective, and when they saw Africans organizing political parties and trade unions after the war, the weight of their pressure became even heavier. What is more, in 1948 the Afrikaner Nationalists gained power in South Africa, facing Southern Rhodesians with the price of Afrikaner domination for joining the Union. Southern Rhodesia, therefore, attracted even more by the copper revenues of the north and fearing the Afrikaners of the south, saw Greater Rhodesia as their one salvation. The whites in Northern Rhodesia, though suspicious of the economic designs of the Southern Rhodesians, were nevertheless more fearful that the rise of African politics and trade union organization was endangering their supremacy; they saw closer association with the southerners as their best chance of breaking Colonial Office control, which they identified with African advancement.

By this time the European leaders of both Rhodesias, plus some of their brethren in Nyasaland, had seized on 'federation' in place of amalgamation, held a conference to discuss their tactics at Victoria Falls in 1949, and brought heavy pressure to bear on the British Government.

Thus the federal scheme, first published in 1951 and brought into effect two years later, represented a victory for the Rhodesian white leaders over the pretensions of the African masses to any representative share in the government of their country.

When Federation was established in 1953 against the wishes of the Africans and the opposition of the Labour and Liberal Parties and even some sections of the Conservative press in Britain, its leaders had two choices. They could either continue in their drive to create a permanent hegemony, or they could try to achieve the much more difficult task of persuading Africans to co-operate with them in building some form of new structure by giving them the opportunities of advancement in the political, economic, and social life of their countries. Everything that has happened since Federation proves that the first choice was the only one ever seriously considered. This indeed was inevitable, as was seen by the critics of Federation at the time. The white leaders of the Federation realized more clearly than any other Europeans in Africa, except the South Africans, that once the principle of African advancement is admitted there can be no halt in its progress to eventual majority rule. Such an outcome is entirely inconsistent with the European conception of Central African society.

The basic folly of the federal structure was that it forced this policy of white domination into association with the British Colonial Office policy of gradual African advancement. Federal leaders no doubt hoped either to be able to discard the Colonial Office or to persuade it to change its policy. To some extent they have succeeded, but opposition from the Africans and in Britain has prevented their complete success. Thus, although the Federal and Northern Rhodesian franchises and methods of representation have been conditioned very largely by the policy of the Federal Government, even the Government could hardly contemplate imposing white minority rule on Nyasaland. It is in this context that the events of 1959 should be seen. The shadow of the 1960 conference, to be held for the purpose of reviewing the Federal constitution, was growing rapidly darker. The European leaders were mounting their claim for supremacy over all three territories, and the Africans were growing ever more fearful that it would be met. Faced with the continual retreat of the British Government in the face of Federal pressure, the Africans believed that only strong resistance could save them from the South African fate. In this they were probably correct. The return of Dr Hastings Banda to Nyasaland had resulted in a tremendous increase in organization of the Congress, and although the Congress Movement in Northern Rhodesia was weak and divided and was still young in Southern Rhodesia, there was no question that the African masses in all three territories were becoming increasingly frightened of ultimate betrayal and were prepared to act against it. The new Northern Rhodesian constitution showed the pattern they could expect— majority power in both legislature and executive for the small European community, with only a slight, specious veneer of African representation.

At the same time, the European leaders were themselves organizing for a showdown with the Africans. The object was to crush the Congress Movement before it could create further African hostility towards any advance in Federal powers. With every sign that the British Government was steadily capitulating to Federal demands and deliberately conditioning its policy in Northern Rhodesia and Nyasaland to white Rhodesian influences, the Africans increasingly felt themselves on the verge of betrayal. Every indication pointed to the British Government being prepared in 1960, if not to grant complete independence, at least to hand over so much power to the Federal Government as would have given it an irresistible leverage towards a complete supremacy. Many Africans must have asked themselves what could prevent this catastrophe other than a display of violent resistance. It would not be easy to give them an answer.

The white leaders miscalculated. They were able, without the slightest evidence of violence, to suppress the Congress in Southern Rhodesia and arbitrarily remove its leaders. With the assistance of the Colonial Office, they were able to ban the Congress in Nyasaland and put all the leading politicians in detention camps. In Northern Rhodesia the new Zambia Congress was banned, and its leaders exiled to remote rural districts.

But what the white leaders did not recognize was the force of public opinion in Britain and elsewhere. By taking these actions, they had exposed their real intentions. The first casualty of the crisis was not African politics but the Federal hope of independence in 1960. They had, in fact, convinced the British people and the world that the mass of people living in Central Africa were implacably hostile to Federal intentions. The British Government, by its incredible naïvety in appointing the Devlin Commission under the chairmanship of a High Court Judge, with four widely experienced and conservative members, simply exposed its appalling ignorance of Central African realities. For the Devlin Commission inevitably further exposed the disastrous folly of British as well as Federal policies, and even though the British Government with unparalleled effrontery then rejected its own Commission's analysis, the exposé was there for the world to see.

Thus the real objective of this whole history of white Rhodesian policy—the establishment of an independent state giving the white minority absolute power to determine its policy without interference from Britain—has for the time being been both exposed and destroyed. Sir Roy Welensky, the Federal Prime Minister, had to retract very quickly his previous claim for independence in 1960, and although he made a desperate attempt to switch his policy to one of increasing territorial instead of Federal powers, his bluff was immediately called. It is quite clear that, under the present constitutions, additional territorial powers would simply mean handing over further authority to the white leaders in their separate states.

These events—which involved African deaths, imprisonment,

detention, and proscription of political organizations—even had an effect on some white opinion in Central Africa itself. The intelligent Europeans, many of whom previously concentrated simply on making a good living and avoided public affairs, have become conscious of their isolated position as a tiny minority in a huge black continent and have begun to realize that only by active association with Africans can the European settlement survive. In Southern Rhodesia a few minor gestures towards liberalism were made by the Government, but much more important was the formation of the new Central African Party under the leadership of Mr Garfield Todd, former Prime Minister of Southern Rhodesia, and Sir John Moffat of Northern Rhodesia. This was a deliberate attempt to organize a political party on a non-racial basis, and it immediately gained some African support, particularly from Southern Rhodesia. Its problem is how to influence constitutional developments with an electorate almost entirely confined to Europeans, most of whom still believe in white supremacy. Its only hope is that by mobilizing Africans and liberal Europeans, it may create a climate of opinion in which the constitutions themselves will be changed and the franchise radically broadened.

Nyasaland has been left in a hopeless vacuum, with the Africans quite uncowed and the Government myopically trying to act as if nothing had happened. Its proposal to increase the number of Africans in the Legislative Council by nomination and to admit two to the Executive Council will certainly not divert the mass of Africans from their determination to be represented in all stages of government by their own elected members. This is a point of agreement among all African political organizations. Ultimately, of course, it is inevitable that the detained African leaders—particularly Dr Hastings Banda—will have to be released and negotiations conducted with them. The success of these negotiations depends a great deal on how early this step is taken and what is done in the meantime.

In many respects Northern Rhodesia is the key to the whole future of Central Africa. Although there has not been the same degree of trouble here as in Nyasaland, the hostility of the Africans to Federation and to the present Northern Rhodesian constitution is just as strong, though not so well organized. The only difference between Northern Rhodesia and Nyasaland politically is that there are more Europeans, with a stronger voice, in the former territory. Despite the fact that they are still a tiny minority community, they have been given a major voice in the Government, and once the Africans find the means of united organization this position will be challenged just as fiercely as it was in Nyasaland. Northern Rhodesia is certainly heading for a constitutional crisis, and perhaps for a revolution. In its Executive Council the official members can now be outvoted by the unofficials, who are dominated by the Northern Rhodesian branch of Sir Roy Welensky's United Federal Party. Meanwhile, African hostility to the constitution and the administration is rapidly growing, and unless the Africans are quickly able to see the constitutional means towards controlling their own government, they will be forced, as in Nyasaland, to use unconstitutional methods.

The whole lesson of the Federation is that in a society where any sensitivity to democratic principle still remains—in short, in a society which is not completely totalitarian—it is impossible to base government permanently on force instead of on consent. The white inhabitants of Central Africa have to make the choice. Either they can continue to try to use all their powers to establish a virtually white dictatorship, or they will have to reconcile themselves to a rapid increase in African advancement, which must lead to African majority government. If they wish to retain a stake in the country, their only hope of doing so is to prove to the Africans that they are willing to assist them in establishing good government which can ensure guaranteed human rights for all and a rising standard of living.

It may well be too late for the Federation, as it is presently constituted, to achieve this end. The African mind is so completely hostile to Federation that even a radical change in political policy would be met with suspicion. In any event, the Federal constitution is such that it would be virtually impossible for Africans ever to believe that it offered them an untrammelled opportunity for the political progress which is their right. It would therefore seem that the most constructive task for those in and outside Central Africa who want to see a happy society develop there is to examine other methods of association among the three states. Government by consent must inevitably include the right of any of the three territories to secede from the Federation. This would be an admission of failure on the part of those who believe that the three communities can find added strength in unity. Unless this failure is to be final, a new start will have to be made in discovering a structure of association capable of removing the African fears of permanent white supremacy, and ensuring that government by consent on a genuine democratic basis is to be the foundation of such association.

South Africa

Although South Africa is often in the news, there is rarely anything basically new to say about it. Absolute power has been in the hands of the white community for the past fifty years. The Nationalist Government, in following its policy of apartheid, is simply working out the logic of this half-century.

In 1959 the Government took its policy of entrenching white supremacy a number of steps further. It passed an Act to prevent Non-European students from attending the two 'open' universities of Cape Town and Witwatersrand, making provision for separate colleges for Africans, Cape Coloureds, and Indians. Its Bantu Self-Government Act abolished the representation of Africans in the Parliament, setting up separate African states with certain legislative authority but subject to Government control.

Thus the Nationalists continue to impose racial segregation at every possible turn, always giving the Non-Europeans lower facilities than the Europeans, and strengthening Government control over them. What the Government never does, of course, is to interfere seriously with the flow of Africans to serve European interests on the farms, in industry, or in domestic service. Nor has it any intention of allowing Africans in their own areas to conduct their own affairs, except under the vigilant control of the Government.

Meanwhile, the opposition United Party is becoming less and less effective, mainly because the majority of its members accept the principles of apartheid and only really quarrel when their application is liable to harm the economic interests which the party largely represents. There has always been a handful of comparatively liberal-minded members within the United Party, uneasy bed-fellows with the party's conservative outlook. In August 1959 official policy went so far in a conservative direction, particularly on a resolution opposing any extension of African land holdings, that a group of them broke away, loosely calling themselves the Progressives. This once more raised hopes in some minds that the traditional South African coalition might again emerge from the conservative U.P. and the more progressive Nationalist members. There is no reason to suppose that for the foreseeable future such rumours will have any substance. The Nationalists are firmly entrenched and quite convinced that their purpose of segregation is divinely approved; although there has been criticism within their ranks, they are most unlikely to have any desire to share the power they now hold. Criticisms of the Government from within the Nationalists have come largely from certain academic circles, but one Member of Parliament, Jappie Basson, a member from South-West Africa, went so far as to speak against the Bantu Self-Government Act. His opposition and that of his local party—which refused to expel him, in defiance of Dr Verwoerd and the Parliamentary caucus—are largely based on the special circumstances in South-West Africa. There it is known that a large iron field exists and that the Americans, providing for their future needs, are interested in its development. They fear that apartheid would gravely hinder the organization of an efficient labour force; consequently, economic interest conflicts with political policy.

The Africans, their activities increasingly smothered by blanket restrictive legislation, are still searching for effective extra-Parliamentary means of political action. In this they continue to consult the Labour and Liberal Parties, and in the middle of 1959 adopted a policy of boycotting the sale of goods produced by Nationalist firms. This caused some economic fears amongst the Afrikaner community, but it is unlikely to have much political effect. The frustrations provoked by this oppressive system have led to sporadic outbursts of violent protests, particularly amongst

African women and especially in Natal. In this condition of continual frustration, insignificant incidents can cause such outbursts in spite of the weight of power wielded by the Government and its forces. They can be expected to continue spasmodically, for South Africa is marching rapidly on the road towards a revolutionary situation which history has shown as inevitable when the masses are arbitrarily and tyrannically governed by a self-perpetuating oligarchy.

MISCELLANEOUS

Zanzibar

In April the British Resident in Zanzibar, with the approval of the Sultan and the Colonial Secretary, announced an increase from three to five representative members on the Executive Council, with the intention that at least two should be elected members from the Legislative Council. At the same time, he announced that the number of constituencies was to be increased from six to eight—five in Zanzibar and three in Pemba—with a corresponding reduction of appointed members from six to four. The minimum-age qualifications for voters was to be reduced from twenty-five to twenty-one, and the age for exemption from literacy qualifications from forty to thirty. A committee was to be appointed to consider extending the franchise for women, always a delicate point in Arab countries.

Mauritius

The first elections under the new constitution in Mauritius, held in March 1959, were a great success, for 90 per cent of the electorate voted. The Labour Party proved its popularity by winning twenty-three of the forty seats, and their associates gained another eight. Labour members were again appointed to the Executive Council to act as Ministers, and they had to face the growing problems of population pressure, unemployment, and economic dependence on the sugar industry. A new development programme was introduced providing for an expenditure of £16 million over five years for the construction of roads and a new harbour, irrigation and water development, and plans to diversify the economy. The most serious opposition came from the independent Forward bloc, which concentrates on destructive criticism rather than an alternative and constructive policy. Difficulties arose with some sections of the trade union movement, but the basic problem of the party, as in similar circumstances in West Indian islands, will be how to provide the means of life for a population of well over 60,000 people from the resources of a tiny island.

British Somaliland

British Somaliland held its first general election in March 1959, and the moderate National United Front won seven of the thirteen seats to the Legislative Council. Statements from the British Government indicate the intention of speeding up constitutional development so that the choice may be made in 1960 as to whether to join the new state of Somalia. The fact that the very backward Somalis are being encouraged to take political responsibility is used by Africans in other territories as a counter-argument to those who say that Africans are not yet ready for responsibility.

Cameroons

The elections of January 1959 in the Southern Cameroons resulted in a narrow victory for the Kamerun National Democratic Party, led by Mr Foncha. He had a majority of two over the previous Prime Minister, Dr Endeley, who had supported union with Nigeria. Mr Foncha would probably favour his people joining the French Cameroons, which is agitating for the recreation of a united Cameroons state. The choice between these alternatives will now have to be made by plebiscite.

French Africa

The situation in the French African territories is even more fluid than elsewhere in the continent. The French colonial territories in West and Equatorial Africa have set up the eleven republics of Mauritanie, Senegal, Soudan, Volta, the Ivory Coast, Dahomey, Niger, Chad, the Central Africa Republic, Congo, and

Gabon. Madagascar has followed suit. These twelve states are part of the new Community, handling their own internal affairs whilst leaving foreign policy and defence, joint economic and financial policy, and the supervision of justice and higher education to the Community. Their Prime Ministers, along with the French Cabinet, are members of the Executive Council of the Community, which meets in Paris and has also already held one meeting in Tananarive, Madagascar.

Whether this Community, somewhat similar in character to the Commonwealth, is a lasting organism or simply the threshold of African national independence is still to be proved. Within its structure, political conflict among the Africans themselves still flourishes. M. Houphouët-Boigny, the Ivory Coast leader, who has served in many French Cabinets, has made a strong drive towards keeping the African states separate, with allegiance only to the Community itself. He and his party, the *Rassemblement Démocratique Africain* (R.D.A.), were successful in persuading Dahomey and Volta to withdraw from the Mali Federation. His chief opponent, M. Senghor, and Senghor's Parti du Regroupement Africain (P.R.A.) are fighting the battle for federalism and have managed to keep the Mali Federation together, though with only two members, Senegal and Soudan. In the Equatorial area a common customs union has been agreed on, but the central battle for separation or federation has yet to be resolved.

Meanwhile, Guinea, the one state to declare for independence outside the Community, has been rejected by President de Gaulle and has turned to the Czechs, the Soviet Union, and East Germany for economic aid and arms. The state at present is ruled almost solely by M. Sékou Touré, with the right of decree legislation, and continues to show its independence by negotiating with Ghana and Liberia—rather than with the French states—in order to achieve some West African unity.

The future of the North African states continues to revolve around the Algerian war. President de Gaulle has as yet found no means of solving the conflict, which continues to bleed the French economy. It was significant that Algeria took first place on the agenda for President Eisenhower's visit to Paris. President Bour-

guiba of Tunisia has so far managed to withstand the embarrass-
ments of Algeria on the one hand, and the hostility of Cairo on the
other, to establish himself unshakeably in power. The new constitution for Tunisia comes into effect during 1959, based largely on
the American constitution and providing for a President of the
Republic and a National Assembly elected for five years by universal
suffrage, which significantly includes women as well as men.

In Morocco the Algerian war is a more severe embarrassment
and has led to sharp tensions with France. The split in Istiqlal
between M. Allal el Fassi and the traditionalists on the one hand,
and M. Mehdi ben Barka and the progressives and trade unionists
on the other, continues to enliven the political scene. M. Abdullah
Ibrahim's Government is moving leftwards, possibly because of the
severe economic difficulties it has to face. King Mohammed V is
still the main unifying influence, whether it be in the internal
quarrels of the politicians or the external danger of a rupture with
the French over incidents caused by the war in Algeria.

Belgian Congo

The riots at the beginning of 1959 resulted in the banning of
Abako and the imprisonment of its leaders, including Kasavuvu.
Nevertheless, the Belgians showed remarkable foresight in taking
M. Kasavuvu to Belgium and sending him on a study tour of
Belgian institutions. The riots were followed by a sudden increase
in political activity all over the Congo. A Congress of all the
political parties has proclaimed January 1961 as the deadline for
self-government and called for the formation by that date of a
national government with powers to decide the country's future.
The main party to emerge from this new activity is the Mouvement
National Congolais, led by Padrice Lumumba, which has its own
newspaper, has ties with the Belgian Socialist Party, and was
represented at the Nationalist Congress in Accra. The political
position is likely to remain fluid at least until after the elections in
December 1959, but it is now quite clear that the Congo has joined
the rest of Africa in the continent-wide movement towards national
independence. Its future will depend very largely on the extent

to which the Belgians, like the other Europeans in Africa, are prepared to meet this nationalist upsurge.

*   *   *   *   *

All the signs in emergent Africa point to a revolutionary situation. The Africans have begun to move in the same direction as Europeans in the eighteenth and nineteenth centuries, though their progress will be much more rapid, telescoped into a far shorter period. No one can doubt that during the next few years a series of revolutions will occur in every area of the continent—some constitutional, some violent, some in co-operation with the immigrant Europeans and Asians, others characterized by bitter racial antagonism. The struggle for power will be varied. Those who genuinely wish to see a peaceful, constructive society emerge from this period of upheaval will always try to look at the problems through the eyes of the Africans as they enter the difficult world of responsibility, rather than through those of 'superior' European societies. In this respect the interests of Africans and of the immigrant races are identical.   The immigrants can only continue to live in the continent if they are prepared to become full members of the new society; Africans can gain much from European experience and skills. Similarly, it is in the interests of the Western world to show a radical sympathy for African ambitions. If Africa is to join the community of nations in which individual freedom is of first priority, it will only be because those nations regard the individual African as equal in all rights to the citizens of their own countries.

In these struggles for power the principle and practice of individual liberty will be sorely tested. The system of colonialism itself has been a bad predecessor to the establishment of independent libertarian societies. Many specious excuses have been given for interfering with and curtailing individual rights. Those in and outside Africa who genuinely believe in the sanctity of the human personality and the liberty of the human individual will fulfil their responsibility to the Africans best by fearlessly but sympathetically criticising and, indeed, condemning every invasion of personal liberty. This must be genuine, and not hypocritical, if it is practised on all occasions by the colonial powers themselves.

APPENDIX I

SELECTIVE CHRONOLOGY
OF THE MAJOR EVENTS OF AFRICAN HISTORY

1100 B.C.	Erection of Utica in Tunisia by the Phoenicians.
813 B.C.	Founding of Carthage by the Phoenicians.
631 B.C.	City of Cyrene built by Greeks.
470 B.C.	The Carthaginian Hanno claimed to have sailed through the Pillars of Hercules (the Straits of Gibraltar) down the West African coast to the River Gambia.
332 B.C.	Alexander the Great conquered Egypt and built Alexandria.
168 B.C.	Rome colonized Egypt.
A.D. 100	Christianity came to North Africa.
300	Probable founding of Sudanese kingdom of Ghana.
639–681	Moslem conquest of North Africa.
700	Arabs began to colonize East Africa and began slave trading with Asia.
1150	Founding of Timbucktu.
1415	Portuguese under Prince Henry the Navigator began to explore and trade with West Africa.
1441	First African slaves taken to Portugal.
1471	Portuguese reached the Gold Coast; began gold mining.
1481	Portuguese founded first settlement station Elmina on the Gold Coast.
1482	Portugal colonized Angola.
1486	Cape discovered by Portuguese under Bartholomew Diaz.
1491	Roman Catholic missionaries visited the Congo.
1497	Vasco da Gama sailed round South Africa, up the East African coast, and crossed the Indian Ocean to Asia.
1502	First African slaves taken to Haiti.
1505	Portuguese settlement established Mozambique.
1560	Development of Christianity in East Africa by the Jesuits.
1562	Sir John Hawkins began British slave trade between Africa and the Americas.
Seventeenth century	Decline of Portuguese and Spanish empires and rise in succession of Dutch, French, British, and Arab empires.

263

1620	First slaves sold by Dutch to Virginia.
1622	Portuguese missionary Father Lobo reached Ethiopia.
1637	Establishment of first French interests in Cinegal.
1643	French established in Reunion.
1652	Dutch settled at the Cape, led by Jan van Riebeeck. Refreshment station established for ships sailing to East Indies.
1658	First slaves imported to Cape.
1672	Royal Africa Company founded in England as trading venture.
1680 Sqq	Considerable slave trading between Africa and the West Indies.
1688	Huguenot refugees from France arrive at Cape.
1715–1810	French ruled Mauritius.
1770	James Bruce discovered junction of Blue and White Niles at Khartoum.
	Beginnings of constant contact between Cape settlers and Bantu.
1779	First war against Xhosa.
1787	Formation of Sierra Leone Company to resettle freed slaves.
1792	Founding of Freetown.
1795	Expedition of Mungo Park from the mouth of the Gambia to reach the Niger.
	British occupy Cape during Napoleonic wars.
1803	Cape returned to Dutch.
1805	Second expedition of Mungo Park in which he lost his life.
1806	Second British occupation of Cape.
1807	Slave trade made illegal by British Parliament.
1808	Transfer of Sierra Leone from Sierra Leone Company to British Crown.
1809	Pass system introduced for Hottentots.
1814	Cape Colony ceded to Great Britain.
1815	Congress of Vienna, partition of African colonies between European imperial powers.
1820	British settlers land in eastern Cape Province.
1823	Repatriation of freed slaves from America to Liberia.
1828	Citizen rights granted to all free coloured people in the Cape.
1830	French bombarded Algiers into submission.
1833	Abolition of slavery in British colonies.
1836–40	The great trek of the Boers from the Cape Colony to escape from the new liberalism of Cape Government.

1838	Battle of Blood River between Voortrekkers and Zulus under Dingaan.
1840	Appointment of first British Consul at Zanzibar.
1841	French established in Equatorial Africa.
1842	Christian missionaries arrived in Nigeria.
	Non-Europeans in Cape Colony given same rights before the law as whites.
1843	Natal declared British colony.
1844	One hundred years treaty of protectorate signed between Britain and the Gold Coast.
1847	Liberia declared independent.
1849	Livingstone discovered Lake Ngami.
1851	Livingstone reached Upper Zambezi.
	First British invasion of Nigeria.
1852	Transvaal established as independent republic.
1854	Orange Free State declared independent.
	Representative government established at the Cape. Equal political rights for all races.
1855	Livingstone discovered Victoria Falls and reached mouth of Zambezi.
1857	Speke and Burton started expedition from Zanzibar across Tanganyika to East African Rift Valley. Speke discovered Lake Victoria.
1859	Livingstone discovered Lake Nyasa.
1860	Speke and Grant started second expedition, discovering source of Nile in Lake Victoria.
	Indian indentured labourers brought to Natal sugar plantations.
1866	Diamonds discovered in South Africa at Kimberley.
1868	Basutoland becomes British protectorate.
1869	Opening of Suez Canal. Brings decline in importance of Cape route.
1870	British governor appointed over Equatorial provinces including Sudan.
1871	Stanley discovered Livingstone at Ujiji on the shores of Lake Tanganyika.
1872	Responsible government granted to Cape Colony.
1873	British invasion of Ashanti.
1874	Stanley's expedition to the Congo.
1877	Stanley's journey across Africa.
	Transvaal annexed by British.
1878	British–Zulu war.
1879	United African Company formed by British traders.

1880	First Boer war.
1881	French invaded Tunis, established protectorate.
	Restoration of Transvaal independence.
1882	Ivory Coast occupied by French.
	British military intervention in Egypt.
	Revolt of Sudanese.
1884	Establishment of Congo Free State.
	Carl Peters founded German Colonization Society in Berlin; made expedition to East Africa.
	Germany annexed South-West Africa, established control of Cameroons and Togoland.
	British Government established protectorate over British Somaliland.
1885	Berlin conference over Congo dispute; partition of Africa.
	German Government sent fleet to Zanzibar; German East Africa established.
	Death of Gordon at Khartoum.
1885–1914	Imperialist rivalry intensifying between Britain, France, and Germany.
1886	British Royal Niger Company formed.
	Discovery of gold at Witwatersrand, beginnings of Johannesburg.
1888	Formation of British East Africa Company.
	Cecil Rhodes obtained mineral concessions in Rhodesia.
1889	British South Africa Company formed.
	Condominium set up by Britain and Egypt over the Sudan.
1890	British protectorate established over Zanzibar.
	Pioneer column started for Rhodesia. Fort built at Salisbury.
1891	Nyasaland became British protectorate; most of Northern and Southern Rhodesia handed over to British South Africa Company.
	British protectorate declared over Bechuanaland and Matabeleland.
1893	British establish protectorate over Uganda.
	Matabele war.
1894	France annexed Kingdom of Dahomey.
1895	Protectorate established over British East Africa, later known as Kenya.
	Building of Kenya–Uganda railway began.
	Jameson raid.
1896–97	Matabele and Mashona rebellions.

1899–1902	Second Boer war; Transvaal and Orange Free State annexed by Britain.
1900	Nigeria transferred from Royal Niger Company to British Colonial Office.
1904–6	British invasion of Northern Nigeria; Southern Nigeria placed under British Governor.
1905	Italy assumed control of Italian Somaliland.
1906	Indian passive resistance campaign led by Gandhi against pass laws in Transvaal.
1907	Transvaal and Orange Free State restored to responsible government.
1910	Union of South Africa formed. Protectorates proclaimed of Northern and Southern Nigeria.
1911	Italians annexed Libya from Turkey.
1912	Arabs and Spaniards established protectorates in Morocco.
1914	Northern and Southern provinces of Nigeria amalgamated. British protectorate established over Egypt.
1919	German African colonies placed under mandates of the League of Nations to be administered by Britain, France, Belgium, and South Africa.
1920	Dr Aggrey's visit to Africa.
1922	British protectorate in Egypt ended; Egypt became nominally independent.
1923	Responsible government established in Southern Rhodesia.
1924	British Government takes over full administration of Northern Rhodesia from British South Africa Company.
1927	Firestone Rubber plantation begun in Liberia.
1931	Statute of Westminster: South Africa becomes independent of all British control.
1935	Italian invasion of Ethiopia.
1936	Africans removed from common electoral roll in Cape Colony.
1940	First Colonial Development and Welfare Act.
1941	Italians driven out of Ethiopia; Emperor Haile Selassie restored to the throne.
1945	League of Nations mandated territories to be transferred to the trusteeship scheme under the Trusteeship Council of the United Nations.
1948	General election in South Africa—Dr Malan and National Party elected on apartheid programme.
1950	Seretse Khama and Tshekedi Khama exiled.
1951	First general election in the Gold Coast. Dr Nkrumah released from gaol to become virtually the first African Prime Minister.

Nigerian constitution with majority of elected Africans in Legislative and Executive councils.

Beginning of constitutional dispute in South Africa over removal of Cape Coloured voters.

1952   Libya became independent.

Mau Mau rebellion in Kenya started.

1953   Federation of Southern Rhodesia, Northern Rhodesia and Nyasaland.

Kabaka of Buganda exiled.

Dr Malan and National Party re-elected in South African elections.

First federal elections in Central African Federation. Sir Godfrey Huggins first Prime Minister; Sir Roy Welensky Deputy Prime Minister.

1954   Algerian Revolution breaks out.

Lyttleton multi-racial constitution for Kenya.

Second general election in the Gold Coast—Dr Nkrumah and Convention People's Party returned.

Rise of opposition National Liberation Movement in the Gold Coast.

Federal form of government adopted in Nigeria.

Mr J. G. Strijdom takes over from Dr Malan as Prime Minister of South Africa.

1955   Kabaka of Buganda returns with new constitution.

First ministerial system for Uganda.

South African Senate enlarged from forty-eight to eighty-nine members; Appeal Court also increased.

1956   Third general election in the Gold Coast. Dr Nkrumah and the C.P.P. returned again.

Seretse Khama returns to Bechuanaland.

Cape Coloured voters finally removed from Cape electoral roll.

Togoland voted for incorporation with the Gold Coast.

March 1957   First African elections in Kenya.

6 March 1957 Declaration of Ghana, first black Dominion in the Commonwealth.

May 1957   Constitutional conference for Nigeria with offer of self-government to regions.

May 1957   Sierra Leone elections under new constitution with ministerial government.

July 1957   First Zanzibar elections to Legislative Council.

E.A.—Q

Nov. 1957	New Kenya constitution, with increased African representation.
March 1958	Kenya African elections for additional representation under the new constitution.
April 1958	South African elections—Strijdom and Nationalist Party returned with increased majority.
April 1958	Accra Conference of independent African states.
May 1958	Crossbench elections in Kenya Legislative Council.
May 1958	Algerian crisis leading to downfall of the French government; General de Gaulle takes over government.
June 1958	Southern Rhodesian elections won by United Federal Party. Former Prime Minister Garfield Todd defeated.
August 1958	Death of Strijdom; Verwoerd elected Prime Minister of South Africa.
Sept. 1958	Tanganyika African National Union supported candidates win elections in 15 constituencies.
Sept. 1958	French Referendum; Guinea votes for independence from France; other French African territories support constitution of General de Gaulle.
Oct. 1958	Nigerian Constitutional Conference resumed; October 1960 fixed as independence date.
Oct. 1958	First direct elections to Uganda Legislative Council.
Nov. 1958	Sudan coup d'état; military government formed.
	Central African elections under new constitution; Sir Roy Welensky returned as Prime Minister.
	Ghana and Guinea announce intention to form union.
Dec. 1958	New Northern Rhodesian Constitution.
	Accra Conference of African colonial territories.
	Plans for an elected Legislative Council in Basutoland announced.

APPENDIX II

INDEPENDENT STATES IN AFRICA

EGYPT

Area: 386,000 sq miles   *Population*: 22,651,000 (approx.)
Principal Products: Cotton, rice.

Independent; became a republic in June, 1953 when Liberation Rally overthrew monarchy; constitution suspended; government by the Revolutionary Council with President.

ETHIOPIA
(and Eritrea)

Area: 398,350 sq miles   *Population*: 16,000,000 (approx.)
Principal Products: Coffee, tobacco, cattle, hides and skins.

Independent; no political parties; no opposition; government largely in the hands of Emperor Haile Selassie, with elected Lower House of Parliament and Senate nominated by the Emperor.

GHANA

Area: 91,843 sq miles   *Population*: 4,548,000 (1954 est.)
Principal Products: Cocoa, palm products, gold, diamonds, manganese.

Independent (March 1957); includes former Trust Territory of Togoland; National Assembly comprises 104 members elected directly on universal adult suffrage; cabinet system of government; member of Commonwealth.

GUINEA

Area: 97,000 sq miles   *Population:* 2,492,000
Principal Products: Timber, gold, cocoa, bananas.

Became independent in October 1958, after rejecting General de Gaulle's constitution. Territorial assembly of 60 members elected by universal adult suffrage.

LIBERIA

Area: 43,000 sq miles   *Population*: 1,600,000 (approx.)
Principal Products: Rubber, iron ore.

Independent; republic with presidential system of government (modelled on the U.S.A.); it has a Senate of ten members and a House of Representatives with twenty-four members; adult suffrage based on tax payment; sole power lies in President Tubman and his True Whig party.

LIBYA

Area: 679,343 sq miles   *Population*: 1,091,000
Principal Products: Olives, dates.

Independent (December 1951); monarchy; federal constitution; has two-chamber parliament with Senate of twenty-four members nominated by the King and Provincial Legislative Councils, and House of Representatives with fifty-five elected members; formerly an Italian colony and future decided by U.N.

MOROCCO

Area: 173,879 sq miles   *Population:* 10,099,000
Principal Products: Fish, wine, wool, phosphates.

Independent (March 1956); French and Spanish Morocco unified to form new state; no elections held; power lies mainly in Sultan who appoints cabinet.

SUDAN

Area: 967,500 sq miles   *Population*: 10,200,000
Principal Products: Cotton, gum arabic.

Independent (January 1956); Military Government; previously under the Condominium of Britain and Egypt.

TUNISIA

Area: 48,195 sq miles   *Population*: 3,800,000
Principal Products: Olive oil, wine, cork.

Independent (March 1956); first general election held 1956 for Constituent Assembly; all 98 seats won by *Néo-Destour* Party; only Tunisian males have the vote.

UNION OF SOUTH AFRICA

Area: 472,494 sq miles   *Population*: 14,412,000 (Dec. 1957
(excluding S.W. Africa)   est.)

African:	9,600,000
European:	3,011,000
Coloured:	1,360,000
Asian:	441,000

Principal Products: Gold, diamonds, uranium, fruit, wool.

Independent; cabinet system of government; member of Commonwealth.

House of Assembly:
156 elected European members (of which 6 are from S.W. Africa).
3 Europeans for African interests elected by Africans.

Senate:
68 members elected by Provincial Councils.
18 nominated by Gov.-Gen.
3 Europeans elected by and representing Africans.

Franchise: Europeans—universal adult suffrage.

Africans—in the Cape, male franchise on educational income or property qualifications, to elect 3 European Members of the House of Assembly; in other 3 provinces, qualified male franchise for election of 3 Europeans to the Senate.

Cape Coloureds—qualified male franchise for election of 4 Europeans to House of Assembly.

Asians—No franchise.

BRITISH TERRITORIES IN AFRICA

WEST AFRICA

GAMBIA

Area: 4,003 sq miles   *Population*: 275,100 (1956 est.)

Principal Product: Groundnuts.

Political Status: Colony and Protectorate.

Constitution:

  Executive Council:
    The Governor
    5 Official Members
    Not less than 6 Unofficial Members from Legco.

  Legislative Council:
    Speaker
    4 ex-officio Members
    1 Nominated Official
    2 Nominated Unofficials
    14 Elected Members

Franchise: All persons over 25 in the Colony; electoral college system in the Protectorate.

NIGERIA

Area: 373,250 sq miles   *Population*: 31,171,000 (1953 est.)
                                        Northern Region: 16,840,000
                                        Eastern Region: 7,971,000
                                         Western Region: 6,360,000

Principal Products: Groundnuts, palm products

Political Status: Colony and Protectorate (Western and Eastern Regions are self-governing).

Constitution: Federal government, residual powers with Regions.

  Federal Government:
    Council of Ministers:
      Governor-General
      Prime Minister
      Not less than 10 Ministers

House of Representatives:
Speaker
3 ex-officio members
Up to 6 Special Members appointed by Governor-General to represent communities and interests not adequately represented.
184 Elected Members
92 from Northern Region
42 from Eastern Region
42 from Western
6 from S. Cameroons
2 from Lagos

In 1960 the House of Representatives will be extended to 320 members and a Senate will also be created.

Regional Government:

Northern Region:
Executive Council: Governor as President, not less than 12 members of House of Assembly; 3 officials

House of Assembly:
President
4 Officials
5 Nominated Members
131 Elected Members—to be increased to 170

House of Chiefs: All first-class chiefs and 47 other selected chiefs.

The North becomes self-governing in March 1959; colonial officials withdraw.

Eastern Region:
Self-governing with elected House of Assembly (a House of Chiefs will be created); Executive Council presided over by Premier

Western Region:
Self-governing with elected House of Assembly; a House of Chiefs; Executive Council presided over by Premier

Southern Cameroons:
Executive Council:
Commissioner as President
3 ex-officio members
4 unofficials appointed from House of Assembly

House of Assembly:
Commissioner as President
3 ex-officio
6 Native Authority members
No more than 2 Special Members appointed by Governor-General
26 elected members

House of Chiefs with 20 members.

Franchise:
    Eastern and Western Regions: Full adult suffrage
    Northern Region: Confined to men
    Federation: Same electoral arrangements as in
                                    regions

SIERRA LEONE

Area: 27,925 sq miles   *Population*: 2,260,000 (1957 est.)
Principal Products: Palm products, iron ore, diamonds.
Political Status: Colony and Protectorate.
Constitution:
  Executive Council:
    4 ex-officio members
    Not less than 4 unofficial Ministers from elected members of House
      of Representatives (9 Ministers appointed in 1957)
  House of Representatives:
    Speaker
    4 ex-officio members
    2 nominated members (no voting powers)
    51 elected members:
      14 representing Freetown and the Colony
      25 representing Electoral Districts in Protectorate.
      12 Paramount Chiefs elected by 12 District Councils in Protec-
        torate
Franchise: Direct Elections; virtually all adult males and all adult tax-
  paying or property owning females

EAST AFRICA

KENYA

Area: 224,960 sq miles (of which   *Population*: 6,300,000 (July 1957
    5,230 is water)   est.)

1953 estimates	
Africans	5,644,000
Indians/Goans	131,000
Europeans	42,000
Arabs	29,000
Others	4,500

Principal Products: Sisal, coffee, pyrethrum
Political Status: Colony and Protectorate
Constitution:
  Council of Ministers:
    Governor
    Deputy Governor
    6 official members

Minister of Finance
Minister of Forest Develop-   } May be filled from within or with-
   ment, Game and Fisheries   out public service
4 Europeans
2 Africans
2 Asians
Not less than 3, nor more than 5 Assistant Ministers

Legislative Council:

communal seats {
   14 elected European members
   14 elected African members
   6 elected Asian members
   1 elected Arab member
   1 Arab representative

special seats {
   4 Europeans
   4 Africans   } elected by Legco members
   4 Asians

Sufficient nominated members to secure an adequate Government majority

Council of State:
   Chairman
   10 members from outside the Legco (has powers of delay and reservation for H.M.G. in matters deemed differentiating)

Franchise:
   Europeans—adult suffrage
   Asians—adult suffrage
   Arabs—male suffrage
   Africans—qualified suffrage with multiple franchise up to 3 votes per person; qualifications based on education, or service, or income, or age, or decoration, or membership of public body; special qualifications of loyalty test for members of Kikuyu, Meru and Embu tribes.

TANGANYIKA

Area: 362,688 sq miles
   (of which 19,982 is water)

Population: 8,456,000 (mid-1956 est.)

African:	8,329,000
European:	28,000
Indian/Goan:	76,000
Arab:	17,000
Others:	6,000

Principal Products: Sisal, coffee, cotton, diamonds
Political Status: U.N. Trust Territory
Constitution:
   Executive Council:
      9 official members

　　　6 nominated unofficial members
　　　　2 Europeans
　　　　2 Asians
　　　　2 Africans
　　Legislative Council:
　　　Government side:
　　　　3 ex-officio Ministers
　　　　6 nominated Ministers
　　　　6 unofficial Assistant Ministers
　　　　19 nominated members
　　　Representative side:
　　　　10 Africans ⎫
　　　　10 Europeans ⎬ 5 nominated, to be elected in 1959, and 5 elected
　　　　10 Asians ⎭
　　　　1 African ⎫
　　　　1 Asian ⎬ Representing general territorial interests
　　　　1 European ⎭

Franchise: First elections took place in 5 Constituencies in 1958, and in remaining 5 in 1959, on a common roll, each person having 3 votes (for a European, African and Asian candidate in each constituency); qualifications are based on residence, education, or office, or income, or property.

SOMALILAND

Area: 67,936 sq miles　　　　　　*Population*: 650,000 (estimate)
Principal Products: Millet, hides, skins, gum, guano.
Political Status: Protectorate
Constitution:
　Executive Council:
　　3 ex-officio members
　　such official and unofficial members as appointed by the Governor
　Legislative Council:
　　Governor as President
　　3 ex-officio members
　　no more than 5 official members
　　no more than 6 unofficial members
Franchise: There is no franchise
　New constitutional statement, 1959.

UGANDA

Area: 93,981 sq miles (of which 13,689 is water and swamp)　　*Population*: 5,593,000 (1956 est.)

　　　　　　　　　　　　1948 census:
　　　　　　　　　　　　　Africans:　4,917,000 (approx.)
　　　　　　　　　　　　　Indians:　　33,500
　　　　　　　　　　　　　Europeans:　3,500
　　　　　　　　　　　　　Arabs:　　　1,500
　　　　　　　　　　　　　Others:　　　2,000

Principal Products: Cotton, coffee, groundnuts, maize

Political Status: Protectorate

Constitution:

Executive Council:
   Governor as President
   13 members (of whom 10 are Ministers)

Legislative Council:
   Speaker
   3 ex-officio members
   13 Government Ministers and officials
   16 nominated Government members
   30 Representative members:
     18 Africans
     6 Europeans
     6 Asians

Franchise: Direct elections for 10 African representative members of the Legislative Council were held for the first time in 1958. Buganda did not participate in these elections, but continues to elect its representatives in the Council through an electoral college. The elections were held on a qualitative franchise, with land ownership, occupation, literacy, public service, and income qualifications.

ZANZIBAR

Area: 1,020 sq miles

Population: 282,000 (est.)
1948 census:

Africans	75.6 per cent
Arabs	16.9 per cent
Indians	6.1 per cent
Europeans	0.1 per cent
Others	1.3 per cent

Principal Products: Cloves, coconuts

Political Status: Protectorate

Constitution:

Privy Council:
(to advise Sultan)   Sultan as President
                     British Resident
                     Heir Apparent to the Throne
                     Chief Secretary
                     Attorney General

Executive Council:
   British Resident as President
   4 ex-officio members
   3 official members
   3 representative members

Legislative Council:
British Resident as President
  4 ex-officio members
  9 officials
 12 unofficial members (6 elected and 6 appointed by Sultan)

Franchise: Common roll; male franchise based on educational and economic qualifications; must be subjects of the Sultan. First election held
July 1957 for 6 of the 12 unofficial seats in the Legco.

CENTRAL AFRICA

FEDERATION OF RHODESIA AND NYASALAND

Area: 488,060 sq miles

Population: 7,071,600 (est.)	
Africans:	6,810,000
Europeans:	233,600
Asians:	18,400
Coloured:	9,600

Political Status: Self-governing colony

Constitution: (Matters not on the Concurrent or Executive Lists are
reserved to the Territorial Governments)
Governor General:
  has power to reserve any Bill for H.M. Pleasure and must do this for
  Bills referred by the African Affairs Board.

Cabinet system:
  on British model
Federal Assembly:

  44 elected members:
        24 from Southern Rhodesia
        14 from Northern Rhodesia
        6 from Nyasaland

  8 African elected members:
        4 from Southern Rhodesia
        2 from Northern Rhodesia
        2 from Nyasaland

  *4 specially elected African members
        2 from Northern Rhodesia
        2 from Nyasaland

  3 European members for African interests:
        1 from Southern Rhodesia
        *1 from Northern Rhodesia
        *1 from Nyasaland

*These will eventually be replaced by ordinary elected members, of
unspecified race

Franchise: There are two electoral rolls, the General and the Special
Roll. Voters on the General Roll elect the 44 elected members and

combine with Special Roll electors in voting for the 8 African elected members and 1 European representative from Southern Rhodesia. Voters on the Special Roll elect the 8 African elected members and 1 European in Southern Rhodesia.

Qualifications for the two rolls are as follows:

General Roll

Rhodesian subject or British protected person; over 21 years of age; resident in Federation for 2 years; literate in English and able to complete application form unaided.

Either:—
Income of £720 p.a. or ownership of land worth £1,500.

Or—
Income of £480 p.a. or ownership of land worth £1,000 together with approved primary education

Or—
Income of £300 p.a. or ownership of land worth £500 together with approved secondary education (4 years)

Special Roll

Rhodesian subject or British protected person; over 21 years of age; resident in Federation for 2 years: literate in English and able to complete application form unaided.

Income of £150 p.a. or ownership of land worth £500.

Or—
Income of £120 p.a. together with approved secondary education (2 years)

NORTHERN RHODESIA

Area: 288,130 sq miles (of which 3,000 is water)

Population: 2,218,400 (Dec. 1956 est.)

African:	2,140,000
European:	71,000
Asian:	5,800
Coloured:	1,600

Principal Products: Copper, zinc, lead, tobacco.

Political Status: Protectorate

Constitution:

Executive Council:
Govenor as President
4 ex-officio Ministers
6 Other Ministers (2 Africans and 4 Europeans)

Legislative Council:
Speaker
22 Elected Members
12 from "ordinary" single-member constituencies, covering Crown land adjacent to railway line and surrounding Native Trust land and Reserves

6 from "special" single-member constituencies covering the rest of the country

2 Europeans from 2 constituencies covering total area of "special" constituencies

2 Africans from 2 constituencies covering "ordinary" constituencies

6 Official Members

2 Nominated Members

Franchise: There are 2 electoral rolls, an ordinary and a special roll. In the 12 ordinary and the 2 amalgamated constituencies electing European members, the total of special votes may not count more than one-third of the ordinary votes cast.

Qualifications for the 2 rolls are as follows:

All voters must be able to complete application form unaided, be literate in English, be a British or Central African citizen or a British protected person, over 21 years of age and have 2 years residence in the Federation and 3 months in the constituency.

Ordinary Roll

Either:—

£720 p.a. or ownership of land worth £1,500

or—

£480 p.a. plus primary education

or—

£300 p.a. or property worth £500 plus 4 years secondary edution

or—

Ministers of religion, sisters and lay brothers of religious orders fulfilling certain training and service and who follow no other profession

or—

Paramount Chiefs, chiefs recognized by the Governor, including those certified to be of equivalent status in Barotseland

Special Roll

Either:—

£150 p.a. or property worth £500

or—

£120 p.a. plus 2 years secondary education

or—

Certain headmen or hereditary councillors, who are recognized as such by their chiefs

or—

Persons receiving a pension earned after 20 years service with one employer

or—

The wife (only one wife of a polygamous marriage) of a person in any one of the above categories if she has the residential and literacy qualifications

The special roll qualifications will be gradually raised over the next ten years, until they merge with the ordinary roll.

In the twelve ordinary constituencies and in the two amalgamated constituencies electing European members the total of special roll votes will not be allowed to count for more than one-third of the total number of ordinary votes cast.

NYASALAND

Area: 49,177 sq miles (of which   *Population*: 2,647,900 (June 1957 est.)
11,600 is water)

Africans:	2,630,000
Europeans:	7,500
Others:	10,400

Principal Products: Tobacco, tea, maize, millet

Political Status: Protectorate

Constitution:

Executive Council:
   3 ex-officio members
   2 official members
   2 unofficial members

Legislative Council:
   4 ex-officio members
   8 official members
   6 Non-African elected members (Europeans, Asians and Coloureds on common roll)
   5 African indirectly elected members

Franchise: Franchise for non-Africans based on English language, property and residence qualifications. No franchise for Africans.

SOUTHERN RHODESIA

Area: 150,333 sq miles   *Population*: 2,481,200 (mid.-1957 est)

African:	2,290,000
European:	178,000
Asian:	5,100
Coloured:	8,100

Principal Products: Tobacco, chrome, coal

Political Status: Colony—internally self-governing subject to provisos relating to differential legislation.

Constitution: Cabinet system
              Legislative Council of 30 elected members

Franchise: Dual roll franchise with following qualifications:

Ordinary Roll	Special Roll
Ability to speak, read, write and comprehend English, and to complete enrolment form unaided.	Ability to speak, read, write and comprehend English and to complete enrolment form unaided.
either:	either:
Income of £720 p.a. or ownership of immovable property worth £1,500	Income of £240 p.a.

or:

Income of £480 p.a. or ownership of property worth
£1,000 together with six
years' primary education.

or:

Income of £300 p.a. or ownership of property worth £500
with four years' secondary
education.

or:

Income of £120 p.a. and two years'
secondary education.

Voters on the Special Roll will enjoy same voting rights as those on the
Ordinary Roll, but if at any stage the number of such voters registered exceeds one-fifth of the Ordinary Roll electorate, no further
enrolment on the Special Roll will be allowed.

SOUTHERN AFRICA

BASUTOLAND

Area: 11,716 sq miles

Population: 641,674 (1957 census)
Africans: 638,857
Europeans: 1,926
Asians: 247
Persons of
Mixed
Descent: 644

Principal Products: Wool and mohair

Political Status: Protectorate

Constitution: Resident Commissioner responsible to the High Commissioner for the 3 Protectorates.
No Legislative Council; the all-African Basutoland Council is advisory.

Franchise: None

Proposals for elected Legislative Council were published in December
1958

BECHUANALAND

Area: 275,000 sq miles

Population: 296,310 (1946)
Africans: 292,755
Europeans: 2,379
Mixed
descent: 1,082
Asians: 94

Principal Products: Cattle

Political Status: Protectorate

Constitution: Resident Commissioner responsible to the High Commissioner for the 3 Protectorates

African Advisory Council (chiefs and tribal representatives) meets once a year

European Advisory Council (8 elected members) meets twice a year

Joint Advisory Council (with equal African and European membership) meets twice a year.

Franchise: None

SWAZILAND

Area: 6,704 sq miles

Population: 185,215 (1946)
Africans: 181,269
Europeans: 3,201
Mixed
descent: 745

Principal products: Cattle, asbestos

Political Status: Protectorate

Constitution: Resident Commissioner responsible to the High Commissioner for the 3 Protectorates

No Legislative Council—government is through the Paramount Chief and Council

For administrative purposes there is an Advisory Council of 10 elected representatives of the Europeans which advises the Commissioner on European matters.

Franchise: None

SOUTH-WEST AFRICA

Area: 317,725 sq miles

Population: 414,601
Europeans: 48,588
Africans and
Coloureds: 366,013

Political Status: Mandated territory under Union of South Africa

Constitution: Legislative Assembly of 18 directly elected Members, with similar jurisdiction to Provincial Councils of the Union of South Africa, but with financial autonomy. Six representatives are elected to Union House of Assembly and 4 Senators are in the South African Senate.

Constitutional status in dispute between Union and United Nations.

Franchise: Universal adult suffrage for Europeans. No franchise for non-Europeans.

MAURITIUS

Area: 720 sq miles

Population: 579,123 (1956 Dec. est.)

Europeans
and
Coloureds: 29 per cent
Indo-
Mauritian: 67 per cent
Chinese: 4 per cent

Principal Products: Sugar cane, fibre, tea, tobacco, cattle, fish

Political Status: Colony

Constitution:

Executive Council:
Governor as President
3 ex-officio
7 elected by Legco
2 nominated members

Legislative Council:
Governor as President
3 ex-officio
19 elected members
12 nominated members

In 1958 the Electoral Boundary Commission recommended that the colony be divided into 40 single member constituencies; and that the Governor should nominate 12 extra members to the Legco to ensure that representation is in proportion to the communities on the island.

Franchise: Elections are due to be held in 1959 with universal suffrage

OTHER EUROPEAN TERRITORIES IN AFRICA

FRENCH TERRITORIES

ALGERIA

Area: 847,500 sq miles

Population: 10,010,000
French number about 1,250,000

Principal Products: Wine, figs, iron ore, phosphates

Political Status: Part of France

FRENCH CAMEROONS

Area: 166,800 sq miles

Population: 3,065,000

Principal Products: Cocoa, Bananas, coffee, palm products

Political Status: U.N. Trust Territory under French Administration

E.A.–R

FRENCH EQUATORIAL AFRICA

Area: 969,111 sq miles   *Population*: 4,436,500
Principal Products: Cotton, timber, cocoa, diamonds, gold
Political Status: French 'overseas territory'; member of French Union;
   new developments in 1959

FRENCH WEST AFRICA

Area: 1,718,768 sq miles   *Population*: 14,000,000
Principal Products: Peanuts, palm kernels, coffee, groundnut oil
Political Status: French 'overseas territory'; member of French Union;
   new developments in 1959

MADAGASCAR

Area: 229,438 sq miles   *Population*: 4,913,000
Principal Products: Coffee, cloves, vanilla
Political Status: French 'overseas territory'; member of French Union

FRENCH SOMALILAND

Area: 8,376 sq miles   *Population*: 62,000
Principal Products: Hides, salt
Political Status: French 'overseas territory'; member of French Union

FRENCH TOGOLAND

Area: 21,235 sq miles   *Population*: 1,015,000
Principal Products: Cocoa, coffee, palm products
Political Status: U.N. Trust Territory under French Administration

PORTUGUESE TERRITORIES

ANGOLA

Area: 481,351   *Population*: 4,145,000
Principal Products: Coffee, maize, sugar, palm oil
Political Status: Portuguese overseas province

MOZAMBIQUE

Area: 297,731 sq miles   *Population*: 5,732,767
Principal Products: Sugar, maize, cotton
Political Status: Portuguese overseas province

PORTUGUESE GUINEA

Area: 13,948 sq miles   *Population*: 511,000
Principal Products: Rice, palm oil
Political Status: Portuguese overseas province

BELGIAN TERRITORIES

CONGO

Area: 904,974 sq miles   *Population*: 12,000,000 (approx.)
Principal Products: Palm oil, cotton, copper, diamonds, gold, uranium
Political Status: Belgian colony

RUANDA-URUNDI

Area: 20,120 sq miles   *Population*: 4,425,000
Principal Products: Tin, coffee, gold
Political Status: U.N. Trust Territory under Belgian Administration

ITALIAN TERRITORIES

ITALIAN SOMALILAND

Area: 220,000   *Population*: 1,264,000
Principal Products: Skins, hides and frankincense
Somaliland was transferred to Italy by the U.K. in 1950. It is to become an independent sovereign state on 2 December 1960.

INDEX

Date Due